your cosmic kids

Books by the Author

As Trish MacGregor

The Everything Astrology Book
Power Tarot, Simon & Schuster
    (co-author, Phyllis Vega)
The Everything Dreams Book, Adarns,
    (co-author, Rob MacGregor)

As Trish Janeshutz

The Making of Miami Vice
In Shadow
Hidden Lake

As T .J. MacGregor

Hanged Man
The Seventh Sense
Dark Fields
Kill Flash
Death Sweet
On Ice
Kin Dread
Death Flats
Spree
Storm Surge
Blue Pearl
Mistress of the Bones

As Alison Drake

Tango Key
Fevered
Black Moon
Lagoon
High Strangeness

YOUR COSMIC KIDS

using astrology to understand your children

TRISH MACGREGOR

HAMPTON ROADS

PUBLISHING COMPANY, INC.

Cover design by Marjoram Productions
Cover art by Francine Barbet

For information write:

Hampton Roads Publishing Company, Inc.
134 Burgess Lane
Charlottesville, VA 22902

Or call: 804-296-2772
FAX: 804-296-5096

e-mail: hrpc@hrpub.com
Web site: http://www.hrpub.com

If you are unable to order this book from your local
bookseller, you may order directly from the publisher.
Quantity discounts for organizations are available.

Call 1-800-766-8009, toll-free.

Library of Congress Catalog Card Number: 98-73903

ISBN 1-57174-127-5

10 9 8 7 6 5 4 3 2 1

Printed on acid-free recycled paper in Canada

Dedication

With love for Megan,

the double Virgo who transformed my life.

Eu coosi dao, Suki

Table of Contents

Part Three: Your Child's Ascendant

Introduction

Your Kids & the Stars

Is your Aries toddler running the neighborhood? Is your Sagittarian second grader rounding up the stray cats on your block and bringing them home? Has your Aquarian teenager started a donation program for the homeless in your town?

As a parent, you undoubtedly recognized your child's uniqueness at a very young age. Perhaps your child spoke before her first birthday or didn't speak until she was four. Maybe your son or daughter skipped the crawling stage altogether and went straight from the crib to an upright walk. Perhaps your four-year-old daughter is painting like Van Gogh or playing the piano like Mozart. Maybe your son has a magical way with animals.

Your child's uniqueness, however it shows up, is often apparent in her birth chart, as a *pattern* depicted by a particular arrangement of planets.

Your Aries toddler, for instance, may have his Moon in Cancer, which makes him fiercely attached to his home, his neighborhood, his turf. Your Sagittarian second grader may have her Moon in Pisces, which fills her with compassion for strays and outcasts of any species. And if your

11

humanitarian Aquarian has her Moon in Leo, it might explain why her donation program for the homeless hit the front page of your local newspaper.

While the Sun represents your child's overall personality, his ego, his outer radiance, the Moon symbolizes his emotions. It describes his emotional temperament, how he acts and reacts emotionally, what kind of relationship he has with his mother. It also provides hints about his early childhood, his domestic situation later in life, even the state of his health and the kind of work at which he may excel. The sign of your child's Moon gives you, as a parent, insight into his inner world, into what makes him tick. Your child's rising sign or ascendant is the face he shows to the rest of the world. When it is combined with your child's Sun/Moon pairing, you have a powerful and insightful tool for guiding your child toward his fulfillment.

Birth Data

If you're not sure of your child's birth sign, look at table 1 in the text. To derive maximum benefit from *Cosmic Kids*, you'll also need to know the sign of your child's Moon and his ascendant, derived from his birth date and time and place of birth. Most New Age bookstores provide computerized natal charts for about $5.00.

This chart is unique to your child, pegged specifically to his birth data. It depicts talents and tendencies with which your child was born—and yet nothing is written in stone. Astrology isn't about fate or destiny; it's about free will and how that will is brought to bear on the *pattern* depicted in the natal chart.

In other words, your little Lydia may very well be the next Marie Curie. But if she doesn't have the opportunity or the environment in which such a talent can flourish, then it benefits none of us and she may end up blocked creatively. If she's lazy, if she's unmotivated, her genius remains nothing more than a seed.

A child whose chart indicates genius may use it to cruise through life, living off others, or she might find a cure for cancer. A child with a compassion for animals may take in so many strays that he eventually goes bankrupt. Or he may become a vet and write best-selling books about his adventures as a vet for exotic animals. There's no telling where a child's free will might take him. Any astrologer who tells you otherwise is playing God.

The Tribes

Cosmic Kids focuses on the signs of the Sun, Moon, and ascendant, a fraction of a complete natal chart. But these are the three most important elements, because they show who your child thinks she is, how she feels about herself, and how other people perceive her.

Parts of the various descriptions will fit your child, others won't seem to apply at all. And that's as it should be. Each child is unique and yet each child holds membership in a particular tribe that exhibits certain personality and behavioral tendencies.

My Experience

When my daughter was born in 1989, I didn't have an astrology software program. But I had her exact time of birth, so I headed over to the local New Age bookstore for a computerized birth chart. I then asked an astrologer friend to interpret it, because I felt that I, as her mother, might read things into her chart that weren't there.

"She's going to have terrible colic," said Renie, the astrologer.

Megan was only two days old at the time, but I hadn't seen any indication of colic. "Tell me something good."

"She's very bright."

That sounded better. But it seemed rather, well, generic, something a good friend would tell a new mother. "What else?"

"She's artistic, very psychic, and she's going to love animals."

Great. Things were improving. Then again, maybe Renie was just being nice. "Go on."

"Her health is directly linked to her emotions."

"That's true of everyone."

"It's especially true for her. Just be aware of it."

I didn't like the sound of that, but before I could question Renie, she went on. "She's going to be fussy about details, but that fussiness will be selective."

"What do you mean by that?"

"Oh, you know, a messy room, but her art will have to be perfect in every way."

At this point, I took the chart from Renie and studied it, trying to find the part about the messy room and the perfectionism about art. I didn't see it. "Where're you getting this stuff, anyway?"

She pointed at the Sun and Moon, both in Virgo in the sixth house of health and work. "These ground her and force her to pay attention to details, but her rising in Pisces sweeps in and connects her to much deeper levels and makes her a dreamer." Renie paused and looked up. "You should massage her feet, she'll like that, it'll calm her."

By now I was taking notes. "So what else is in there?"

"Her art will be rendered in miniature."

Now, nine years later, most of what Renie told me then has proven true. I still don't know where she got the part about miniature art, but Megan's little drawings and paintings are posted all over our house.

And that, really, is the ultimate riddle about astrology. Does a child grow up to become a particular type of person because his environment was conducive to it or because he was born with a particular agenda? Personally, I think it's more complex than anything we can imagine, that it's ultimately a spiritual choice that the soul makes before birth.

But even if you remove the cosmic slant from the equation, one salient fact remains. Astrology is a practical tool that you can use to guide your child through the labyrinth of life and help him fulfill his greatest potential.

Part One

The
Solar Tribes

1

Vitality

Without the Sun, the world as we know it would not exist. This is an obvious statement until a child asks you what would happen if the Sun didn't rise tomorrow.

So what, exactly, do you say? That the planet and everyone on it would die? That it won't happen and there's no point worrying about it?

This simple question threw me into chaos the day my daughter asked it. I didn't want to be facile or glib about it, but I wasn't up to a science lesson, either. My response was to walk outside where the yard grows wild and to ask her to imagine all the green turned to brown. "The life would go out," she said, with a stricken expression on her face.

I think she meant to say that the lights would go out, but she said "life." She was, inadvertently, referring to vitality.

And that's what your child's Sun sign means. Vitality. It represents her fundamental identity, her ego. It's the source that fuels her and the primary lens through which she filters her experience of the world.

In ordinary, everyday reality, this can mean the difference between a child who leaps out of bed when the alarm shrieks on a school morning and one who snoozes right through it. It can mean differences as pronounced as the tortoise and the hare.

Your Sagittarian daughter, for instance, may seize every opportunity to travel, while your Cancerian son may prefer sticking close to the familiar turf of his own neighborhood. Nothing moves your Taurus teen when he's made up his mind about something; your Pisces college student, however, may waffle back and forth before he decides what his major will be. While the broad traits of each Sun sign generally fit, the specifics may not fit, because every child's vitality is expressed uniquely.

Virgos, for example, are supposedly tidy individuals. But I know plenty of Virgo kids, my daughter among them, who consider a messy room its natural state. Cancer kids should be nurturing, but I've met some who are bullies through and through.

When you look at a group of kids who share the same Sun sign, the diversity among them is staggering. But beneath the surface of it all, you'll find similarities, a certain perception that unites them, a common thread of passions.

Children Born on the Cusp

A cusp is the point between one sign and another. A child born on the last day or two of a particular sign often exhibits as many characteristics of that sign as he does of the next sign. Take August 22, the last day of Leo.

A child with this birth date may have the Leo flair for drama, the need for being the center of attention. But she may also have Virgo's penchant for self-criticism and may not think she's worthy of being the center of attention. She's a confusing mixture of both signs, a perplexing mystery to herself and to everyone who knows her.

If you're not sure about the sign into which your child falls, table 1 will clarify it.

Table 1: Sun Signs

Sign	Symbol	Dates
Aries	♈	March 21–April 19
Taurus	♉	April 20–May 20
Gemini	♊	May 21–June 21
Cancer	♋	June 22–July 22
Leo	♌	July 23–August 22
Virgo	♍	August 23–September 22
Libra	♎	September 23–October 22
Scorpio	♏	October 23–November 21
Sagittarius	♐	November 22–December 21
Capricorn	♑	December 22–January 19
Aquarius	♒	January 20–February 18
Pisces	♓	February 19–March 20

Grouping the Signs

Our neighborhood has a hundred and thirty-five homes, most of them occupied by families with children who range in age from infants to teens. It's a kid's paradise because there's always someone to play with.

We've lived here for nearly ten years, since our daughter was six weeks old, so many of her friends are kids she has known all her life. From the time she was old enough to understand the concept of friend, I noticed certain patterns in Megan's friendships. I began to collect the birth dates of her playmates and, eventually, I collected their times and places of birth as well.

The picture that emerged deepened my appreciation of astrology as a tool for depicting broad personality patterns. In terms of specifics, I found myself paying closer attention to two distinct groupings of Sun signs: the elements—fire, air, earth, and water—and the qualities—cardinal, fixed, and mutable, which describe how we approach and react to circumstances in our lives.

I realized that, in terms of Sun signs, the kids Megan gets along with the best have Sun signs that complement her Sun in Virgo (earth) or who share the same quality as Virgo (mutable). In some instances, her closest buddies have their Moons or ascendants in signs that complement her Virgo Moon and Pisces ascendant.

When you begin to notice the deeper patterns that operate in your child's life, it enriches your experience as a parent and your appreciation of your child. Table 2 summarizes the attributes of each element.

Elements or Triplicities

Each of the four elements is associated with a sign of the zodiac, so that three signs share the same element. It doesn't take a physicist to understand how compatibility—or its opposite—works with elements.

Fire feeds fire, air fuels fire, water feeds earth, earth extinguishes fire, air and water tolerate each other but exist independently of each other. You get the general idea.

The important thing to remember about elements is that each one has a particular attribute.

Fire signs are enthusiastic and impulsive. They're terrific at starting projects, but they sometimes have a tough time finishing what they start. Earth signs tend to be grounded, focused, stable. They don't sweep through a project; they plod, they plan. They're often concerned about financial security. Air signs are mental, studious, often intellectual. They are also flighty at times, living in their own private worlds of ideas. Water signs are intuitive, sensitive, emotional.

These are only general attributes. I've met a number of children who don't seem to fit the parameters at all. Nine-year-old Samantha, for example, is obsessive about rules. She reminds other kids that they should wear their helmets when they ride their bikes, adheres strictly to the rules in any game, and is the first kid on the block to report an encephalitis scare at Disney World, even though it's four hours north of where she lives. I figured Sam for a Capricorn, an earth sign concerned with structures, parameters, limitations. When I found out she was a Sagittarius (fire), I was floored.

Sagittarians tend to be free-spirited rebels who go their own way, with little regard for what authority claims is the right way. I finally asked her mother for her birth data and discovered she has a Capricorn ascendant, with five planets in that sign. It means her rebellious Sun, her need for travel and independent thought, constantly struggle against a basic thrust in her nature for practicality, rules, structure.

Once you have your child's natal chart, the astrologer will note the distribution of the ten planets through the elements. A preponderance of any single element will amplify the attributes of that element, particularly if that element applies to the Sun, Moon, *and* the ascendant.

The absence of an element among the planets is also significant and several things may result. The child might gravitate toward children who have a lot of that missing element—or the missing element will never be a big deal. It depends on whether the characteristics of that element were mastered or avoided in other lives. You'll know which it is by the time your child is old enough to get around on his own.

My daughter has no planets in fire. One astrologer interpreted this to mean that she wouldn't have much initiative or impetus to act on her convictions. But so far, this gloomy prediction hasn't panned out. If anything, she seems to be the opposite.

In table 2, the attributes listed for each element are general. If they don't seem to fit your child, then dig deeper. Check out the signs of your child's Moon and ascendant.

Table 2: Elements

Fire: (Inspiration) Aries, Leo, Sagittarius

Primarily interested in immediate action. They are enthusiastic, courageous, spontaneous, outspoken, and blunt. Fire signs need space to grow, evolve, to find their own path. They tend to be spirited kids, the kind that teachers with thirty or more children to a classroom sometimes find irritating. They can rebel against authority, particularly if the basic rules haven't been explained to them. They usually seek independence at a young age.

Earth: (Physical) Taurus, Virgo, Capricorn

Rooted in the here and now. They seek stability, are security minded, practical, and reliable. They can be possessive and often have an attitude that says, "Prove it to me." These kids are quieter than fire. They usually develop a practical and stable approach to life at a young age. They also tend to be quite serious and need to be reminded that magic exists in everything!

Air: (Mental) Gemini, Libra, Aquarius

Concerned with the future. They are curious, logical, rational, sometimes intellectual. They travel through the world of ideas and usually communicate what they learn in some fashion. They tend to be popular children because they're adaptable and usually are gregarious. Air sign kids may seem insensitive to other people's feelings. It's not that they're less compassionate, only that they are sometimes out of touch with their own feelings.

Water: (Emotions) Cancer, Scorpio, Pisces

Feelings are their domain. They are intuitive, sensitive, psychic, receptive. They connect to the personal unconscious and express themselves best through their emotions. These kids tend to absorb the emotions in their immediate environment, so it's important that they associate with positive, upbeat people. They have an uncanny ability to size up strangers accurately and quickly. Stability of early childhood is important to a water child.

Qualities or Quadruplicities

There are only three terms to remember with quadruplicities: cardinal, fixed, and mutable. Each grouping, as you'll see in table 3, has four signs.

These qualities describe how we approach and react to circumstances in our lives. Cardinal signs act quickly. Fixed signs don't adapt well to change, especially sudden, unexpected change. Mutable signs are adaptable. The trick is how these qualities integrate with other facets of your child's chart.

Take Jenny, a nine-year-old Virgo. On the surface, it would seem that her Virgo Sun (earth), a Moon in Libra (air), and an ascendant in Leo (fire), might create some fundamental conflicts in who she is and how she perceives herself.

Her practical, earthbound ego wants things spelled out quickly and efficiently. But her emotions, with that Libra Moon, force her to carefully weigh and balance every decision before she makes up her mind. She may try to keep the peace at any cost. Her Leo ascendant, on the other hand, demands drama and the limelight and demands it now—this instant, not tomorrow, not next year. It would seem that her Leo rising would be constantly trying to squelch that earthbound Sun.

And yet, in terms of elements and qualities, the mix works amazingly well. Her Virgo Sun (mutable) allows her to change her mind when she sees fit. Her Libra Moon (cardinal) allows her to do this tactfully, gracefully, but with determination. Her Leo ascendant (fixed) gives her the persistence to get what she wants.

Table 3: Qualities or Quadruplicities

Cardinal Signs: Aries, Cancer, Libra, Capricorn

Initiates action, but may not follow through. They are creators, they plant the seeds. They tend to be enthusiastic and independent.

Fixed: Taurus, Leo, Scorpio, Aquarius

Stabilizes, sustains, preserves. They seek stability through what the cardinal signs have initiated and resist change. They have fixed opinions and don't change their minds easily. Most have terrific memories.

Mutable: Gemini, Virgo, Sagittarius, Pisces

Adapt and transform what the fixed signs seek to stabilize. Their focus is knowledge, communication. They tend to be changeable and intuitive.

As a rule, people who have signs that share the same quality don't get along well because they're so much alike. "Mix and match" seems to be what works best because there's a balance of strengths and weaknesses.

As you read through the interpretations in the following chapters, keep in mind that a birth chart doesn't create your child's personality or the events in his life. It only depicts patterns that your child's free will sculpts and molds and arranges to suit his soul's higher purpose.

2

The Tribes

All of us are members of a tribe. As young children, our tribe is our immediate family. As adolescents, our tribe includes our friends, the people we hang out with. As adults, our tribe expands continually and encompasses our own families, our neighborhood, our community, the people with whom we work, relatives, even newsgroups on the Web.

But from the moment we draw our first breath, we belong to a particular tribe of the zodiac. We come in with certain qualities and attributes that are intrinsic to that tribe. We are doers, dreamers, worriers, builders. We are cool or passionate, teachers or students. We may identify with other members of our tribe—or we may never think about membership in any tribe. We may not even be aware of the existence of tribes because we just don't think in those terms. But the attributes of our particular tribe remain an intractable part of who and what we are and what we hope to become, attain, and contribute.

Solar Sleuthing

A Few Guidelines

Several years ago, in Georgia, my husband interviewed a woman who claimed to have been closely associated with Carlos Castaneda during his apprenticeship to don Juan. It was the last day of a booksellers' convention and we sat, the three of us, in a cold, impersonal room in the convention center.

I listened to the interview for two hours, intrigued by the driving intensity of the woman's story, the intimate details she provided. It smacked of truth. But before I could make up my mind, I wanted to see her birth chart. So I asked what her birth date was. "Why?" she asked.

"I'd like to do your birth chart."

She smiled, a soft, knowing smile. "But if I give you my birth information, I'm giving away part of my personal power."

Her words stuck with me. Even though I don't believe that "personal power" can be given away through birth data, she believed it. I respected her belief and backed off.

Another time, my daughter went to play at a new friend's house. I learned that she and her two siblings were all in the gifted program, and I asked the mother for their birth data.

There was a long pause and I thought, "Uh-oh." Sure enough, she replied that she had "problems with the origin of astrology" and would prefer not to have anything to do with my research. At first, I thought she might have a scientific bias against it. But it turned out to be the usual thing, a religious bias.

And that's one of the points I consider now before asking anyone for a birth date. Will my request offend the other person? Children usually are intrigued, but their parents might not be. So when I'm in doubt, I either don't ask or ask in such a way so that it seems like a casual question.

Even when you remove the element of religious beliefs, the skeptics remain. Since you probably aren't going to change someone else's beliefs, you gain nothing by arguing about the validity of astrology. And that's my second rule. I don't try to convince people whose minds are already made up.

Although astrology in general seems to be gaining a wider acceptance as a valid tool for self-knowledge, the narrower paradigm persists. Astrology challenges you to explore your own potential, to uncover your soul's intent. But once your curiosity extends to other people's birth charts, boundaries must be respected. I now always try to get a sense of the person before I ask.

Teachers & Other Adults in Your Child's Life

From the time my daughter entered kindergarten, I've made it a point to find out her teacher's Sun signs. This information is useful to me as a parent, because it gives me a general idea of what I can expect from the teacher and how he or she is likely to interact with Megan.

Her first teacher was a young woman who had a warm, gregarious personality and who obviously loved kids and wanted children of her own. She was a nurturer, the ideal teacher for a child's introduction to the school system. I pegged her as a Cancer because her soft, rounded face and her nurturing are classic Cancer traits. But before I asked her birth date, I got to know her and felt reasonably sure that the question wouldn't offend her.

Megan's first grade teacher had the same nurturing quality, but physically she was slender, a brunette with beautiful dark eyes. I thought she was a Libra because she had a wonderful sense of balance and harmony. But I didn't feel comfortable asking her birth date until several months into the school year. We were on a class field trip and she happened to mention that her lower back had been bothering her. Libra rules the lower back, so I immediately seized on this and asked if she was born in October.

How'd you know that?" she asked, surprised—but not offended.

"Your back. That's a Libra thing."

"But I'm a Scorpio."

It turns out she was born on the cusp, so that she possessed attributes of both Scorpio and Libra.

When my daughter was in second grade, I thought her teacher was a Leo because she had a mane of lovely hair, thick and shiny, a trait of Leos. She also possessed Leo's great enthusiasm and obvious affection for children. But I noticed that, although she was great at starting projects, she had problems with completing them—an Aries trait. Midway through the school year, I casually worked my question into a conversation one afternoon. She wasn't offended at all; in fact, she enjoyed talking about herself. It turned out that she was an Aries with a Leo ascendant. Since the ascendant rules your appearance, the luxurious hair fit!

This solar sleuthing paid off in unexpected ways with the Aries teacher. When Megan came home with weekly writing projects, I suggested she try something heroic with a touch of magic, elements that appeal to an Aries. Sure enough, she and the teacher got along famously when it came to Megan's writing.

And that's exactly the point. Astrology, even if you're just dealing with solar tribes, is an *information tool*, nothing more and nothing less. It provides you, as a parent, with an immediate overview of the people who are significant in your child's life. It makes certain questions less difficult to answer.

Take babysitters. Would you leave your two-year-old Libra son in the care of a teenage Leo? Definitely. Leos of any age generally love children. And all that fire is certain to mix well with Libra's air. The Leo would indulge in kid stuff with your son, who would reciprocate and probably beg to have the Leo sitter come back.

Would you leave your Capricorn daughter in the care of a Sagittarian teenager? Doubtful. The fire of adolescence in a Sagittarian is considerable; she would be more interested in talking on the phone with her boyfriends than in watching your daughter. For an Aries boy, this probably wouldn't be a big deal. But for a Capricorn girl, it would be a very big deal.

The Horoscope

As you read the descriptions of the solar tribes, keep in mind that a Sun sign is only part of the picture. The attributes of any sign are influenced by the entire birth horoscope. Even though horoscope interpretation lies beyond the scope of *Cosmic Kids*, it's important that you know what you're looking at when you obtain a copy of your child's birth chart.

The first thing you'll notice in the chart is that nothing seems to be written in English; the language is symbols and numbers, an astrological shorthand. Just as astrological signs are represented by the symbols given in table 1, the planets also have symbols, which are depicted in table 4.

In addition to the Sun and the Moon, which are treated like planets, a birth chart includes the signs and house placements of Mercury, Venus, Mars, Jupiter, Saturn, Uranus, Neptune, and Pluto. Many charts also show the nodes of the Moon, the Part of Fortune, the Vertex, Aries point, Equatorial ascendant, and a handful of asteroids.

Table 4: Planetary Symbols

Sun	☉
Moon	☽
Mercury	☿
Venus	♀
Mars	♂
Jupiter	♃
Saturn	♄
Uranus	♅
Neptune	♆
Pluto	♇
South Node	☋
North Node	☊
Ascendant	Asc (cusp of first house)
Descendant	Ds (cusp of seventh house)
Imum Coeli	Ic (cusp of fourth house)
Medium Coeli	Mc (midheaven or cusp of tenth house)
Other Symbols	
Part of Fortune	⊗ or PF
Vertex	Vtx
Aries Point	00♈00
Equatorial Ascendant	Eq

Chiron	⚷
Vesta	⚶
Ceres	⚳
Pallas Athene	⚴
Juno	⚵
Transpluto	♇

Looks Like Greek to Me

Take a look at the chart in figure 1-1. The first time I saw one of these, it was my own chart. I took one look at it, decided I didn't have the patience to learn the language, and tossed it aside. But the next day I dug the chart out of the garbage and headed to the library to find an astrology book. I then spent the next few days trying to decipher the astrological code of who I am.

The horizontal line that cuts through the middle of the horoscope circle is the rising, or ascendant. This literally means the sign that was rising as you were born.

If you had Aries rising at the time of your birth, then Aries rules your first house, Taurus your second, Gemini your third, and on around the horoscope. If Libra was rising as you were born, then it rules your first house, Scorpio rules your second, one sign following the other around the circle. The signs always begin with Aries and end with Pisces, just as they're listed in table 1. The exception occurs when a sign is intercepted—or totally contained within another sign.

The twelve wedge shapes into which the circle is divided are called houses. They represent different areas of life and are divided according to their degrees. Houses 1, 4, 7, and 10 are called *angular* houses; their focus is *action*. Houses 2, 5, 8, and 11 are *succedent* houses; their focus is on security. Houses 3, 6, 9, and 12 are *cadent* houses; their focus is on learning.

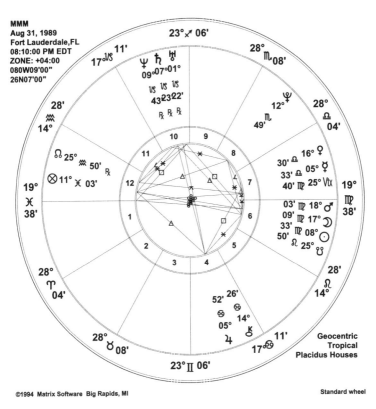

Figure 1-1

Entire books have been written on the astrological houses, but the basics are simple:

House 1: You, your physical appearance, your general health

House 2: Your money and financial resources, your material security

House 3: Communication skills, siblings, short trips, the conscious mind in the everyday world, the exchange of information in all its forms

House 4: Your home, the early part of your life, the latter part of your life, the nurturing parent, your roots

House 5: Creativity, pleasurable pursuits, your first-born child, pets

House 6: Health and work, specifically the work environment, employees; small pets can be included here as well

House 7: Partnerships (romantic, business), your spouse, open enemies

House 8: Joint finances, taxes, death, insurance, sex, metaphysics (yes, this house is loaded!)

House 9: Higher mind, higher education, foreign cultures and journeys, film, publishing, religious and spiritual pursuits and interests

House 10: Profession and career, authority figures, authoritarian parent

House 11: Friends, group associations, wishes and ambitions

House 12: Your personal unconscious, the parts of your identity that have not been integrated, hidden enemies, karma

In the chart in figure 1-1, for instance, the ascendant (Asc) is 19✶38, or nineteen degrees and thirty eight minutes of Pisces, which governs the first house. Its opposite point, the descendant, rules the seventh house and lies in Virgo, in the same degree.

At the bottom of the chart lies the Ic, the Imum Coeli, which in Latin literally means the bottom of the heavens. It lies at 23♊06, or twenty-three degrees and six minutes of Gemini, and forms the cusp of the fourth house. Directly opposite, at the top of the chart, you'll see the sign for Sagittarius, ♐, which rules the cusp of the tenth house, or the Midheaven (Mc). These four ninety-degree angles are important points in a horoscope, and any planet that falls near or directly on them assumes enormous importance.

Notice that in figure 1-1, two planets fall near the critical angles. In the sixth house, Mars (♂) and the Moon (☽) fall close to the cusp of the seventh house. Mars lies at 18♍03 and the Moon at 17♍09, both within two degrees of the descendant at 19♍38. In the chart interpretation, these planets would be given extra emphasis.

Figure 1-2 is a graph called an aspectarian. On some computerized charts, it appears in the lower right-hand corner. This indicates the relationship or aspects among the various planets in the chart, which is determined by the

MMM

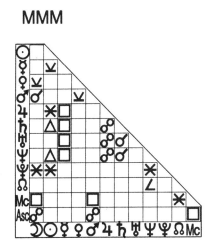

Figure 1-2

angle of separation between the planets. Some astrologers use very small orbs—one to three degrees—to determine the aspects. The norm is five to eight degrees, with the higher end used in charts that have few aspects and for aspects to the Sun and Moon.

The symbols in the squares (I know, more symbols) represent the aspects. Entire books have also been written on aspects, but for the scope of *Cosmic Kids*, the definitions lists in table 5 should suffice.

At some point, you may want to have a professional astrologer interpret your child's entire birth chart. Or you may decide to explore it on your own. Either way, you'll embark on a fascinating journey into the heart of who your child is and might become.

Table 5: Aspect Symbols & Definitions		
Conjunction	☌	0 degrees: an intense concentration of energy, focus, drive. Considered a major hard aspect
Sextile	✶	60 degrees: favorable, helpful, confers ease similar to a trine. Considered a major easy aspect
Square	□	90 degrees: friction, tension. Considered a major hard aspect
Trine	△	120 degrees: ease, harmony, smooth expression of energies. Considered a major easy aspect
Opposition	☍	180 degrees: think polarity, think magnets, think about the laws of repulsion and attraction. A major hard aspect nearly as powerful as the conjunction

3

The Aries Tribe

The Ram ♈

Dates: March 21–April 19
Element: Fire
Quality: Cardinal
Ruler: Mars

A pioneering spirit characterizes this tribe. As youngsters, they strike out to explore new worlds, even if those worlds extend no farther then their back yards. These kids are leaders. They love to be in charge.

In a group of children, the Aries is the one who decides what game will be played, then delegates tasks, assigns roles, and appoints helpers to do his bidding. He's the little emperor, overseeing an empire.

Aries is symbolized by the ram, the animal that leads its flock. The planet Mars, Roman god of war, rules the tribe and brings its characteristics to the sign: aggression, a courage that often borders on fearlessness, impulsiveness, spontaneity. Even though the Aries temper is easily aroused, it burns out just as fast as it surfaces. He isn't the type to hold a grudge.

These kids are instigators who get things moving, whether it's an adventure, a project, or mischief. They're also innovators who gravitate toward the new, the adventurous, the unusual. Their perceptions are usually razor sharp, instinctive.

Both the boys and girls of this tribe tend to be impatient, especially with other children who don't catch on as quickly as they do. Their directness can border on bluntness, which may hurt the feelings of children or adults who don't understand that, for an Aries, it's nothing personal. Their charm and charisma, however, attract many friends of varying backgrounds.

If your Aries is accident prone, injuries are likely to be to the head and face. When ill, he may run a high fever. Try to get him to talk about the underlying problem. What angers him? Is something not going right at school? With his friends? As he matures, he benefits from any kind of relaxation technique—meditation, physical exercise that allows him to release tension, even a walk in the woods.

Son: Straight talk, that's what you get from your Aries son. Ask him a question and he tells you the truth as he sees it, even if it's something you may not want to hear, even if it infuriates you. But in the next moment, he compliments you on something you've done or the way you look or he gives you the best hug of your life and your heart melts away. That's life with an Aries boy.

Your son is fearless, and he has been like that since he was old enough to walk. He's the type who, on his first day at the beach, runs right up to the edge of the water, then hurls himself into the ocean whether he can swim or not. He brings home bugs to show you, delighted with the perfect symmetry of what they are, their very *bugness*. On Christmas morning, he leaps onto his new two-wheeler and speeds off without a lesson, only to take a spill seconds later. Instead of wailing, instead of avoiding the bike for several months, he rises to the challenge, jumps back on, and keeps going until he gets it right.

Aries boys aren't afraid of new situations. One five-year-old, for instance, while visiting his father's family in Venezuela, refused to allow the difference in language to deter him from playing with kids his own age. He simply explained, in English, that, even though he didn't speak much Spanish, he was going to be in charge. He then spent the next week directing play time for a neighborhood of Venezuelan kids.

Make no mistake about it: an Aries son may turn you gray before your time. His temper, his demands, and his impatience may disrupt your household. If you're an overly protective parent, he'll drive you half nuts with his eagerness to explore, to experience. As he matures and begins to dabble in whatever captures his passion and attention, just hope that he doesn't blow up your basement with his latest chemistry experiment.

In his utter relish for life, for living, he'll force you to perceive yourself and your world in an entirely new and different way. You can't fight it, so you might as well try to go with the rhythm that he establishes. The limits you impose should be firm but not rigid; clear but organic. Help him to see the larger picture. Help him to understand the importance of pursuing an endeavor to the end.

Daughter: From the moment she draws her first breath, she breaks rules, parameters, established truths. She's atypical. Pay close attention to the details of her birth; in retrospect, these details may offer intimate hints about who she is and what she aspires to become.

If you're hoping for a daughter who is into dolls and dress up and little girl frills and stuff, then you better readjust your thinking very quickly. While these elements may be part of your daughter's early life, they won't be major parts. She's much too interested in the real thing. Give her a real baby, real clothes, real frills—a sister or a brother, a role in a play, a hot air balloon ride. Expect demands for the tangible and the more intense, the better.

Your Aries daughter has definite and very personal ideas about how things work, and she won't hesitate to let you know what she thinks. This will be true of her as a youngster, a teen, an adult. Her greatest frustration in life is why other people *just don't get it*. If you, as a parent, can instill tolerance in her at a young age, then she'll be better equipped at every stage of the game.

Tell her, "It's like this, sweet pea: We don't all have your drive, instinct, courage, or passion. So lighten up."

You'll know early on that your Aries daughter, like her male counterpart, has issues with completion. That she loses interest. That she's impatient to move onto something else before she has finished what she has started. So help her out. Stress the importance of follow-through in every facet of her life. You'll be doing her a favor. You'll be showing her a way out of her troubles.

As your Aries daughter grows up, she's going to be fickle. Expect it. Embrace it. Accept it. You aren't going to change it. But know this: once she finds the right balance in a mate, she plays for keeps.

Aries Stages

Infancy to seven: Before verbal skills are developed, your Aries child makes his will known through his temper. He cries, he fusses. Interesting visuals distract him, however, so decorate his room with plenty of mobiles and colorful posters.

Aries is so impatient to explore his environment that he benefits from a walker or early attempts to crawl. He's into everything—dirt that the houseplants grow in, the dog food, the cabinets and drawers. Keep locks on things he can reach. These children are sometimes too restless to be early readers. But if they're surrounded by books from a very young age, they gravitate toward stories with rhymes and colorful pictures.

Once these kids acquire verbal and physical skills that allow them to function on their own, they're sociable, friendly, and very independent. And watch out. They'll ask you about everything, from why the sky is blue to why boys stand up to go to the bathroom and why girls sit. They expect straight answers, too, so be prepared. Male or female, they benefit through physical exercise and team sports, which also allow them to blow off steam and energy.

It's a good idea to establish parameters and rules early on. An Aries has an easier time once he knows what is expected of him.

Seven to fourteen: Regardless of Sun sign, this stage is always marked by a thrust for independence. But, with an Aries child, the thrust is more pronounced. This is the time when he ventures more deeply into the world, testing what he has learned in his home environment. He holds on to what works and discards what doesn't.

Rebellion in an Aries teen is likely to be swift and brutal. But don't take it personally. This is simply the way an Aries evolves and sculpts his identity. Look to the Sun/Moon combination for the emotional nuances associated with this particular stage.

Fourteen to twenty-one: In the earlier part of this stage, your Aries is probably consumed by tremendous energy. He starts a hundred projects that he doesn't finish; his friendships begin and end abruptly; and his school grades suffer from precipitous ups and downs. As a parent, you need to understand this is the way he learns who he is, his process of individuation.

By the time he enters college, this phase has evened out

considerably. Your Aries may still be sampling majors the way the rest of us sample foods, but don't worry about it. If you've instilled the importance of patience and tolerance, he'll get to where he's going in one piece.

Twenty-one and beyond: An Aries child follows the same rule as wine or scotch: He improves with age. By the time he hits his twenties, he has a clear understanding of the society in which he lives. His patience has improved; he has learned to temper his impulsiveness. He is probably much closer to knowing what his niche is, too. Once he finds that groove, watch out! There's no limit to what he can accomplish.

The Cosmic Aries

Be prepared to provide concrete answers to the many questions your Aries is certain to ask about spiritual issues. For some Aries kids, these questions begin as soon as they can verbalize what they feel and are couched in simplistic terms: What is God? What are angels? What are spirits? Do trees have spirits? Where do pets go when they die?

Regardless of the age, however, the Aries approach to spirituality is likely to entail a sampling of many different belief systems and creeds, from the totally nontraditional to the very traditional. One month he's into paganism and the next he's discovered Catholicism. He dabbles. In this way, his restless mentality picks and chooses what suits him—a little of this, a little of that.

The secret with the Aries child lies in not denying him exposure to a particular spiritual belief system because you don't agree with it. All this does is fuel the Aries need to *know* and creates a seductive mystique about what is denied.

The inspiration and creativity of this sign is best served by open discussion and honesty concerning all things, but spiritual issues in particular. If your Aries, for instance, re-calls his dreams and nightmares, don't shrug off his need to talk about them or tell him they're "just dreams." Question him. Ask what frightened him or made him feel good about the dream. If he tells you about another life he lived, encourage him to share the details. Suggest that he draw or write a story about that life.

Your Aries is first and foremost an explorer and some of his explorations take place in inner realms. By encouraging him to share these sacred journeys, you establish an unbreakable bond and rapport that will endure through rougher times.

4

The Taurus Tribe

The Bull ♉

April 20–May 20
Element: Earth
Quality: Fixed
Ruler: Venus

What Aries pioneers, Taurus tames and cultivates. They can't help it, they need roots. They need to see the tangible results of their labors, even if it's nothing more than a little garden that is all theirs.

In a group of kids, the Taurus observes, measures, internalizes before she joins the others. This may happen in the space of a single breath or it may take several days. It depends on how quickly and thoroughly your Taurus processes social information. She needs to understand how and where or even *if* she fits in.

Once she connects with the group and accepts the leader, she still holds back part of herself. She retains something that is private, sacred, uniquely hers. A Taurus child doesn't make snap judgments. She moves at her own pace and, ultimately, she follows her own agenda even when it appears that she's following someone else's agenda.

Remember the story about Ferdinand the Bull? He preferred smelling flowers to fighting in the ring. That typifies a Taurus child. Ruled by Venus, the goddess of love and beauty, your Taurus child flourishes within a harmonious and secure environment. So if you and your significant other argue or disagree, do it when your Taurus child isn't around.

Some Taurus children can be remarkably selfish. They don't like to share, they think of themselves first. But they also can display enormous compassion at times.

All Taureans enjoy aesthetics—colorful mobiles, comforting textures, art that resonates at a personal level, books where the language flows. As earth signs, they also take to activities that appeal to their tactile senses—gardening, weaving, painting, writing, travel, sex.

Forget about rushing her. Forget pushing her, pigeonholing her. If you try to make her do what you want, she refuses unless you can convince her absolutely that your way is better. This kid redefines the word stubborn.

Both genders of this sign seem to be born with an instinctive knowledge about what is right for them. Even when their instincts are wrong, however, they're slow to change their opinions. It's not that they're calculating or manipulative; they simply demand that it be proven. Even then, their change, if and when it comes, tries the patience of Job.

The Taurus child is usually well coordinated. Her neck, however, is the weakest part of her body, the place where tension and stress show up first. Even as a youngster, she benefits from massage and periodic chiropractic adjustments. If your Taurus kid doesn't gravitate toward team sports, she should be involved in some type of regular physical activity, because she may have a tendency to gain weight. She enjoys good food.

Son: Reticence may be your Taurus son's middle name. Don't expect him to spill his most private thoughts and feelings. You have to earn his trust first, just like anyone else in his life. But even when you do, there will be many points in your relationship that are marked by silence, by a verbal stillness.

Instead of fretting about it, seek communication through the other venues that appeal to him—camping, hiking, canoeing, sitting by a lake at sunset. He enjoys the outdoors and appreciates anyone who enjoys it with him.

Your Taurus son possesses great patience. But if you abuse it, if you push him to his breaking point, you unleash "the bull's rush," a fierce temper that mows down anyone and everything in its path. He doesn't hold grudges, though. He's basically too affectionate and loving for that.

Taurus boys, like their female counterparts, are notoriously stubborn, and this tendency suffuses everything in their lives. You see it if you cook something for dinner that your Taurus son detests and you see it if you try to push him into doing something that he absolutely doesn't want to do. No threat, no punishment, will force him to do, eat, watch, or engage in what he finds abhorrent. Remember: His sign is fixed. He's slow to change. And his patience is practically infinite; he'll simply outwait you.

As your son matures, he's going to be fickle. But once he settles, he usually settles for good, unless his significant other nags and bullies and basically makes life so inharmonious that he simply can't stand it. In affairs of the heart, the best advice you can give your Taurus son is open honesty. He'll carry that with him throughout his life.

Daughter: Like ice cream, she comes in many flavors. She may be quiet or rowdy, shy or forward, serious or funny. But she is always stubborn, fixed in her opinions, and infinitely patient. She gives you and everyone close to her the benefit of the doubt—until you corner her. Then she refuses to budge. She turns inward. She gets moody and seeks solitude.

Your Taurus daughter probably doesn't mind being alone. As a youngster, she may spend long hours playing by herself, watching movies, reading, whatever moves her. One Taurus girl, whose father got off work at about the same time her mother went to work, used to sit at the foot of her parent's bed as her father slept, watching movies and playing until her Dad woke up.

This penchant for solitude sometimes lends new meaning to the adage that still waters run deep. Your daughter's periodic retreats may allow her to bolster her immune system, to process new information, or to delve into past life memories that have some connection to her present life.

Eight-year-old Jessie, for example, turned to her grandmother one day and told her in elaborate detail about a life she and her brother had lived in Egypt. In that life, she had failed to help him in some way, so this time they were born as brother and sister so she would learn to share.

At any age, your Taurus daughter can be a real charmer. How could it be otherwise with Venus ruling her sign? At times like this, you marvel at her ease in social situations. Her eagerness to explore the larger world prompts her to spend weekends with friends, to get involved in sports, to become firmly enmeshed in anything physical.

Like her male counterpart, she needs physical outlets—karate lessons, softball, swimming. Give her the chance and she flourishes in nature.

As she matures, her fundamentally sensitive nature leaves her open for emotional hurts. When she trusts someone and that trust is betrayed, there's no consoling her. You hurt along with her and can try to talk her through it, but your words won't do much. She has to retreat into that deep and private inner place to lick her wounds, to make sense of what has happened, to heal.

Months or even years later, she may refer to the incident. What you thought was just part of growing up turned out to be, for her, a major turning point in life. With a Taurus daughter, you rarely see the full picture.

Taurus Stages

Infancy to seven: Usually, this period is easy sailing. Your Taurus infant probably sleeps through the night from an early age and doesn't fuss very much. There are always exceptions, of course, but generally the Taurus infant is fairly content with whatever is available.

Once your Taurus child learns to crawl and then walk, however, his abundant patience may vanish faster than an endangered species. It's as if he's compelled to make up for lost time and now wants everything at once. At this stage, your best bet lies in the art of distraction—books, paints, chalk for the sidewalk out front, friends, family outings. Above all, make your Taurus child feel loved and secure.

Seven to fourteen: Sometimes, this period is marked by reticence and sometimes its hallmark is incessant chatter. The Moon combination usually reveals what is *really* going on. As a parent, your job in this crucial period is to make sure your Taurus knows that you support her, that you're willing to listen without judgment or criticism.

Rebellion in a Taurus teen is apt to be kept under wraps. It's a secret. For one Taurus seventh grader I taught, rebellion took a creative form. She wrote intricate and beautiful poems and stories that she never showed either of her parents. For another Taurus teen I taught, rebellion meant sneaking out after his parents had gone to bed to feed and spend time with a stray dog. In other words, these kids usually don't rebel in the way you expect for teens. They have a very personal agenda.

Fourteen to twenty-one: Individuation for a Taurus usually happens slowly, much more slowly than it does for other Sun signs. Remember that these kids are fixed earth signs; they aren't crazy about abrupt change.

If they try drugs, it's not a total immersion in the drug culture; it's merely to experiment, to see what a high feels like. The same may be true for sex, except that sex involves emotion and that muddles the picture considerably for a Taurus. He feels deeply, he hurts deeply. Be aware of it and encourage your Taurus child to talk about what he feels.

Twenty-one and beyond: The Taurus child is probably seriously committed or married by now. Despite the need for solitude, both males and females of the sign enjoy companionship and the security that commitment brings. And yet, for a Taurean, the lure of greener pastures always looms. Travel, other lovers, other lifestyles, other everything: How can it all be fitted into just one life? He wants to love and be loved in return, he wants a family and stability and security, but the seduction of the unknown beckons. What will he miss if he continues on his present path? What might he become if his life veers toward something else? Can he ever really know? Does he dare find out?

The Cosmic Taurus

For the Taurus child, the cosmic stuff often happens under the surface, in private, out of sight. You may never hear about it or you may stumble across this side of your Taurus quite by accident, as Jessie's grandmother did.

If your Taurus does open up to you about her cosmic musings, encourage her to talk, to ask questions. Answer her questions honestly. Bring her books to read on the subject or take her on a canoeing or hiking trip, where your solitude together encourages discussion.

A Taurus child's approach to spiritual issues is usually practical and grounded. She may initially enjoy the ritual of organized religion, the commitment to a particular faith or practice. It provides her with the fundamentals, with a basis for comparison. But don't be surprised if she strikes out on her own spiritual exploration once she's old enough to think for herself.

The Taurus child's spiritual pursuits may be found most intimately through nature, particularly if she's made aware at a young age that all life is connected. She feels this most deeply when she's out in nature, doing whatever she loves best, whether it's rock climbing or merely walking. A park will do just as nicely as the real woods, and if neither of those is available, then a lush summer garden would be okay, too.

The most important thing to remember with a Taurus child is that her opinions are formed early on and she won't change them without a fight. If you try to push her into a particular spiritual niche, if you force feed her, she simply shuts you out. But work with her, meet her at least halfway, and your own spiritual path will be enriched beyond measure.

5

The Gemini Tribe

The Twins ♊

Dates: May 21–June 21
Element: Air
Quality: Mutable
Ruler: Mercury

Once Taurus has tamed and cultivated, Gemini sweeps in. This tribe gathers and disseminates information, starts schools and newspapers, and is concerned with communication in general. They keep things stirred up so the other tribes don't become too complacent.

In a group of kids, spotting a Gemini child can be tricky. It depends on which twin is dominant at a given time—the one who is fun-loving and buoyant or the one who is moody and introspective. And that's really the bottom line with this tribe. As a parent, you aren't just raising one child; you've got twins who are often literal opposites of each other.

One twin, possessed of seemingly endless energy, flits about like some magnificent butterfly, sampling a little of this, a little of that. He's fun, he's funny, his mouth moves nearly as fast as his mind, at the speed of light. The other twin is more circumspect, moodier, more bookish. And yet, both twins are contained within the same body, and some days you wake up wondering which twin you're going to meet on the way to breakfast.

The Gemini tribe is ruled by Mercury, the mythological god known as the messenger. And, like Mercury, most Geminis tend to move, think, and speak quickly. They absorb information like little sponges. Tell a Gemini child something once and she'll remember it fifty years later. The Moon combination is important with this child. A Moon in earth grounds him; air makes him more intellectual; water brings more intuition; and fire may blow you out of the water.

Even though their nervous energy seems to make them scattered at times, there's a filing cabinet in their restless minds that stores facts, statistics, figures, stories. They're masters of trivia.

These kids generally enjoy travel, even if it's just to the corner drug store. They like the hustle and bustle of daily life, the diversity among people, and they usually have friends from a variety of backgrounds. They're genuinely curious about other people and, depending on which twin is dominant on a given day, they can be good listeners.

Listening is one of the ways a Gemini child learns. But any vehicle will do, particularly if it's related to the intellect and to communication. Books, movies, TV, newspapers, comic books, the back of a cereal box: It's all fair game to a Gemini. One of the best gifts you can give your Gemini child is early exposure to the written word.

The weakest part of a Gemini's body is the lungs. When your twin is stressed, it's likely to show up in respiratory infections—colds, the flu, bronchitis. And that's when your Gemini needs a lot of parental TLC—hugs, watching old TV shows, reading books to each other on a rainy day. That's the stuff your twin will remember when he's got kids of his own.

Son: Despite his rhetoric and willingness to talk, your Gemini son may not offer much insight into what really makes him tick. He excels at assuming roles and often reflects whatever a situation calls for at a given moment. Remember: One of his greatest assets is his adaptability. Put him in unfamiliar terrain and that lightning quick mind instantly assesses the details, then proceeds to do whatever is necessary to adapt.

From a very young age, your Gemini son is affable, outgoing, social. He gravitates toward people and flourishes in a group. It doesn't seem to matter whether the group consists of kids or adults; either way, he has fun. He also has moments, though, when he's perfectly content to play alone, paging through books, showering attention on the household pets, or studying some oddity outside in the yard.

Gemini boys, like their female counterparts, form their opinions early on about themselves and the world in which they live. Their relentless curiosity takes them into countries of the mind where you may not be able to follow. These mental forays can consume them so deeply at times that they don't pay enough attention to their physical surroundings. The Gemini boy suddenly looks up and finds himself in the middle of a busy highway or knee deep in a lake.

One ten-year-old Gemini boy was so intrigued by his father's new computer that he inadvertently deleted files in the operating system, which resulted in the crash of the hard drive. He didn't mean any harm; his curiosity simply drew him deeper and deeper into the computer's programs.

Your Gemini son may lack tact. In his eagerness to *know,* he can be too blunt. He may ask, for instance, why Uncle Todd is bald and may do it in front of Uncle Todd! It's really nothing personal. It's just that restless Gemini intellect trying to fit all the pieces together. If you scold him, he'll grow to resent Uncle Todd. But if you set him straight about etiquette and compassion, the lesson will stick.

When stress hits your Gemini son, it's likely to be manifested in several ways. He may became unbearably moody, withdrawing into himself like a snail into a shell, or he may get "hyper," or he may just get sick.

In the first instance, try to draw him out gently. Get him to talk about what's wrong. *Communicate* with him. In the second instance, let him blow off steam through physical activity. A baseball game. Swimming. Skiing. Then try to talk to him about what's bothering him. In the last instance, make sure he knows you're there for him, supportive and loving.

Daughter: For the most part, she's an enigma. Everything about her puzzles you—her conception, her birth, the patterns of temperament and behavior in her early life. She may sleep through the night from the time she's two days old—or not until she's nearly ready for kindergarten. She's probably an early talker; she desperately needs to communicate. But nothing else is predictable about your Gemini daughter.

As a youngster, she's easily distracted by anything unusual or different. Bold colors, rain shimmering against a rooftop, exotic animals, books, and movies and people that bring her closer to worlds other than the one she knows. This tendency probably extends into her early school years as well. She delves into the topics that interest her and couldn't care less about all the rest of it.

The Gemini mind is often so quick that subtlety and nuance escape it. In practical terms, this means that your Gemini daughter may perceive the broad strokes of a given situation but not understand how the pieces fit together. Explain these small details to her, help her to connect the dots, illustrate the importance of nuance. This applies not only in terms of her schoolwork, but her friendships as well.

As she matures, you may find that your daughter's bluntness embarrasses you. She seems to lack tact or compassion or both. But what you need to understand is that, with your Gemini daughter, these remarks shouldn't be taken personally. She's speaking strictly from the intellect, the left brain. So when you ask her how she likes your new haircut and she replies that you looked better with long hair, don't be offended. You asked her opinion and she gave it.

The popular opinion of Geminis, both males and females, is that they're fickle when it comes to love. This is supposedly connected to the duality of the sign. But your Gemini's capacity for love and the way she expresses it is best encompassed by the signs of her Moon and Venus and their house placements.

Since Geminis tend to live very much in their own heads, exercise grounds them, makes them more aware of their bodies. Encourage your Gemini daughter to participate in sports that require mental strategy or mental discipline and chances are good she'll participate with the same intensity with which she experiences her internal world.

Gemini Stages

Infancy to seven: There are usually several extremes with Geminis at this stage. They either fit the textbook specifications about how an infant and child should sleep, eat, and act, or they don't. And sometimes they seem to fit both extremes. It depends, again, on which twin surfaces on a given day.

From quite early on, though, your Gemini probably is consistently restless and keeping him occupied may tax your creativity. Just remember that Gemini is a mental sign; books, games, and puzzles intrigue him. And in a real pinch, a loyal pet can go a long ways toward mitigating that restlessness.

Seven to fourteen: At any age, boredom can plague a Gemini. But at this stage, when a thrust for independence begins and hormones start to change, boredom can send your Gemini child places you would rather he didn't go. As a parent, make sure that, by the time your Gemini reaches second grade, he has something that is uniquely his—a family newspaper that he writes, an instrument that he plays, an artistic pursuit that he loves. This will mitigate much of the adolescent confusion that accompanies the stage and will make peer pressure less important.

Always remember that, by triggering your Gemini's natural mental curiosity, by engaging his intellect, you're one step ahead of the game.

Fourteen to twenty-one: No two ways about it: this stage can test the patience of a saint. When you tell your Gemini that he can't do something or if you limit him in some way, he wants to know why. It isn't enough for him that you're the adult and therefore in charge.

If your explanation doesn't make sense to him, he'll bug you about it until you explain it to his satisfaction. If you can't convince him you know best, you had better rethink your game plan, reevaluate your goals as a parent, and come up with something that works. Otherwise, these seven years may feel like an exile.

Twenty-one and beyond: At some point, you're bound to hear that Geminis tend to marry more than once or that they're likely to have twins. This kind of conclusion can best be found by an analysis of the entire natal chart. However, one thing is certain about Geminis at this stage: They're seeking intellectual communion in their partners and intellectual satisfaction in their professional lives.

It's vital to your Gemini's fulfillment that he find both.

The Cosmic Gemini

There's no telling where a Gemini may ultimately take cosmic issues. He certainly mulls them over, however, and does his research.

He may, for example, conduct an extensive analysis of the similarities and differences in the world's spiritual beliefs, absorbing every nuance but never incorporating any particular spiritual practice into his life. He may sample various religions and practices before he finds what suits him. He may follow an organized religion or become a shaman or a Wiccan. He may not find any spiritual belief. But the usual pattern for Gemini is that he explores his options.

Thanks to the versatility of the sign, Geminis can live a long time with a contradiction in their core beliefs. But at some point, contradictions may begin to catch up with them. The animal lover, for instance, may find he can no longer stomach meat, so he becomes a vegetarian. The smoker can't reconcile his environmental concerns with his habit, so he quits.

At the heart of such drastic reversals lies your Gemini child's greatest strength: his intellect. It's his filter, the lens through which he perceives and understands the world. It's his vehicle of evolution and transformation.

6

The Cancer Tribe

The Crab ♋

Dates: June 22–July 22
Element: Water
Quality: Cardinal
Ruler: Moon

With this sign, think of hearth and home, domesticity, the need for roots and personal history. These kids are emotional, sensitive, and attuned to their personal environment. They need the emotional support and unconditional love of their families, especially of their mother.

In a group of kids, the Cancer child stands out because of her appearance—a face as round as a full Moon, eyes like liquid. She may be rowdy or quiet within the group, but she generally wants to be *part* of the group, as opposed, for instance, to a Taurus, who generally couldn't care less.

Even though Cancer kids tend to be emotional and sensitive, they may withdraw into themselves when confronted with an issue they don't want to deal with. They then move like the crab that symbolizes their sign, darting to the right or left to avoid a head-on confrontation.

At times like this, even threats won't force them to spill what's bothering them; they'll tell you when they're good and ready. They become like the Moon that governs their sign, silent and mysterious, a mirror that reflects their surroundings.

Your Cancer child is apt to be a homebody. In practical terms, that means you can expect the neighborhood gang to play at *your* house, in *your* yard, trampling your new bed of impatiens. Her home is as important to her now as it will be twenty or thirty years from now. It's her harbor, her refuge, her nest, and she fills it with people and animals and experiences that please her.

It's here, in the embrace of her family, where she first defines what security means to her. As a parent, your most important gift to this child is to make sure that her sense of security is solid. A Moon child who knows such security is free to offer compassion and love to others; an insecure Cancer always tries to fill that early void.

As a water sign, your Cancer child, male or female, feels things deeply. Emotions are her intuitive connection to life. In some Cancers, this intuition proves to be highly developed and may manifest in some type of psychic ability—clairvoyance, precognition, telepathy.

At first, this ability probably concerns her immediate family; but as she matures, it can extend outward until she's able to psychically read complete strangers. It all depends on how secure she feels and has felt from her earliest days.

Cancer children are unusually sympathetic, kind, and compassionate, unless they're hurt. Then they can be vindictive, sharp tongued, and quite selfish. As a parent, you usually don't have to shout or get angry with a Cancer child to make the rules clear. Say it once, say it firmly, and be sure you spell out the consequences if the rules are broken. Once your Cancer child understands the parameters, she usually stays inside of them.

As a cardinal sign, your Cancer child has the same drive and initiative as Aries. But because Cancer is ruled by the Moon, these traits tend to be more subtle.

Son: He's private, often quiet, and observant. He lives in his own world, where he digs into his passions with the tenacity of a crab burrowing into wet sand. The things he knows best are the things he feels; his emotions speak to him and are his vehicle for navigating his experiences. He can enter a room, for instance, and immediately sense the emotional nuances; if something is wrong, he feels it.

Your Cancer son learns and experiences at his own pace. He can't be forced to rush into something if it doesn't feel right to him. At a carnival, he's the kid who walks around for awhile, observing the rides, mulling them over, before he decides which one to try out first. At the beach, while the rest of the kids gallop toward the water, your Cancer son lags behind, digging his feet into the warm sand, glancing around at people on the beach, acutely aware of the smell of the air. He heads for the water only when he has fully absorbed his surroundings. He doesn't act this way out of fear; he's simply more cautious than those under other cardinal signs.

Cancer boys, like their female counterparts, are sometimes so sensitive their feelings are easily hurt. This is particularly true when they're quite young, before they've learned not to take everything so personally. At times like this, they need to work through the emotion and release it. If the emotional release is stymied or the emotion itself is shoved underground, health problems could be caused later on. This is also true of female Cancers, but the release can be more difficult for a male simply because of cultural biases.

Cancer males may suffer feelings of inferiority and a lack of confidence if their early relationships with their family are emotionally detached or rift with tension. They benefit from positive reinforcement.

A natural assumption about Cancers, males and females, is that they will have traditional domestic lives as adults because of their need for roots. But Cancer's usual characteristic can manifest in any number of ways. Your son, for instance, may satisfy his yearning for a home by living out of his van and house-sitting for other people.

Daughter: As a youngster, she is probably the proverbial good kid, quiet and respectful in school, attentive and respectful out of school. She has her little group of neighborhood friends, her pets, her *things*. She can be quite possessive about everything having to do with her home and private world. She may not readily share her toys with playmates and can be quite fussy about the placement of objects in her room. She may have a deep attachment to some of her personal belongings—a favorite stuffed animal, a favorite doll.

Your Cancer daughter is more of a homebody than is a Cancer son. She may not like spending the night elsewhere and, even if she thinks she can do it, you may get a call in the middle of the night. One Cancer child that my daughter plays with always has the best intentions about spending the night. Invariably, though, she begins to feel sick sometime after dinner and usually heads home before ten.

She can be quite moody. Even though she isn't as close-mouthed as her Cancer brother, you should encourage her to talk about what she feels. Because of the influence of the Moon that rules Cancer, your daughter's moodiness may follow her throughout her life. Regular exercise and good nutrition can go a long way toward mitigating the moodiness and any tendency she may have for menstrual irregularity and female problems later on.

If your Cancer daughter isn't a mother herself, her nurturing qualities find expression in other areas of her life. She might care for animals or the homeless. She might teach school. Maybe she's a doctor. The bottom line is that she must have emotional security to be able to extend herself to others.

Cancer Stages

Infancy to seven: Overall, the temperament at this age tends to be pleasant. Even before verbal skills are developed, it's unlikely that a Cancer child experiences the frustration of an Aries or a Gemini. But if she does, the sound of water and soft music calm her. Her room should feel like a cocoon to her, a safe, secure niche from which she can venture out into the world when she learns to crawl and, later, to walk.

If exposed to books at a young age, Cancers can be early readers. This quiet, personal pleasure suits their temperaments. They tend to enjoy stories, and it doesn't matter whether these are stories they hear, read, or make up.

Once Cancers hit school age, they gravitate toward small groups of friends that reflect their emotional needs and concerns. They get along well with Pisces, but Scorpio's intensity may overwhelm them. Earth signs—Taurus, Virgo, and Capricorn—complement them and they probably get along well with Aries and Libra, fellow cardinal signs.

Seven to fourteen: Cancer children often come into their own during this period. They have a clearer sense of how they fit into the larger world and, up until the age of twelve or so, are better able to cope with their emotional swings and sensitivity. Then, along comes puberty, a period of emotional extremes for a Cancer. The child either dives within and attempts to order her world through some type of artistic expression or her personality becomes more externalized, more tribal in terms of friends. The ideal, naturally, is a balance.

If you nurture any talents your child has before she hits the teen years, she is better able to cope with her emotional extremes. She has something to fall back on that is uniquely her own.

Fourteen to twenty-one: Individuation for this sign occurs through emotions. As your Cancer child enters this period of her life, emotional nuances take on new meaning. She learns to read small details about other people through body language and by reading between the lines. She grows more adept at understanding her own emotional needs and conflicts.

By the time she's preparing for college, she usually has a clear sense of who she is, but she may not yet understand how she fits into the world outside her immediate environment. Her tribal affiliations have begun to change. Her new roots may lie with a particular group of friends or an organization or cause that reflects her beliefs.

Twenty-one and beyond: By now, your Cancer has been in or is involved in a committed relationship. She's testing the parameters of who she is and what she wants in intimate relationships with others. While a Taurus is seduced by greener pastures, a Cancer usually realizes that the greenest pastures are those that exist in this moment.

Even if her outward independence is fully established by now, she still feels the tug of home, parents, childhood. She may even have several childhood objects that she keeps for nostalgic reasons, because they remind her of her roots. It's through the past that the Cancer child defines her present and her future.

Since the fourth house is Cancer's natural home, these individuals find their greatest fulfillment in any profession where their nurturing qualities shine. Cancers are also successful in real estate and any business dealing with foods, gardening, and the sea.

Cosmic Cancer

The cosmic connection for a Cancer occurs through the tribal mind. It begins in childhood with her family and gradually expands to include her immediate community, the society in which she lives, and quite often her country as well. It is through this tribal association that she expresses her spirituality.

She's the type who may start a food drive for the homeless in her community. She may be an animal rights activist or be involved in political issues that directly reflect her nurturing qualities.

Cancer pursues her spiritual beliefs wholeheartedly, regardless of what they are. If she attends a particular church, then she's as dedicated to it as she is to her family. If her beliefs are nontraditional, then she explores them in depth, through books, workshops, seminars. Her natural intuition flourishes and deepens once she realizes that her emotions are her conduit to spiritual evolution and transformation.

7

The Leo Tribe

The Lion ♌

Dates: July 23–August 22
Element: Fire
Quality: Fixed
Ruler: Sun

Leo kids enjoy being in the spotlight, right smack on center stage. They're actors, comedians, dancers, singers, whatever it takes to grab attention. It's part of what makes a Leo child easy to spot in a crowd of kids.

He's the one around whom the others congregate. He's at the heart of the action. In fact, he may be directing the action, unless an Aries is present, and then the two of them will have to fight it out. They could come to literal blows, but probably won't. Aries, after all, is more interested in competition and Leo, despite his fierce roar, wants to be liked and appreciated.

The Sun, as ruler of this sign, confers optimism and innate cheerfulness, a certain egotism and bravado, and true courage. An adage for Leos might read a little like the original Star Trek slogan: ". . . boldly goes where no man has gone before. . . ." As corny as it sounds, it fits the sign.

As a fixed sign, Leo children usually know what they want, and one of the things they want very much is acknowledgment by others. For this approval, for this recognition as a sovereign being, a Leo child may go to great lengths. One Leo I knew, a twelve-year-old girl, was so afraid of other people's disapproval that her usual response to the simplest questions (Would you like a peanut butter sandwich, Amanda? Would you like to go to the zoo?) was a shrug, usually followed by, "I don't know." Or, even worse, "I don't care."

As a parent, you can coerce your Leo into doing what you want him to do simply by withholding your approval. But that's a powerful and detrimental weapon to use against a Leo child. In his huge and generous heart, he knows his success in life is best found in being true to himself.

A Leo child's self-expression is vital to his fulfillment. He's a natural actor and dramatic training bolsters his confidence and self-respect. Regardless of what his talent proves to be, it should be nurtured and applauded at a young age, so that he carries the confidence with him as he matures.

He's a persistent child, this one, and once he sets his sights on something, he goes after it with everything he has. In this sense, his nature is as fixed and relentless as Taurus. But he lacks Taurus's slow plodding; Leo's drive is dashing and dramatic, and sometimes arrogant and selfish. And when he's in that mode, he mows you down if you get in his way.

Son: He's opinionated. At times it may seem that he was born that way. But unlike Scorpio, another fixed sign, your Leo son isn't dogmatic about his opinions. He doesn't bludgeon you or anyone else with his beliefs in an attempt to convert you. In fact, he's so cheerful about his opinions you can't hold anything against him.

Leo boys enjoy spectator sports—football, baseball, hockey, anything that draws crowds. Actually, the sport itself isn't as important as the crowds. Leos play to the crowds. It's part of what makes them natural actors and entertainers. They bask in the attention.

As a youngster, your Leo son may organize elaborate theatrical productions with the other kids on the block—puppet shows, plays, dances. He'll organize rehearsals, sell tickets, and he'll direct, produce, and star in the production. If he has brothers or sisters, he gets them involved, too.

Your Leo son is always generous with his siblings. He genuinely likes children and the more the merrier. This holds over into his adult life, when he either works with children in some capacity or has children of his own. If it's the latter, then he considers his family his kingdom, the place where he rules absolutely. This can get tedious for the people he thinks he rules. Some of his greatest challenges may revolve around what children ultimately teach him about himself.

A Leo son, after all, really does want to be noble. He truly cares about what others think of him and wants to do the right thing so others will hold him in high esteem. It's through this need that he evolves and reinvents himself.

Leo boys, like their Leo sisters, have a soft spot in their hearts for animals. Maybe it's the lion in them; maybe it's just that animals love you no matter what. Your son may not limit his love of animals to just domestic pets. He likes exotic animals as well, the bigger the better. Given his preference, he tends to injured wildlife and strays that he encounters. His heart is large enough to feel concern for the wounded of any species.

As a parent, the greatest service you can perform for your Leo son is to acknowledge and appreciate him at a young age. Applaud his efforts, whatever they are. This foundation allows him to move through his life relatively unencumbered by emotional baggage.

Daughter: She has hair like Jackie Onassis's, thick and stunning, the kind of hair other females probably envy. And like Onassis, a classic Leo, she may find herself in the spotlight even if she hasn't sought it.

Her disposition is basically optimistic and cheerful. She plays hard, but she works just as hard to attain whatever she wants. Her magnetic personality makes her popular and attractive to the opposite sex. This may stir a bit of jealousy in other girls her own age. Your Leo daughter, however, manages to make friends with the very people who envy her.

Your Leo daughter, like her male counterpart, may have quite a temper. But once she explodes, that's it. She doesn't hold grudges and usually doesn't nurse old wounds. There's too much else to do.

Her temper shows when she's stressed out, which is often related to other people's opinion of her or to an accretion of small details in her life that have slipped through the cracks. If she doesn't blow up, her natural bravado and courage carry her forward even under trying circumstances.

Honesty is a hallmark of this sign. But both male and female Leos can be braggarts, especially when they're trying to impress someone. At best, this tendency is merely irritating; at worst, it drives friends away. Leo daughters can be just as bossy, stubborn, and egotistical as their male counterparts. It behooves them to periodically evaluate who they are.

Leo females dislike being subordinate just as deeply as their male counterparts do. This is true whether it's in a job or at home, in the family hierarchy. If you're too rigid with her, she rebels in a major way. The best approach is to be firm but flexible and make her feel that she's part of a democratic process. In the workplace, your Leo daughter aims for the top and probably gets there eventually simply because she's so persistent and ambitious.

Leo rules the heart, which is the location of the heart chakra. The heart chakra is about love, giving and receiving it, and Leos excel at both. Even at a young age, however, Leo females may love unwisely and too readily.

Leo Stages

Infancy to seven: As a fire sign, Leo comes into life with a need for action. Since action is stymied in infancy by obvious physical limitations, a Leo baby can be incredibly fussy. If he learns that loud crying in the middle of the night brings mom or dad loping into his room, he'll cry even louder the next night. If he learns that a temper tantrum results in his being picked up so that he can see his immediate surroundings better, his tantrums will get worse.

As soon as Leo learns to crawl and then walk, much of his frustration eases. He's into everything—not with the reckless fearlessness of his fire cousin, Aries, but with the bold courage that marks a true Leo. This courage sees him into his early school years, when he suffers little if any separation anxiety from his parents. He's eager to explore, to learn, to move forward. There's simply no time to look back.

Seven to fourteen: Leo's boldness can be troublesome to teachers and other authority figures. These kids don't believe everything they hear even when it comes from someone who is supposed to have all the answers. They ask a lot of questions and expect illuminating responses.

Although Leos aren't particularly introspective, they need consistency in their evolving world view. When something doesn't fit, they need to know why and they will go looking for the answer. If that search takes your Leo places where you, as a parent, can't follow, you simply have to trust that his heart will guide him to where he finds his greatest fulfillment. Anything less than that is just window dressing.

Fourteen to twenty-one: This period of individuation is when Leo rediscovers what he knew as a child, that he can change his life through his own intent, desires, and initiative. Once he understands this, it becomes easier for him to manifest what he needs.

The process itself may take Leo through a variety of painful experiences, but he rarely suffers very long. His essential nature is simply too optimistic and buoyant for self-pity.

Twenty-one and beyond: Leo really begins to shine once he's completely on his own. By now, his egocentric tendencies are tempered somewhat. He begins to realize that his capacity for love and compassion are his greatest vehicle to self-fulfillment.

He probably has found his professional niche, and even if he hasn't made it to the top yet, he feels fairly confident that he will. For Leos in the arts, this is the critical period when they put what they know to work for them. They hone their skills and talents. They hunger for the reality of whatever their vision happens to be.

Since the fifth house is the natural home for Leos, their lives are geared toward creativity, children, pleasurable pursuits of all shapes and sizes. If their creativity makes them money and never ceases to be fun, they excel at it.

Cosmic Leos

A Leo's date with the cosmos unfolds dramatically, with flamboyance and style. His need for creative expression, whatever form it takes, is the fuel that propels him to achieve. Action and initiative are the vehicles that get him to where he wants to go.

If Leo's ego plows toward his goals with all the subtlety of a semi, he won't get anywhere fast. Something unexpected trips him up. He backslides. He stagnates. Fortunately, Leo despises stagnation. It's the place where he dies a piece at a time. It gets him moving again and he does so with a renewed sense of what is important and how he can attain it without compromising the best of who he is.

8

The Virgo Tribe

The Virgin ♍

Dates: August 23–September 22
Element: Earth
Quality: Mutable
Ruler: Mercury

Members of this tribe are tireless workers. Give them a task that stimulates or interests them, and they are consumed by it. They seem to instinctively know how to create order out of chaos.

In a crowd of kids, Virgos tend to blend in. They're quiet or boisterous, flamboyant or invisible, whatever is required. That's their mutable quality kicking in, which allows them, like their Gemini cousins, to adapt readily to most group situations. But on a deeper, personal level, they're seeking an idealized version of whatever they tackle.

Virgo, like Gemini, is ruled by Mercury. This makes them good communicators. But because they tend to be so picky, so obsessed with perfection, they often get mired in their own best intentions. Instead of saying what they mean, they say what they *think* they mean and that isn't always quite right, either.

If you have three Virgo kids in a room and ask them what color the sky is, all three will tell you the sky is blue, of course. But as soon as you leave the room, they'll begin to doubt the answer. Exactly what shade is the blue? Like the sea? Like a sapphire? Like a bird? They'll go on like this until some other topic seizes their attention and then later, in the privacy of their own heads, they'll mull over this puzzle about the blue sky until they arrive at an answer that suits them.

This relentless striving is precisely what motivates Virgo. My daughter, a double Virgo, with both Sun and Moon in the sign, spends hours perfecting her miniature drawings and writing stories about these tiny beings in their tiny worlds. The people in these stories reflect real life in all its vagaries—divorce, death, struggle—but always, an *ideal* version of life is found in their lives as well.

Her characters may live on a farm, surrounded by animals. They may live in a castle or in a kingdom where the subjects always love and revere the princess. They invariably possess some individual passion that propels them forward.

Virgos are supposed to be neat freaks. This may be true for some of them. The majority I've known, though, are more concerned about order, specifically order in their work. For Virgo kids, work encompasses school and hobbies. They take great pride in their work and are usually careful and precise about details. They are also very critical of themselves when their work doesn't meet their high standards. They can also be critical of others for the same reasons.

Virgo kids are often so tough on themselves that it can affect them physically. It's as if their bodies absorb the brunt of their striving for perfection. For this reason, they benefit from physical exercise that allows them to vent energy that might otherwise be turned inward. They also benefit from sound nutrition and health awareness, a topic that typically interests them as they get older.

Your best gift to your Virgo child is to teach her at a young age that perfection isn't a prerequisite for your love.

Son: From the time he's quite young, he finds fault with people he cares about. These faults usually reflect facets of himself that he doesn't like, that he chips away at with his sharp and critical intellect. This fault finding eventually extends to the friends in his life and, later, to girlfriends. In this sense, he can be difficult to live with. But once he realizes that these unsolicited critiques of other people don't endear him to anyone, his natural charm has a chance to shine.

Virgos seek mental stimulation in the same way that Geminis do. This can make them early and avid readers as well as excellent students. The males, like the females, usually have good memories, especially for small details, and excel at puzzles and games. Word games may be of particular interest to your son—Scrabble, computer word games, Spill & Spell. He may enjoy working with his hands in pursuits like carpentry, sculpture, even building computers. Encourage him in this type of artistic expression. It bridges his restless mentality with a physical outlet and will be something he carries with him throughout his life.

Daughter: She's like the little girl in the nursery rhyme. When she's good, she's very good. When she's bad, you would rather be elsewhere.

Her bad moments, however, aren't the result of maliciousness or a blatant disregard for rules. It just goes back to that Virgo quest for perfection. Whatever she takes on, she wants to do it perfectly the first time. When she realizes the project may need another pass, her frustration erupts into tears or anger or both. As she matures, the tears disappear and the anger transmutes into frustration.

Even at a young age, Virgos enjoy helping other people. It's part of the "service" orientation associated with the sign. Your daughter may be terrific with kids less fortunate than she is. Or she may feel a particular kinship with her grandparents. Her compassion doesn't discriminate. She feels just as deeply for the homeless person on the corner as she does for her friend whose parents are getting divorced. This compassion is often directed toward animals as well and may result in strays calling your place home.

Virgos are often depicted as such tireless workers that it sounds as if they lack humor and the capacity for fun. This simply isn't true. The Mercury influence gives both males and females a sharp wit and their capacity for fun is as deep as that of any other sign. Your daughter may even be mischievous at times, especially when she's younger. It's just her way of telling you how special you are in her life.

Virgo Stages

Infancy to seven: At this stage, Virgos have some of the same frustrations at Geminis. As infants, they need stimulation in their immediate environment—bright colors and interesting shapes, soft music, the purring of a contented cat.

Some Virgos are fussy sleepers, who refuse to sleep through the night until they're old enough to walk and wear themselves out. This type may suffers from colic. My daughter fell into this category. But other Virgo infants sleep through the night almost from the day they're brought home.

Both types—and their parents—find that life is easier when they begin to crawl and walk. By the time your Virgo is able to articulate what she feels and thinks, she may go through periods when she talks nonstop. Her questions aren't casual and shouldn't be shrugged off with canned responses. Virgo orders her internal world with the same precision that she brings to her external life. She needs your clarity and honesty to do that.

Seven to fourteen: This period is when she is most likely to be hardest on herself. She is learning to define who she is through social interactions with friends, schoolmates, and the various authority figures in her life.

She may feel that she's not good enough in some way—not as smart, attractive, or popular as other kids. These kinds of issues, of course, are endemic to most of us during our individuation process. But to a Virgo, these feelings can have long-lasting affects. During this seven-year period, do whatever you have to do to maintain an honest and open relationship with your Virgo.

Fourteen to twenty-one: I've yet to meet a parent who claims that teens are easy to deal with. But a Virgo at this stage is likely to be less troublesome than, say, a Scorpio or an Aries. Virgo rebels through the mind, usually the critical, nitpicky, and logical left brain.

This is the period when Virgo demands, "Prove it to me." Prove that you're wiser, Mom. Prove that you've got it together, Dad. Prove that what you're saying is the right path, the right answer. Yes, this period can be incredibly trying. But if you've maintained an open and honest relationship with your Virgo up to this point, then she knows she can come home when she hurts. And that goes a long way toward mitigating the unpleasantness.

Twenty-one and beyond: Once Virgo finds the work that pleases and fulfills her, her life stabilizes. She may still be hard on herself, expecting perfection in whatever she tackles. But she also has learned that she is, after all, only human and that a balanced approach to work will take her where she wants to go much faster.

Virgo subjects her romantic relationships to the same scrutiny that she brings to other facets of her life. Problems develop when her partner fails to live up to her expectations. This can cause her repeated heartbreak. Once she realizes that none of us is here to live up to anyone else's expectations, her love life unfolds much more smoothly.

Virgo's capacity for careful work and dedication is apparent in her relationship with her children—flesh and blood offspring as well as artistic creations.

Cosmic Virgo

As an earth sign, Virgo's approach to spirituality is apt to be practical. But pragmatism doesn't prevent her from delving into the invisible, more mystical realms. As a child, she is naturally open to them and unconsciously seeks a holistic framework for the left-brain concerns that often rule her life.

As Virgo learns to use her critical thinking to explore spiritual issues, inner doorways open. She discovers that intuition can be developed, relied upon, and used to enhance the quality of her life. By recognizing intuition as a viable tool, her confidence blooms, her path expands, and she truly begins to shine.

As a parent, one of the ways you can encourage your Virgo to develop her intuition is through simple games. My daughter and I have played a color game since she was old enough to identify colors,. In this game, one of us acts as the sender and the other is the receiver. The sender thinks of a color and tries to communicate it the receiver. This works best when we're both relaxed, but we've even played it in the car with astonishing results. Intuition is like a muscle; the more you exercise it, the stronger it grows.

By learning to recognize and act on hunches, your Virgo child's inner and outer worlds flow into alignment.

9

The Libra Tribe

The Scales ♎

Dates: September 23–October 22
Element: Air
Quality: Cardinal
Ruler: Venus

The children of this tribe are the true peace lovers of the zodiac. They're cooperative, like harmony, and find violence completely repulsive.

In a group of children, a Libra isn't easy to pick out unless a disagreement or a fight is in progress. Then Libra is at the forefront, trying to negotiate a treaty. This is something they do very well because they understand both sides of an issue. It makes them excellent strategists, too, which is how they prefer to win their battles in life.

As a cardinal cousin of Aries, Libra initiates action, but in a far more subtle way. Instead of plowing ahead with reckless fearlessness, Libra negotiates, arbitrates, and suggests, seeding ideas so skillfully that his opponent plays right into the strategy. Even young children display this talent, perhaps by keeping peace in their families, among their friends, or in their neighborhoods.

Venus-ruled Libra has a finely developed aesthetic sense that hungers for art, music, good books. Take a Libra child to a museum, a bookstore, or a record store, and he's content to wander around for hours, absorbing and sampling everything. Libra children like pleasant, tasteful surroundings, nice clothes, anything that is refined and gracious.

As social creatures, Libra children define themselves through their relationships. They need friends and companionship and work well as part of a team. In fact, they would rather work with other people than work alone. Their friends, like their possessions, reflect their love of refinement. Even very young Libra kids dislike vulgarity and a lack of good taste in others.

One of my daughter's Libra friends refuses to go to the community pool in our neighborhood whenever a particular group of vulgar boys is there. She simply removes herself from any situation that holds the potential for vulgarity or dissension.

When a Libra is an only child, you can expect his friends to congregate in your home, particularly if you've made his room an aesthetically pleasing sanctuary. When he doesn't have his friends around, puzzles, games, and books keep him occupied. He probably likes chess and word games, too.

Most Libras are so polite and softly spoken that other people consider them pushovers. But this simply isn't so. Libras fight if a principle is at stake, and although it takes a lot to anger them, get out of their way when they blow.

As your Libra son or daughter matures, romance is highlighted. Libras are romantics in the truest sense of the word—candlelight dinners, walks on a moonlit beach, soft music. All the clichés for romance apply to them. They need a partner and most marry at least once in their lives.

Son: As a youngster, he's a breeze. He's so easy, in fact, that you're the envy of every other parent on the block. He wants to please you and to cooperate with whatever your household agenda is.

Even though he's generally quite agreeable, his mood can suddenly change. It's nothing as overt as you would see with his cardinal cousins. You won't see an explosion, as you would with an Aries, or an emotional withdrawal, as you would with Capricorn. Instead, he makes subtle suggestions. He slides into his negotiating mode and turns on the charm. If the charm doesn't work, he debates the issue until he wins you over or you end the discussion.

If your Libra son has artistic talent, by all means nurture it. Many Libras have an excellent ear for music and enjoy dance. Even if they don't have those talents themselves, they appreciate the aesthetics. Whatever his talents, encourage him to join a group of like mind—a band, for instance, or a dance troupe.

Libra males are easily seduced by refinement and a graciousness in manners. They may be so seduced that they don't peer beyond the surface to find unpleasantness in another person.

While I'm not suggesting that anyone should look for shortcomings in people they love, your Libra can spare himself considerable heartache by not jumping into relationships. Advise him to take things slowly, a step at a time. He may not listen to you, but at some point he'll learn the lesson on his own.

Daughter: She's pretty. She's diplomatic. She's fair. Like her Libra brother, she instinctively grasps the duality of any issue, and because of it, she vacillates at times about making decisions. It isn't just important decisions, either. It can be something as simple as whether she should play with Annie down the street or go shopping with you.

Your Libra daughter loves pretty things—attractive clothes, furnishings, dolls, even animals. Forget the common tabby; give her a Persian cat any day. The animal shelter mutt doesn't go with the decor in her room, but the golden retriever does.

Although she usually doesn't judge people solely by how they look, appearances certainly play a major role in her choice of friends. But for a Libra, appearance goes well beyond a person's physical characteristics; it has to do with style. With panache.

One of the most memorable Libra students I had, who was all of thirteen at the time, surrounded herself with friends who weren't particularly attractive or scholarly or even well dressed. But they all had a special artistic talent. By associating with them, she was making a statement about herself. In the adult world, she would be considered a "patron of the arts."

Your Libra daughter may be fickle when it comes to love. In her teen years, you probably dismiss this as hormones and youth. But later on, when she's trying to juggle two or more relationships simultaneously, hormones and youth are beside the point. It seems to you that she's just indecisive.

In reality it's not that way at all. In affairs of the heart, her innate sense of fairness and deep compassion make her incapable of hurting anyone.

Libras of both genders should be encouraged to find their individual passions rather than falling into the habit of supporting other people's passions and artistic endeavors. The tendency with this sign is for the latter, which may lead to frustration later in life.

Libra Stages

Infancy to seven: As an infant, he's a dream. He sleeps through the night from a very young age, coos with contentment over the smallest things, and seems happiest when surrounded by other people.

Libra takes to school like the proverbial duck to water. It's not school, per se, that entrances him, but the contact with other people his own age. From kindergarten through second grade, he blossoms socially, redefining himself through his new friendships.

Seven to fourteen: During this period of individuation, Libra clarifies his needs in terms of his relationships with others. He may not go along with the household agenda quite as cheerfully as he once did. His suggestions and strategies may be convoluted or less subtle. His hobbies and interests are likely to change during this period and so will some of his friendships. Certain people will drop out of his life and new people will enter.

During this period, your Libra is likely to be more talkative and open about what he feels. Through your support, he's able to bridge the gaps in his experiential knowledge.

Fourteen to twenty-one: Rebellion for a Libra isn't as overt as it can be for other signs. It's likely to occur through his relationships. Maybe he starts hanging out with the wrong group or falls head over heels for a girl with a pierced nose. You may not like what's going on, but if you're dogmatic about it you'll only drive a wedge between the two of you. Offer advice and give your opinion when asked. Otherwise, keep your own counsel and remember that this, too, shall pass.

Twenty-one and beyond: Your Libra may be seriously committed or married by now. If not, he may be married to some artistic endeavor and most certainly has a wide circle of friends and acquaintances who support his interests and passions. He probably enjoys opera, ballet, and museums and may live in an area that offers an abundance of cultural activities.

If he's working in a job that he dislikes, he won't be there long. This is often a period when an unsettled Libra goes from job to job, seeking an elusive fulfillment in his external world. But Libra is rarely nomadic or alone for long. He prospers through marriage and committed relationships and, one way or another, settles in for the long haul.

Cosmic Libra

Some Libras take to organized religion. They enjoy the beauty of the ritual and tradition and like the social interaction that grows from a common belief system. Other Libras couldn't care less about religion and seek spiritual fulfillment through nontraditional venues. They may infuse their marriage or their art with spirituality.

Sometimes, an especially intense relationship or event forces Libra to examine his deepest beliefs and he subsequently develops an interest in metaphysics. His focus initially may be past-life connections between himself and a partner.

As a cardinal air sign, Libra's approach to spiritual issues is apt to be intellectual, motivated by his questions about his relationships. At first, he culls information through books and the Web, then he ventures out into the social arena, where he attends workshops and lectures and talks with other people who hold similar beliefs. He weighs and evaluates everything, always aware of all sides of the issue. Then he makes up his own mind. Libra rarely tries to push his spiritual beliefs on anyone else. He hopes, of course, that his partner shares his beliefs, but if not, that's okay, too.

Libra can be as intuitive as any other sign. But his intuition is likely to develop quite strongly in regard to the people he loves. So if your Libra one day blurts that his little sister is in trouble at preschool, don't laugh it off.

10

The Scorpio Tribe

The Scorpion ♏

Dates: October 23–November 21
Element: Water
Quality: Fixed
Ruler: Pluto

Intense. Passionate. Fearless. These are some of the adjectives that apply to a Scorpio child, but they barely scrape the surface. These kids are complex, mysterious, and often a complete enigma even to the people who love and know them best.

In a group of peers, Scorpio is the solitary brooder, the one with the soulful eyes who appears to be lost in her own thoughts. She actually is observing everything around her quite carefully and has learned to do this without seeming to do so. If she joins in the activities at all, it is with a few close friends who are as loyal to her as she is to them.

As a fixed water sign, Scorpio's emotions are her primary vehicles for experiencing and exploring the world. But unlike her water cousins, Cancer and Pisces, her emotions possess a driving intensity that often overpowers kids her own age.

As her parent, you undoubtedly find this quality over-whelming at times, too. The best way to deal with it is to allow her to vent the full range of her emotions, whatever they are, and to encourage her to talk about what she feels. If her powerful emotions aren't permitted a venue for expression, they turn inward and may cause health problems farther down the road.

These outbursts are rarely temper tantrums; Scorpio doesn't blow unless she's pushed to the absolute edge. She simply needs help understanding why she feels so deeply about so many things when other kids her age go on their merry way.

Many Scorpio children discover emotional release and fulfillment through the arts—music, painting, writing. Some have so much talent that they don't need formal lessons, for example, to play an instrument or draw or paint. One eighteen-year-old Scorpio I knew had never taken a piano lesson in his life, couldn't read a note of music, but could play virtually anything you requested. He had an ear for music.

Since Scorpio is a naturally intuitive sign, these kids enjoy games in which they need to use their intuition. If the talent isn't squashed by religious beliefs or superstitions, it can easily develop into an impressive psychic ability.

Pluto, as ruler of the sign, gives Scorpios a deep interest in *big* questions that demand honest, thoughtful questions. Where did I come from? Where will I go when I die? Did I have a life before this one? Who was I in that other life? Who were you? Life with a Scorpio child is many things, but it's never boring. As astrologer Grant Lewi wrote: "Scorpio is the only sign that never produces a shallow person."

When I taught seventh grade Spanish, I used to reserve one class a week for experiments and discussions about psychic phenomena. I had several Scorpios in my class who weren't the least bit interested in Spanish but who really woke up when we talked about psi. It was as if they had lived their first twelve or thirteen years with an entire portion of their personalities split off from ordinary life and now, suddenly, had an opportunity to talk about some of their experiences.

These kids excelled at everything we tried—reading auras, recollection of their dreams, telepathy. One Scorpio boy began to have out-of-body experiences (OBEs) that he told his parents about. His mother, who equated OBEs with an aberrant mental condition, expressed her concern to me. I tried to explain it to her but realized that she simply wasn't going to get it. So I stopped talking about OBEs in class and the boy and I confined our discussions to after-school hours.

Son: He's as opinionated as his Leo cousin. But you won't know about it unless it involves what he perceives as a violation of one of his principles. Then you won't hear the end of it. He talks circles around you at times like this, wanting to know why you believe what you do and why you did what you did and how this compares to what he believes and does.

Scorpios of either gender rarely have many friends. But the ones they have are probably friends for life. They are extremely loyal to people they love unless they are crossed. Then watch out. The scorpion's sting can be brutal and the slight is never forgotten.

Your Scorpio son is as serious about his love life as he is about his spiritual ideals and his relentless drive to achieve his dream, whatever it might be. When he loves he does so profoundly, intensely, to the utter depths of his soul. If the relationship falls apart, he is wounded just as deeply. The good news is that he won't try a rerun with the person who hurt him. Once the tie is broken, it's broken for good.

As he matures, his sexuality is often as intense and powerful as the other facets of his personality. This is also true for the females of the sign, and in either case, control may become an issue. If your son, however, is allowed to own his power as a child, then he won't need to control other people as an adult.

Daughter: If you're hoping for a daughter who is all sweetness and light, this girl isn't it. From the first breath she draws, you know there's something very different about her.

When she cries, she cries as if her heart is broken. When she smiles and coos, lights come on in the world. Even as an infant, the power she emanates rises from someplace so deep you know you'll never be able to follow her there unless you, too, are a Scorpio.

The females of this sign are more enigmatic than the males. Even as youngsters, they have a certain look about them that hints at knowledge so ancient it can't be articulated. It can only be felt. It's like the current you feel when you're waist deep in the ocean, a kind of rippling, mounting pressure. Except it's not coming from the ocean; it's coming from your daughter.

All Scorpios, of course, aren't mystical or filled with ancient knowledge. Some are sexually obsessed, like the woman in *Fatal Attraction*. Some are criminals. Blame Pluto for that. But because Pluto rules this sign, all Scorpios have the capacity for spiritual transformation through a plundering of the soul's darker terrains. If they aren't made aware of this as children, then they will find it out on their own as they mature. Life, however, is much easier for this child if she grows up with the knowledge of her own power.

Once you accept the fact that your daughter isn't like other kids you may know, you're able to embrace the wisdom she brings into your life.

Scorpio Stages

Infancy to seven: Long before your Scorpio starts school, you have some inkling of the energy this child has brought into life with her. People of all ages are drawn to her, from doting grandmothers to young kids. Her charisma is apparent right from the start.

In school, the friendships she forges are neither frivolous nor quick. She may enjoy art and music more than she likes the three Rs, but she's a conscientious student. Even at this young age, Scorpios take life seriously. You should encourage her to lighten up on herself. The sooner she learns how to do that, the easier her life will be.

Seven to fourteen: Scorpio's thrust for independence during this stage usually happens on a deep, unconscious level. For some kids, this involves nightmares, dreams of flying, perhaps even a confession that she has had an imaginary playmate for years. She may become incredibly stubborn. Her questions revolve around weighty issues—life after death, sex, the soul. For some Scorpios, experimentation with sex is a distinct possibility, especially at the onset of puberty.

Rules are needed and parameters should be redefined during this stage. But if you impose stringent restrictions and limitations on your Scorpio, expect rebellion. Strive for honest communication and do things as a family. Travel. Go camping. Go to an amusement park. Do whatever you can to make sure your Scorpio knows she is loved.

Fourteen to twenty-one: This stage may get worse before it gets better. Most parents may feel this way about teenagers, but one father with a Scorpio son put it this way: "At times, I felt like abdicating from the family. Other times, I knew I'd been blessed." Either/or, black or white: that's how it invariably is with a Scorpio child. And this stage usually underscores the extremes.

If your Scorpio child has a special interest, hobby, or talent, all that Scorpio passion can then be channeled into more constructive venues and much of the excess of this stage is mitigated.

Twenty-one and beyond: Your Scorpio child is now pretty much on her own and is seriously committed or married. If she's one of those Scorpios who has always known what she wants to do with her life, then she probably is embarked on her path. If she has had only vague goals, then she may be floundering, moving from one job and relationship to another. Either way, though, she conducts her life with utter seriousness.

Cosmic Scorpio

In less evolved Scorpios, spirituality may be a moot issue. The emphasis in life falls on the sign's darker side, sex, drugs, a fast, noir life with a morbid edge to it. This can be said of any Sun sign, but it seems to be especially true of Scorpios.

In an evolved Scorpio soul, spirituality is the primary focus. Its manifestation varies, of course, but these people are usually deeply intuitive and concerned with unraveling profound mysteries. Their capacity for personal transformation is tremendous.

11

The Sagittarius Tribe

Centaur-Archer ♐

Dates: November 22–December 21
Element: Fire
Quality: Mutable
Ruler: Jupiter

These children value freedom above all else. They're imbued with energy, are direct and honest in their dealings with others, and enjoy people from every walk of life.

In a group of kids, Sagittarius is the one having the most fun. His exuberance infects everyone around him and he's always in great demand for group games and activities. All this fun comes to an abrupt halt, however, if someone attempts to make Sag compromise his integrity or tries to impose unreasonable restrictions on him.

As a mutable fire sign, Sagittarius is as restless and impatient as Gemini, his polar opposite in the zodiac. He is often in such a hurry that he overlooks details or shrugs them off as unimportant. He's more concerned with the large picture and prefers to leave the details to other people.

Most of these kids are great travelers and enjoy exposure to foreign countries and cultures. This is right in line with the areas ruled by the ninth house, Sagittarius's natural home. They also like expounding on what they know and believe. This tendency can get tedious for a parent; Sagittarius sometimes thinks he knows more than he actually does.

Kids born under this sign have a natural affinity for animals. In more highly evolved children, the household pets usually aren't merely pets; they're part of the family. In the less highly evolved types, household pets are considered important only within the hierarchy. In either case, animals can act as healers for a Sagittarian child who is in pain.

The expansive nature of the sign naturally embraces humanitarian causes. This magnanimity is often apparent in young children through concern about the environment, animal and human rights, and spiritual freedom.

When you encounter a Sagittarius child who seems to contradict all this through narrow religious beliefs or racial prejudice, then the parents probably have an overwhelming influence. The good news is that the bias won't endure. Once the child is old enough to form his own opinions about such issues, he breaks free of parental conditioning and forges his own path.

These kids tend to be athletic. Any kind of regular physical activity helps bleed off some of that tremendous energy and calms their restlessness. Because of their social natures, they prefer team sports and many have the physical build and stamina, as well as the ambition, to tackle professional sports.

Sagittarius is ambitious, but not in a conventional sense. He won't compromise his principles or step on anyone else to get ahead. He relies on his own ability and has the self-confidence to get him where he wants to be.

Son: He's a charmer. He knows instinctively what to say or do to turn your insides to mush. "You're the greatest, Mom. You're the best, Dad." And he means every word of it until tomorrow or the next day, when you ask him to clean his room or to do something else that he doesn't feel like doing. Then the charm disappears in a flash, his bluntness cuts deeply, and you're left with a kid who seems merely selfish and self-centered.

Both faces fit Sagittarius, but the characteristics show up differently in males and females of the sign. With a son, the best way to temper his selfishness is to praise his compassion.

When your son is deeply hurt, you may not know about it until he blows up over something unrelated to the incident that hurt him. Then the whole story of what's bothering him comes out piece by painful piece. It's difficult for your Sagittarian son to admit that his life isn't exactly the way he would like it to be. But once he learns it's okay to admit that he, too, is learning to exist in an imperfect world, life becomes infinitely easier for both of you.

Your son is probably athletic and enjoys any kind of team sports. Besides the physical benefits that he derives, he learns the importance of group cooperation. This, in turn, helps him get along within his family as well.

Daughter: She's a charmer, too, buoyant and clever, the kind of person everyone enjoys being around. But when she pontificates about what she thinks she knows and adamantly defends her position, all that charm collapses. At moments like this, your first instinct is probably to argue with her, but it would be futile. Even though she's adaptable in most situations, she clings to her opinions about what is true and right. In many instances, she probably *is* correct, which only fuels her certainty that she is *always* correct.

From the time she's quite small, your Sagittarian daughter attracts friends. They come from every social, religious, and racial strata and all of them expand your daughter's perceptions in some way.

Unlike some kids, your daughter is rarely timid about leaving home, starting with the journey down the block to spend the night at a friend's house. Travel of any sort feeds her restless quest for knowledge. She enjoys being outside and gains immeasurably from camping trips, canoeing, kayaking, or just basking under the stars.

Like her male counterpart, she finds a distinct pleasure in learning about things that interest her. It's all a kind of journey for her. A telescope, for instance, allows her to travel into outer space; a microscope is her vehicle into smaller worlds; books and movies reflect her forays into the ordinary world. Animals feed her soul. It's all fodder for Sagittarius.

With Sagittarians of either gender, the Sun/Moon combination often explains certain riddles in the child's personality.

Sagittarius Stages

Infancy to seven: Your Sagittarius seems to be born with a love-filled heart. As an infant, his smile lights up a room and he's quick to learn which parent is most likely to be bewitched by that smile. He's anxious to move around on his own and may try to crawl before his body is physically strong enough to sustain him. Once he's walking, watch out! This is the kid who is out of the house and down the street before you turn around.

In school, Sagittarius is usually in his element. His love of learning, however, is heavily influenced by the teacher. If he has a petty tyrant whose demands compromise or violate his principles, he shuts down. And then no threat will force him back into the fold.

Seven to fourteen: At this stage, Sagittarius may begin to feel unsettled and increasingly restless. If his world has been too narrow, he actively seeks to expand it in some way. New friends. New interests. He may express a desire to attend a different school. If his world is already broad, he may intentionally contract it, pulling the walls inward.

Even though change marks this age group in any Sun sign, for a Sagittarian this period can be one of major transition, a vital step in inner growth and understanding.

Fourteen to twenty-one: These seven years deepen a Sagittarian's compassion or his selfishness. At times, he seems almost angelic, acting out of a pure and unmitigated joy. Other times, he seems to be motivated primarily by selfishness and has grandiose plans and schemes that he probably doesn't share with you.

The real trick at this stage is to remain nonjudgmental. Don't criticize him. Be a good listener. Offer advice when asked. Be a worthy role model.

Twenty-one and beyond: Sagittarius usually hits his stride once he's on his own. The world seems to lie at his feet. There's so much to do—pursue his passions, fall in love, travel. If he's committed to a relationship, he may be uncertain whether he wants to carry the commitment any farther. He may decide to travel for a while before committing himself to a job, relationship, or even a particular place. Travel, in fact, may be just what he needs right out of college because it helps him clarify his goals and needs.

Cosmic Sagittarius

Jupiter and the ninth house, the ruling planet and natural home for Sagittarius, confer an innate interest in spiritual and philosophical issues. Sagittarians attempt to see the larger picture but often get locked into a narrow expression of spirituality because of their tendency to believe their way is the right way. In practical terms, this can produce a religious fanatic or a spiritual pioneer.

The Sagittarian religious fanatic tends to bludgeon other people with his view. Believe as he does or he doesn't want to know you. Tolerance goes straight out the window. His home is highly repressive, with his spouse and children urged to tow the religious line. In this type of Sagittarian, the underlying issue is one of control that probably stems from some deep fear that originated in childhood.

The spiritual pioneer is a true seeker. His spiritual beliefs may involve foreign cultures: gurus in India, missionary work, the study of mythology in far-flung corners of the world. Even astral travel is fair game to him.

Sagittarians possess the innate capacity to develop psychically. Many of the Sagittarians I know are involved in metaphysics. Several are excellent psychics, capable of penetrating insights and clairvoyance. Others are astrologers who are able to wed intuition and science in their astrological interpretations. Most seem to share psychic links with animals.

For a Sagittarian, the Moon sign will provide deep insight into what motivates the child. Paired with a Scorpio Moon, the tendency for control may be greater and there can be greed as well. A Libra Moon softens the bluntness and brings an aesthetic quality to the spiritual search.

12

The Capricorn Tribe

The Goat ♑

Dates: December 22–January 19
Element: Earth
Quality: Cardinal
Ruler: Saturn

Life is serious business for these kids. There are parameters to respect, rules to follow, goals to accomplish.

In a group of children, the Capricorn is the child who spells out the rules of the game to everyone else and who makes sure these rules are followed to the letter. She's the responsible team leader or the leader's most prized assistant. Authority figures love her because she doesn't make trouble.

As a cardinal earth sign, the typical Capricorn is a realist. She values what is tangible and practical. She doesn't sit around waiting for opportunities to come to her; she actively pursues what she wants. This drive gives her an entrepreneurial edge over other kids, because if she can't afford what she wants, she does something about it. She sets up a lemonade stand, washes cars, babysits, whatever it takes.

Saturn, Capricorn's ruler, represents limitations and restrictions in life. Its influence has a lot to do with how serious and hard working these kids are. They often shoulder more than their share of family responsibility and may feel some resentment about it. If they aren't allowed to vent their frustration openly, it may fester and cause health problems later. These kids benefit from regular physical exercise, and it doesn't matter whether it's a solitary pursuit or a team sport. The point is to get out from under all that responsibility.

The typical Capricorn child is emotionally reserved, unless she learns at a young age that it's okay to express emotion, even emotions like anger. Otherwise, she tends to repress the vast potential of her inner life. If she does that, it may mean that she'll cut off access to her dreams, too, and be unable to remember them. Dreams can be a vast wealth of information for this child and she should be encouraged to remember them.

Capricorns seem to be born with a need and desire to become someone important or to achieve something in the larger world. Their ambition sometimes blinds them to the fact that the achievement of any goal requires appropriate training and education. They are excellent, however, at making long-range goals and sticking to them.

Even a young Capricorn benefits from setting goals and taking steps to achieve them. The challenge for parents, though, is that the child becomes consumed by the goal. Be careful about assigning too much responsibility to your Capricorn child. Even though she takes it on gladly because it's her nature to do so, you may be stealing a bit of her childhood.

Son: He enjoys sports, preferably team sports with clearly defined rules. He works hard at perfecting his athletic skill and likes the physical reality of his own body, the way it moves and reacts.

Your son may not have hordes of friends, but the friends he has are usually loyal and steadfast. They also may represent unexpressed parts of himself. If he's demonstrative, for example, he may have a close friend who isn't. Or vice versa. He learns vicariously through his observations of other people.

Capricorn's respect for authority can sometimes boomerang, creating a petty tyrant who orders his siblings and friends around. The good news is that it's a transitory phase, a time when he's trying to define his role in the overall scheme of things. It may also be a reaction to excessive responsibility.

Males and females of this sign need to feel financially secure. Even at a young age, they understand that money is power and they like handling it, earning it, saving and spending it. The seduction of money, in fact, may prompt them to formulate goals rather early on. My Capricorn nephew decided at the ripe old age of nine or ten that he wanted to be a stockbroker when he grew up "because they make a lot of money." By the time he was eleven, he'd decided that he would be an entrepreneur because they made a lot of money, too, and worked for themselves. Next year, it may be something different. But whatever he finally decides to be, it will certainly be a profession with a great potential to make money and call his own shots.

Your son is loyal to people he loves. This allows him to commit to another for the long haul, but it can work against him when he can't release a bad relationship. Then he gets stuck—stuck in a relationship that doesn't work, in a pattern that is ultimately damaging to him. To break this pattern, he may need the insight of someone he trusts—and it is hoped that this person is you, his parent.

Daughter: Through her early teens, she probably sticks closely to the family agenda. She gets along well with people who are older than she is, and because of this, she seems to have a sage-like quality about her. She's actually quite comfortable in the company of adults and converses well with them. But she's still a kid and needs to do kid things–pretend games, sleepovers, Girl Scouts, giggling about boys.

Like the males of the sign, your Capricorn daughter often attracts people who represent unexpressed parts of herself. This may be true of all of us regardless of when we were born. But Saturn's influence on Capricorns inhibits elements of their personalities more than the rulers of other signs do. The people who act as mirrors in your daughter's life may be people she loves, people she barely knows, or complete strangers. If she is athletically gifted, she may have a friend who is handicapped in some way. If she's too rigid in her beliefs, she may attract someone who forces her to loosen up.

If she learns to recognize and use this type of "personality message," she makes a quantum leap in her understanding of herself and what motivates her. For her, however, the challenge may be in learning to recognize such messages. If she learns at a young age that such messages exist, life for her will be considerably easier.

Capricorn Stages

Infancy to seven: As an infant, she gazes at you with eyes that seem old somehow, as though she were born with the memory of the past life connections between you. As she learns to talk and express herself, you experience many moments when you're certain that she sees what she shouldn't be able to see, that she penetrates what is hidden in you, your spouse, and your family.

By the time she hits school age, most of that piercing insight has worn off. She's involved in the excitement of her new friends and environment and her soul has forgotten what it once knew.

Seven to fourteen: You probably won't go through out-right rebellion with your Capricorn; even their individuation is governed by their respect for rules. But you can expect considerable resistance as Capricorn seeks her own code and set of rules. And be prepared for blunt questions about why *your* way is right. Remember: This is the future CEO speaking, the entrepreneur who sees a gap in the consumer market and fills it.

Fourteen to twenty-one: Just when you think you've got your kid figured out, she hits puberty. Belief systems with a lot of rules and regulations appeal to her. One month she considers becoming a nun; the next month, she decides to be a cop. You can't fight it. You won't win an argument with her.

But you can attempt to make her aware of the deeper order that operates in her life. Once she recognizes the importance of meaningful coincidences, everything begins to click for her. She meets people who help her fulfill her greatest potential. She finds the inner security that carries her through to the end of her life.

Twenty-one and beyond: At some point during her college years, she becomes committed to a person, ideal, life-style, or profession. Or all of the above. Her commitment, loyalty, and inner strength sustain her through rough times.

In the romance department, she seeks a partner whose ambition matches her own. The challenge in such partnerships, however, is that ambition may form the core of the relationship and she becomes blinded to her own material-ism. This makes her vulnerable to potential partners who may deceive her.

Cosmic Capricorn

This sign's need for structure dictates her approach to spiritual issues. If she pursues organized religion, then she does it with full commitment and involvement. If she follows a nontraditional course, she establishes her own parameters and rules. Either way, the point for Capricorn is to somehow use her spiritual explorations to deepen her understanding of herself and her role in the larger world.

When Capricorns nurture their intuition and allow it to flourish, they make excellent psychics. In this capacity, they might be found working as clairvoyants with police, as healers, or as intuitive counselors. Whatever course they choose, they work within established boundaries and rules.

An evolved Capricorn possesses the stamina and drive to achieve change in the world. But to do this she must first harness Saturn's restrictive nature so that it works for her rather than against her. With Saturn ruling her Sun sign, she may feel that she's struggling upstream at times, unable to see or effect any change in her own life.

But once she realizes it's possible to pour her energy into her vision, she achieves her ambitions.

13

The Aquarius Tribe

The Water Bearer ♒

Dates: January 20–February 18
Element: Air
Quality: Fixed
Ruler: Uranus

These kids are the individualists of the zodiac, the rebels and anarchists who usher in new ideas and unique ways of doing things. Yet, they are also social, vivacious, and group-minded. They are paradoxes even to themselves.

In a crowd of children, the Aquarian is the kid who insists on equality and fairness for all. He defends the underdog and works for the good of the collective group. Other children depend on him.

As a fixed air sign, the typical Aquarius embraces unique ideas. He enjoys science, technology, computers, electronics—virtually anything that allows him greater control over his world and access to new information. As an air sign, his interest is in the mind. Despite his fascination with innovative ideas, he's slow to change his mind once his opinions are formed. In this way, he can be as stubborn as his fixed cousins, Taurus and Scorpio.

Uranus, ruler of Aquarius, is the planet of originality, unconventionality, disruption, and genius. These characteristics influence everything your Aquarius child does—or doesn't do. If you try to make this child do something that he perceives as unreasonable or in violation of his principles, he simply won't do it. Even threats won't move him.

Aquarius is deeply compassionate. In practical, everyday life, this means your child may bring home strays. Whether it's a friend whose parents are immersed in divorce or an injured kitten, they're equal in the eyes of Aquarius. As your child matures, this compassion extends to larger causes—speaking out for animals rights, demonstrations against war, picket lines, raising money for the homeless. Whatever his age, the bottom line for Aquarius is to break through social barriers and reform rigid conventions, all of which ultimately benefit society.

The energy that an Aquarian child brings into life with him is quite often the kind of energy that has been lacking in his family up until his birth. If the family is prejudiced, the Aquarian child, one way or another, breaks through those barriers of prejudice. If the family is unconcerned about humanitarian issues, Aquarius changes that.

Given the opportunity and early exposure to technology, Aquarian kids easily become computer savvy. To them, the information highway is just another way to keep in touch with friends.

Son: He isn't the type to compliment you. But he shows his appreciation in other ways—a poem, a bouquet of flowers that he picked, some small gesture that means a lot to you. Most of the time, he's easy to be around, quick-witted and fun, a social creature who enjoys his family's company as much as he does the company of his friends.

Then he hits a pocket of resistance and the whole picture changes. As a parent, you may not be sure what, exactly, triggers the change in his mood. He probably doesn't know himself. It's as if a black veil suddenly falls between him and the rest of the world.

One Aquarian boy in our neighborhood invariably arrives on his bike several afternoons a week to play with my daughter. He's a pleasure to have around, quick to smile, easygoing, willing to go along with whatever develops as more kids show up. Then, for no reason that anyone has ever been able to discern, he abruptly leaves, pedaling off down the street without an explanation to anyone. When I asked him once why he'd left so suddenly, he just shrugged and replied, "I felt like it. "

The call of individualistic freedom is as intrinsic to an Aquarian as the need to communicate is to a Gemini. And when your son hears his call, he's gone like the wind. If you attempt to restrict this trait, you may find yourself in the middle of an outright rebellion.

On the other hand, he needs to learn about socially acceptable and unacceptable behavior. After all, if he answers the call of freedom when he's eighteen and in the middle of a job interview, he probably won't get the job!

Daughter: She's looking for kindred souls who share her interests, passions, and beliefs. Since she doesn't recognize any sort of class, racial, or religious distinctions among people, her friends come from all walks of life.

As an air sign, she likes new and novel ideas and is easily bored when she doesn't have them. Books and movies may satisfy this need to some extent, but for her, it always comes back to people. She needs her friends just as much as they need her.

Your Aquarian daughter accumulates interests the way other kids accumulate clutter. One month a particular series of books might grab her attention; the next month, it could be reincarnation, astrology, or alternative healing. She shares what she learns with friends and vice versa.

The pockets of resistance found in Aquarian boys also exists in girls. The way it is manifested depends to a large extent on her role within her own family. One Aquarian girl in my daughter's circle of friends uses her stubbornness as a way to manipulate other kids into doing what she wants to do. As the middle child in her family, this is how she seizes attention for herself.

Like any child, your Aquarian needs to be recognized and appreciated for who she is. This alone mitigates much of her stubbornness and resistance.

Aquarius Stages

Infancy to seven: The infancy of an Aquarian baby tends to be easier than that of a Mercury-ruled child like Gemini or Virgo. There are always exceptions to this, of course, but generally the Aquarian temperament is content to let things unfold.

Once your child hits the terrible twos, all that can change. He's anxious now to be with other toddlers, to express himself as the social creature he really is. By the time he starts school, the socialization process is well under way.

Seven to fourteen: This is the age when those pockets of resistance first show up. It's also when his friends become the pivot around which his life revolves. His circle of friends at this point is likely to be quite large, which may create chaos in your household unless you set limits on how many children are allowed at a time in your Aquarian's room.

His individuation process occurs primarily through his intellect, in accelerated growth spurts. While these spurts dazzle you, they may annoy his teachers because he has so many questions about such an array of subjects. Encourage his curiosity now and he runs with it the rest of his life.

Fourteen to twenty-one: The more restrictions you place on your Aquarian during this period, the greater his stubbornness and resistance will be. The smoothest way to get through this phase is to provide your Aquarian with tools that feed his intellect and social consciousness. A computer with an on-line service. Books. Team sports. A family activity that involves community service.

By now, you should have a clear idea of the areas in which your Aquarian excels. Whatever his dream, encourage him to pursue it.

Twenty-one and beyond: Love for an Aquarian must include an intellectual attraction and camaraderie. When he finds it in another, he commits himself. And yet, always in the background is that thrust for individuality and freedom. An Aquarian can't be owned, penned in, or possessed in any relationship. But if you give him the freedom he demands, he always comes home again.

Aquarians may have unusual marriages simply because of their need for freedom. If their partners don't understand their need for freedom, then the marriage probably won't work. Or it may stumble along for awhile, each partner trying to adjust and compromise until the whole house of cards collapses.

Aquarians and Sagittarians often attract each other, perhaps because freedom is such an issue for both of them. There's also an attraction between Aquarians and Geminis.

Cosmic Aquarius

The natural home for Aquarius is the eleventh house of friendships and group associations, so this area is vitally important for his spiritual development. Some of his closest friendships are with people whom he has known and loved in past lives.

In many instances, he will recognize these individuals at some level when he meets them. These "karmic appointments" may not always be pleasant, but they are always vital to his evolution as an individual and to his ultimate spiritual fulfillment.

If an Aquarian is raised within an organized religion, it's likely that he breaks free of it at some point in his life. As a parent, this may not be to your liking, but he needs to find his own way, his own path. If you respect his choices, then he respects yours in return and your spiritual differences will never injure your relationship.

Aquarians tend to be nonjudgmental and tolerant of other people's spiritual beliefs. If they don't agree with your beliefs, they won't voice their objections unless you ask. But if you ask, they'll give you the unvarnished truth as they see it.

More than any other sign, Aquarius possesses the innate wisdom and capacity to transform the world, to usher in a new age in which equality exists for all people.

14

The Pisces Tribe

The Fish ♓

Dates: February 19–March 20
Element: Water
Quality: Mutable
Ruler: Neptune

Pisces is the true mystic of the zodiac: sensitive, moody, imaginative, and deeply psychic. She's able to delve into the unconscious river of knowledge that unites all people, and when she surfaces, her imagination spins tales about what she experienced.

In a group of children, a Pisces child doesn't stand out because of the way she acts. It's her magnificent eyes that mark her, liquid pools that gaze serenely from the depths of some other world. Liz Taylor has the quintessential Piscean eyes.

Neptune, as ruler of Pisces, brings distinct and opposing characteristics to the sign. In its least desirable form, Neptune breaks rules by creating confusion and vagueness. In its highest form, it brings great imagination, creativity, and spiritual depth. Your Pisces child probably exhibits both sides of the Neptunian influence.

On a daily basis, this means your little Pisces has trouble making up her mind about the simplest things. Should she have chicken or casserole for dinner? Should she go rollerblading with her friends or to the movies with you? But when it comes to her intuition, she doesn't vacillate. And always she poses large, complex questions that underscore the kind of activity that goes on in her unconscious mind. "What was I before this life? What happens when I die? Do I go somewhere in between lives?"

Pisces kids are like psychic sponges. They easily absorb vibrations from the people around them, so it's important that they have positive, upbeat friends. This psychic sensitivity also makes it easy for them to empathize with others, which is the source of their compassion.

Your child's imagination can work both for and against her. On the positive side, it's one of her greatest tools for learning in that it enables her to see the whole picture. On the negative side, she has more than her share of nightmares and not all of them happen while she sleeps. A noise that she hears while alone in a room might be little green men knocking at the window. Or it might be monsters under her bed or her fairy godmother.

While asleep, her unconscious mind is extremely receptive to suggestion. If she doesn't feel well, for instance, whispered affirmations about healing can boost her immune system. Waking or sleeping, she's open to suggestion and you can easily work with her to banish fears, maintain her health, or whatever else she needs.

Son: The two fish that symbolize Pisces are swimming in opposite directions. This tug-of-war typifies your son's inner life. His head tells him one thing, his heart screams something else. This is part of the reason he has so much trouble making decisions.

Some of this ambivalence is mitigated as he matures, but when he's young, it may drive you crazy. While you're urging him to hurry up and get in the car because you're late for an appointment, he's still deciding whether he wants to go. Once he decides, he changes his mind a dozen times before you even reach the car. If you, as a parent, gently urge him to act on his first hunch, he develops a confidence in his intuition that will follow him through life.

Your son is as sensitive to the subtle moods of his family as he is to his friends. If he tells you that his older sister is feeling blue about her relationship with her boyfriend, believe him even if you see no signs of it.

Male Pisces are as emotional as the females of the sign and get their feelings hurt just as easily. But because of acculturation, they may not express it as readily. This can make them moody and withdrawn, so it's wisest to let them express whatever they're feeling. Pisces of either gender benefit tremendously by remembering and talking about their dreams with people they trust. Encourage it. You're guaranteed to be surprised by what you hear! You may also uncover hints in your son's dreams about what's really bothering him.

Daughter: When your Pisces daughter flashes a quick smile at you, her luminous eyes light up the darkest shadows in your heart. You feel utterly certain that she is your greatest gift, your most profound blessing. Then she pulls back into herself, into one of her dark, puzzling moods, and it seems that no matter what you do or say, you can't reach her.

She's very emotional and this doesn't change as she gets older; she only learns to control her emotions better. As a youngster, she may be reluctant to spend the night away from home, which means that your home is the center of the action on weekends.

One of my daughter's Pisces friends always arrives with the best intentions, her overnight bag crammed with toys and movies to see them through the night. But around nine or ten, homesickness settles in. She gets headaches, her stomach hurts, she feels generally miserable, and she invariably calls her mother and says she wants to go home.

Pisces kids enjoy any kind of story that deals with things that go bump in the night. They also love games that make them stretch their intuitive muscles.

One of the favorite games of my daughter's Pisces friends is a takeoff from the early telepathy experiments conducted at Duke University. Each child draws a shape in one of the primary colors on a piece of paper and seals it in an envelope. The envelopes are tossed in a pile and mixed up. Then each child draws one and tries to see the color in her mind. Pisces are very good at this sort of thing, and once they realize how good they are, it bolsters their self-confidence and makes it easier for them to make decisions.

Pisces Stages

Infancy to seven: This stage is usually fairly easy. Your Pisces infant sleeps well and soundly, slipping back into the mysterious world from which she so recently came. If you do have trouble getting her to sleep, gently rub her feet; this soothes her.

Astral travel is easy for a Pisces during this stage. Unencumbered by society's indoctrination, her soul seeks to return to whatever it knows best. It's during this time that your child may have an imaginary playmate. If she tells you about her friend, try not to dismiss it with the usual parental response. Question her about her friend, have tea with the two of them, acknowledge your child's experience.

Seven to fourteen: School can be something of a shock for a Pisces child. Suddenly, the carefree days of play and imaginary friends are gone and she must deal with classrooms, a teacher, her ABCs, the stuff of the real world. But she makes friends easily and attracts people who share her depth of imagination and intuition. She excels in the subjects that interest her and feed her imagination.

If she has had some abiding passion—art, animals, books—this is the period in which it becomes more pronounced. Her indecisiveness may also be emphasized. As long as she knows she can depend on the people she loves most, however, the early tumult of the teen years can be avoided.

Fourteen to twenty-one: The big danger in this period is escapism. It can show up in any number of Neptunian ways—drugs, alcohol, sex—take your pick of parental nightmares. But if escapism can be constructively channeled, you save yourself and your Pisces child an ocean of heartache. Classes in acting, art, poetry, dance, music, or fiction writing can easily take the place of drugs, alcohol, and sex.

As a parent, your attitude during this phase of your child's life is vital. Remain centered, loving, and supportive. Encourage your Pisces to follow her intuition. Help her fulfill her potential.

Twenty-one and beyond: She can't decide what she wants to do with her life. She has changed her college major so many times that, with another two years in school, she could graduate with a degree in three different areas. She doesn't know if the guy she has been seeing is the right guy for her and she isn't about to take your advice to heart. When she calls in hysterics, you just roll your eyes and listen. Actually, you feel like hanging up.

Take a deep breath. Think before your speak. Remind your Pisces that she already has the answers she needs. All she has to do is listen to her heart—and then act.

Cosmic Pisces

The natural home for Pisces is the twelfth house, where the disowned parts of ourselves are stashed away. No matter how great a job you do as the parent of a Pisces child, she will have twelfth house stuff to work through in her life. She will have *issues.*

Some of these issues may be worked out within institutional settings. She may, for instance, work for a time in a prison, hospital, nursing home, or similar environment in which service and a degree of martyrdom are required. She may work behind the scenes in some artistic endeavor, as a ghostwriter, a movie director, a set designer. She may write murder mysteries or read tarot cards. Whatever form her work takes, it somehow allows her to confront the buried issues in her life, to unravel them and finally put them to rest.

Metaphysics are a part of her life at one level or another. If she doesn't explore this area, then time and again certain patterns are repeated that force her to rely on her intuition, to develop and embrace it. Like her water cousin, Scorpio, she possesses a tremendous capacity for personal transformation. But unlike Scorpio, she can be so adaptable that she becomes a chameleon and loses herself in the process of transforming.

This is the kid, after all, who may tap into her past lives with the ease the rest of us bring to driving the interstate. She has the ability to slip out of her body at will and map the world she encounters. She has the potential to break barriers in the arts. If only she can make up her mind.

15

Sun through the Houses

The house placement of your child's Sun sign tells you a great deal about the area of life in which he expresses his physical energy, will, and vitality, as well as his conscious intentions. The Sun is considered strongest in the angular houses—first, fourth, seventh, and tenth.

When you interpret the placement, do so according to the Sun sign descriptions. If your child's Sun sign is Gemini, for instance, and the Sun appears in the third house, then he expresses himself well and may be an exceptionally strong speaker or writer. He also has warm and congenial relationships with his siblings and neighbors. Some form of communication will figure prominently in his career.

Before reading this section, refer back to the section on houses in Chapter 2.

First house: His personality is so powerful it's impossible to ignore this child, even if you want to. He radiates self-confidence; sometimes it seems he was born with that confidence. Forget bending his will to your own. It just isn't going to happen. At best, you'll learn how to coax him to come around to your way of thinking. Other people are attracted to his radiance, so he never has a shortage of friends. Even as a youngster, his ambitions are clear to him.

Second house: Beware taking this child to the mall! He's a consumer who loves to spend money. Conversely, even when he's young, he shows initiative in making money. He's acquisitive and enjoys collecting things just to possess them. This is the kid, for example, who has to have every new toy on the market. He has strong values, but the trick for a parent is to make sure those values extend beyond materialism.

Third house: You won't ever have to guess what he's thinking about because he talks about it constantly. He's also eager to learn and his quick, restless mind absorbs information like a sponge. He needs to develop discipline about learning, though, because he's too restless to stick to one thing for very long. His facility with language is impressive and communication of some kind is likely to figure in his profession. He gets along great with his siblings and neighbors.

Fourth house: His home and family are his sanctuary, the basis for his security in life. You, as parents, are extremely important to him, and your attitudes and beliefs have a long-lasting effect on him. Your child finds his greatest expression through his home and family, and later in life, his home will be his showcase. The Sun here is a promising indicator of professional success.

Fifth house: He's competitive, particularly in sports, the theater, and arts in general. He loves having an audience and possesses true leadership qualities. He can carry these traits to extremes, however, by vying for attention and wanting to be number one in whatever he pursues. This alienates him from other kids. But the Sun here also gives him great warmth and affection toward people. He's a "hugger" and is forever saying his good-byes with an "I love you" attached at the end. As an adult, he may work with children in some capacity.

Sixth house: The emphasis with this placement is on work and health. Your child may be something of a perfectionist, which can inadvertently trigger irritating health problems: sinus headaches, allergies, stomachaches. His health benefits from careful diet and an awareness of how his emotions affect him. He has a quick, agile mind and probably enjoys pursuits like carpentry and sculpture, where he has to use his hands. As he matures, he may be interested in health and medicine.

Seventh house: His friendships are vital to his sense of well-being. He enjoys doing things with other kids and feels that he functions best in partnership with someone else. He needs to develop independence so that he won't surrender everything just to keep a friend. He's cooperative and congenial and, later in life, may work closely with his spouse or significant other.

Eighth house: From his earliest years, he asks penetrating, insightful questions about BIG issues, cosmic issues. And he keeps asking until he gets answers that satisfy him. As a parent, you may sometimes feel overwhelmed or annoyed by his questions. He may need to learn the difference between what is his and what belongs to other people. He may be unusually intuitive and, at times, quite psychic.

Ninth house: The world is literally this child's playground. He's intrigued by geography, world history, foreign cultures and countries, and even foreign books and films. From the time he's old enough to have friends of his own, he isn't reluctant to spend the night elsewhere. He's a planner and is usually well organized. He sees only the best in other people.

Tenth house: He's a leader, the kid on the playground who gives the orders. This may cause problems with authority figures or with his own father, particularly when he's young, because he thinks he already has all the answers. He's more goal oriented than other kids his age and usually has a fairly clear sense of where he's going. The only question in his mind is how he's going to get there. His father or a father-like figure shows him the way.

Eleventh house: Friends are truly important to him. He would rather spend time with them than by himself and is always generous with his friends. He's concerned about what is fair to others and often works at things that benefit everyone, not just himself. He's ambitious, but not to the exclusion of everything and everyone else.

Twelfth house: He illuminates what's hidden, whether it's within himself, his own family, or in working behind the scenes. He may be shy about speaking in front of other people and has a deep sense of privacy. Before the age of two, kids with this placement often have imaginary playmates. At any age, they're fascinated by the supernatural, by other people's motives, and by all that is secret and hidden.

Part Two

Mixed Tribes

16

Emotions

Your twelve-year-old son fishes by the lake at dusk. You watch him from the back porch, his body silhouetted against the twilight, and wonder what he's thinking. If you asked, he probably wouldn't tell you anyway.

You would like to walk down to the lake and sit beside him like you used to do when he was much younger. But you're afraid he might just get up and walk away. It's not that anything is wrong between you; things just aren't like they used to be.

But if you knew that he's also thinking about the way things used to be, wouldn't you march on down there and sit beside him? His Pisces Moon has been playing havoc lately with his emotions and he needs someone to talk to.

Your child's Moon sign holds vital clues about his or her inner life, that private country of the heart that you, as a parent, are often reluctant or forbidden to enter.

On a given day, the Moon fiddles with tides—ocean tides, blood tides, parental tides, unconscious tides, all those emotional tides of how and what and why. It is our link to the collective unconscious, to our early childhood, our unconscious patterns, and to our mother—birth mother, planetary mother—and to the mother that we are to our own children.

If the Sun symbolizes our vitality, then the Moon represents the primal, unconscious force that fuels that vitality. As astrologer Grant Lewi said, the Moon is "our heart's desire."

Mother and Son

In the chart in figure 16-1, the boy's Moon (☽) is 24♉05 (Taurus) in the fourth house. His Sun (☉) lies in 25♐08 (Sagittarius) in the eleventh house. What is immediately apparent is the difference in elements.

His Sun is a fire sign; his Moon is earth. His Sun thrusts him out into the world, his Moon pulls him back into himself. His outward, ego life is expressed through the affairs of his eleventh house—friends, group associations, wishes, and ambitions. His internal life finds expression at home (fourth house) and his mother plays a major role in his life. With that Taurus Moon, his security comes through material resources. He needs a comfortable, aesthetically pleasing home and perceives his mother as a lovely, solid woman who provides the security he needs. This boy may spend his latter years tending the family homestead.

This boy's mother is a Virgo. Her natal chart appears in figure 16-2. In figure 16-3, the boy's natal chart lies in the inner circle, with the mother's natal planets distributed in the outer circle, according to where they fall in her son's chart. Her Sun in Virgo falls in his eighth house of metaphysics, other people's money and resources, inheritances, taxes, insurance. Her Moon in Aquarius falls in his first house of self.

His mother writes mysteries, which would fall under eighth house affairs, and is also a long-time student of the *I*

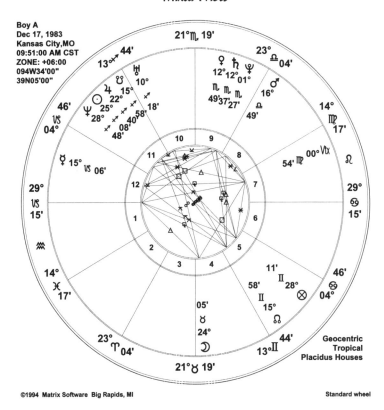

Figure 16-1

Ching. She feeds that part of his Sagittarian nature that seeks larger truths.

His father, who owns his own business, is a Libra. His Sun sign rules the boy's ninth house, which governs, among other things, long-distance travel and foreign cultures. On every school vacation, the boy and his father take off for remote corners of the world. His father feeds that part of his Sagittarian nature that loves foreign travel and learns through exposure to foreign cultures.

It wasn't consciously planned by either parent; it's simply how their interests evolved. This kind of underlying

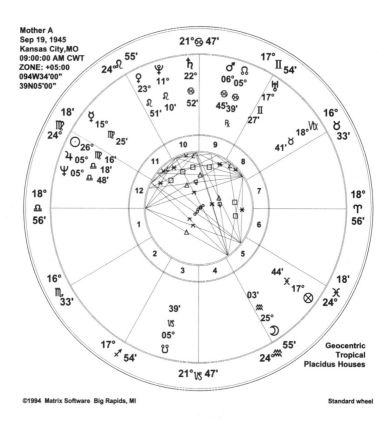

Mother A
Sep 19, 1945
Kansas City, MO
09:00:00 AM CWT
ZONE: +05:00
094W34'00"
39N05'00"

©1994 Matrix Software Big Rapids, MI

Geocentric
Tropical
Placidus Houses

Standard wheel

Figure 16-2

order is often apparent in chart comparisons of children and their parents.

Notice how the boy's Taurus Moon hangs like a pendant at the bottom of his chart. It forms an almost exact conjunction (less than three degrees) with the cusp of his fourth house, or IC. The Moon, which represents the mother, is in the house of the nurturing parent, which makes the placement particularly significant. The boy's mother is influential in his life, particularly in early childhood.

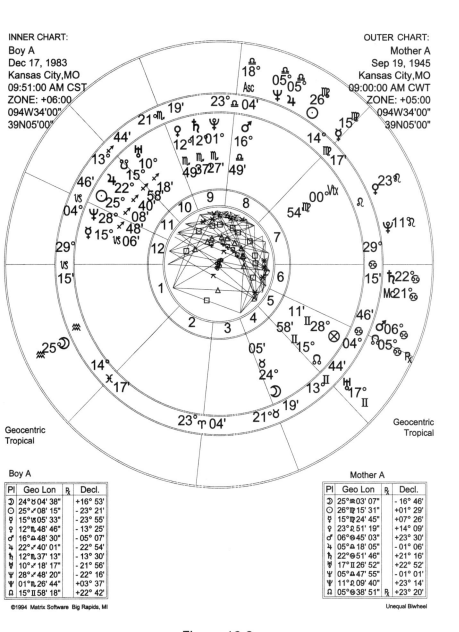

Unequal Biwheel

Boy A

Pl	Geo Lon	℞	Decl.
☽	24° ♉ 04' 38"		+16° 53'
☉	25° ♐ 08' 15"		- 23° 21'
☿	15° ♑ 05' 33"		- 23° 55'
♀	12° ♏ 48' 46"		- 13° 25'
♂	16° ♎ 48' 30"		- 05° 07'
♃	22° ♐ 40' 01"		- 22° 54'
♄	12° ♏ 37' 13"		- 13° 30'
♅	10° ♐ 18' 17"		- 21° 56'
♆	28° ♐ 48' 20"		- 22° 16'
♇	01° ♏ 26' 44"		+03° 37'
☊	15° ♊ 58' 18"		+22° 42'

Mother A

Pl	Geo Lon	℞	Decl.
☽	25° ♒ 03' 07"		- 16° 46'
☉	26° ♍ 15' 31"		+01° 29'
☿	15° ♍ 24' 45"		+07° 26'
♀	23° ♌ 51' 19"		+14° 09'
♂	06° ♎ 45' 03"		+23° 30'
♃	05° ♎ 18' 05"		- 01° 06'
♄	22° ♋ 51' 46"		+21° 16'
♅	17° ♊ 26' 52"		+22° 52'
♆	05° ♎ 47' 55"		- 01° 01'
♇	11° ♌ 09' 40"		+23° 14'
☊	05° ♋ 38' 51"	℞	+23° 20'

Figure 16-3

127

Through her, he identifies with his family's past, his roots, and his family lineage.

With a Taurus Moon, this kid is stubborn and slow to change his opinion about anything. He needs harmonious, pleasant surroundings and a home life that makes him feel secure. He likes to spend money, especially on things that enhance the beauty of his home. His room is a refuge, a haven, a private link to his deeper self.

Because of the fixed earth nature of Taurus, his Moon in this sign and house keep him rooted in the real world. It tempers some of that fiery Sagittarian energy and makes him practical even when he doesn't want to be. With his Sun in the eleventh house, he makes friends easily enough; other people are attracted to his steadfastness, his pleasing personality. But his truly close friends are few, and when one of them hurts him, it wounds him deeply.

The mother's Moon in Aquarius in her son's first house means that she brings Aquarian attributes to her son's sense of self. Through her, he becomes aware of humanitarian ideals, of different types of belief systems, of unique emotional patterns, and an acute awareness of the deeper order of events, relationships, and consciousness.

Moon/Sun Compatibility

When the Moon and Sun are compatible, either because they're well aspected or because they share the same sign and element, the child's inner, emotional life finds easy expression in her external life. She can take on challenges and break through obstacles as a whole person. Her inner and outer selves are in communion. Her intuition has a freer flow and she hears its voice from a young age.

If the Moon and Sun are incompatible, it doesn't spell disaster; it simply means the child has a more difficult time expressing who she is. Quite often, however, an incompatibility creates a tension that helps the child achieve. It grounds her.

Phases of the Moon

It takes the Moon twenty-nine and a half days to go through its cycle from new Moon to new Moon. At the start of the new Moon, the waxing phase, the Sun and Moon are in the same degree. As the Moon separates from the Sun's position, it appears in the sky as a crescent.

About a week after the cycle starts, the first quarter Moon graces the sky. The Moon is now ninety degrees from the position of the Sun, forming a square to it. From here, the Moon swells into a gibbous Moon, which looks roughly like three quarters of a circle. This marks the end of the waxing phase and the beginning of the waning phase.

The gibbous Moon slowly fills out until it's full. The Moon and Sun now lie directly opposite each other in the zodiac, forming an angle known as an opposition. From here, the Moon begins its approach once more toward the position of the Sun, steadily shrinking in view through the disseminating Moon, the last quarter Moon, and the balsamic Moon. Then this slides into the New Moon and the cycle repeats itself.

The phase of the Moon under which your child is born holds an important key to how she resolves emotional conflict. In the chart in figure 1-1, both the Moon and the Sun are in Virgo, in the sixth house. The Moon is seventeen degrees, nine minutes; the Sun is eight degrees, thirty-three minutes, nearly a ten-degree orb. Many astrologers allow a ten-degree orb for aspects between the Moon and the Sun, which would make this a wide conjunction and a new Moon.

New Moon Kids
(Moon conjunct Sun to 45° ahead of Sun)

New Moon kids share some qualities with Aries in that they're terrific at starting projects and eagerly embrace whatever lies in front of them. They're initiators and are typically impulsive and spontaneous. They *emote* great feeling and possess magnetism and charisma, all part of what makes them good actors. They act instinctively. Quite often, they seem to have a lot of fire in their personalities, even if planets in fire signs are absent from their charts.

The closer the conjunction between Moon and Sun, the more likely it is that the new Moon child lives to some extent in the shadow of her mother. Prince William of England is a prime example. He was born with a new Moon in Cancer; his mother, Princess Diana, had a Cancer Sun, emphasizing the importance of their relationship. He certainly lived in her shadow and learned from her example, both in life and in death, about the demands of royalty.

Crescent Moon Kids
(Moon 45° to 90° ahead of Sun)

Crescent Moon kids seek new horizons, just like new Moon children do, but they're forever struggling against old patterns. They may be born into families that are restrictive in some way and spend much of their lives trying to break loose of that old structure. Growth is the key word for these kids.

Elvis Presley and Martin Luther King were crescent Moon types. Presley's early limitation was poverty; King's was his race. Both sought to free themselves from the mold into which they were born and succeeded in breaking new ground in their respective areas.

First Quarter Moon Kids
(Moon 90° to 135° ahead of Sun)

First quarter Moon kids may feel like they are two different people, because at this point, the Moon and Sun are square to each other, creating unease and a certain tension. A child with a Leo Sun and a Scorpio Moon, which are square to each other, feels a constant clash between Leo's need to be in the spotlight and Scorpio's penchant for secrecy and privacy.

This type of Moon is what astrologer Dane Rudhyar calls "crisis of action," resulting in people who work relentlessly to create new frameworks in which social ideals and issues can flourish. The unease between their Moon and Sun creates an inner urge for change.

Gibbous Moon Kids
(Moon 135° to 180° ahead of the Sun)

In the gibbous Moon phase, the Moon looks as if some animal has lopped off a part of it. The Moon and Sun are now four or five signs apart. At four signs apart, the two are in the same element and form an angle, called a trine, which allows them to work smoothly in unison.

A child with a Gemini Sun and a Libra Moon, for instance, is a born diplomat. She intercedes in family disputes, voicing the disagreements for both sides and urging everyone to find a peaceful settlement.

Gibbous Moon kids are anxious to contribute to society. They're doers. They find causes to which they can devote their energies. They're conscious of their actions and are involved in self-analysis for much of their lives.

Full Moon Kids
(Moon opposite to 135° behind the Sun)

It's difficult for full Moon kids to integrate their emotions, because the Moon and Sun are at odds with each other. The closer the opposition, the deeper the conflict. The stress often appears in the child's relationship with others because her inner responses don't coincide with her conscious will.

A child with a Sun in Aquarius and a Moon in Leo, for instance, experiences a constant tug of war to reconcile her humanitarian ideals with her personal needs. Dane Rudhyar identified two types of full Moon people—the enlightened and the emotionally disturbed. Buddha, with his Sun in Taurus and a Moon in Scorpio, represents the enlightened type.

Disseminating Moon
(Moon 135° to 90° behind the Sun)

The disseminating Moon phase looks like the gibbous Moon when seen in the sky, but flipped over, like a mirror image. The Moon is now waning. These kids like to teach others what they know and discover. They disseminate ideas. Some might be crusaders, the type who goes from door to door, collecting signatures to block the erection of a microwave tower near her neighborhood.

Conversely, think of a little Jane Fonda in her political activist days (Sun in Sagittarius, Moon in Leo); at the other end is Marilyn Monroe (Sun in Gemini, Moon in Aquarius).

Last Quarter Moon Kids
(90° to 45° behind the Sun)

If the first quarter Moon is a "crisis of action," the last quarter Moon is what Rudhyar calls a "crisis in consciousness." These kids constantly act out dramas in their lives that result in a realignment of who they are. They continually rewrite the scripts of their lives.

Balsamic Moon
(Moon 45° behind the Conjunction with the Sun)

The Balsamic Moon phase is also called the dark Moon. It occurs during a two-day period every month, when no Moon is visible. At this time, the Moon is either a sign behind the Sun or in the same sign. Kids born under this Moon may have a sense of destiny. They can be visionaries or prophets.

Eclipses

Eclipse literally means to darken, to obscure, to cut short. When a child is born during an eclipse, the influence of the eclipsed celestial body is diminished. A lunar eclipse always takes place during a full Moon, when the Sun and the Moon occupy opposite points in the zodiac. As the Earth passes between the Sun and the Moon, its shadow darkens the lunar surface.

For a child born during a lunar eclipse, the emotions and instincts are affected. It's as if her emotions are never quite in synch with the rest of her life. Or vice versa. Her instinctive reactions, particularly in situations where she needs to act quickly, may be slow. The area of life most affected depends on the house placement of the Moon. The effects of an eclipsed Moon can be softened by positive aspects to the Moon—conjunctions and trines.

When a child is born during a solar eclipse, her general vitality may be depleted. The house placement of the eclipsed Sun is particularly important because the affairs ruled by that house are affected.

The Nodes of the Moon

The first time I heard the term "the nodes of the Moon", I had a vivid mental image of a pair of pimples on the face of the Moon. In reality, of course, nodes have nothing to do with pimples. They are simply points where the orbit of a planet intersect the ecliptic, or orbit, of the Sun.

Just as every parent has his or her own spin on how to raise children, so does every astrologer have a spin on the meaning of the Moon's nodes. Some of the popular theories about the North Node (☊) are that they: indicate areas in which a person finds his greatest potential for growth; point to the karmic lessons we came in to learn this time around; show the areas through which we evolve spiritually in this life; or are points of connection.

So which theory is true? All of them. Astrology is an intuitive, interactive process in which *patterns* are recognized and interpreted. Its symbolic language can be best understood in an organic, holistic way, with the right brain free to wonder and imagine, to dip into the collective ocean and pull out whatever it needs. It does so within the parameters and rules erected by the left brain. Neither the right nor the left brain can interpret alone; this is a duo act.

If we live in a multidimensional universe and there is no such thing as linear time, then the "past life" part of the nodal equation would have to include parallel, probable, and future lives as well. You can see how the whole issue gets complicated. It's simpler to think of the nodes as the soul's intent in this incarnation, distilled from its experience and lessons in many simultaneous lives.

When I look at nodes in a child's chart, I interpret the North Node, or Dragon's Head, as a map to the child's greatest fulfillment as a human being in *this* life. The South Node, or Dragon's Tail, shows what issues and tendencies the child has to come to terms with to reach that fulfillment. The South Node's habitual responses have been built up through previous lives and should be released through activities in the North Node.

In a sense, the North Node represents the future that your child moves toward. The South Node represents habitual, unconscious patterns and the things that come so easily that the child is tempted to take shortcuts.

The Moon's nodes always exist on an axis, an astrological fulcrum. If your child's North Node is in the sixth house, her South Node lies in the twelfth. If her North Node is in Aries, her South Node occupies Libra. Locate the North Node in your child's chart, then look to the house and sign that are directly opposite, or 180° away, to find the South Node. The axis in the above example would be Aries/Libra and houses six/twelve.

The sign of the South Node describes the type of experience that comes easily to your child and what she must release; the house describes the area of life affected. The sign of the North Node describes how the release of the old and evolution toward fulfillment can be accomplished. The house shows what area of life is affected.

Nodes Through the Houses

First and Seventh Houses

First house North Node, seventh house South Node: This placement is about claiming personal power. Your child is tempted to take the easy way out and allow other people to make her decisions for her. To reach her fullest potential, she must develop independence, establish her own identity at a young age, and learn how to balance other people's needs with her own. In other lives, she may have abdicated her power or surrendered it too easily to others.

Seventh house North Node, first house South Node: The emphasis is on relationships. Your child needs to develop more of a team spirit and must learn to cooperate with others. While she may prefer the solo route, she develops most fully when she strives to be considerate of others and to give without reserve. In other lives, she may have been preoccupied with herself to the exclusion of others. By helping others fulfill themselves, she is led to her truest self.

Second and Eighth Houses

Second house North Node, eighth house South Node: She needs to develop her own values. She must understand that she can't depend on other people's resources to make her way in the world. She has to earn what she has, through means that are personally significant to her. When things go wrong in her life, she wants to blame others, but she should look within for the cause. In other lives, she may have used other people's resources for her own gain.

Eighth house North Node, second house South Node: She must learn to respect other people's possessions without coveting them and to be considerate of their values, even if they differ from her own. Once she learns to share her resources with others and to seek deeper meanings and connections in her experiences, she finds the path to her fulfillment. In other lives, she may have been excessively possessive of her belongings, oblivious to other people's values and unaware of how her actions affected others.

Third and Ninth Houses

Third house North Node, ninth house South Node: Education is essential to your child. She may balk at the restrictions imposed on her, but once she realizes the grass is rarely greener elsewhere, she begins to find the happiness she craves. Her restless intellect pulls in information at an astonishing rate, and at some point, she needs to teach what she knows. In other lives, freedom and the development of herself consumed her to the exclusion of everything and everyone else.

Ninth house North Node, third house South Node: The challenge with this placement is to delve deeply into experience. When your child refuses to settle for trivial details and a superficial way of doing things, she begins to uncover the vast, untapped richness within herself that broadens her horizons and deepen her understanding. Foreign travel and cultures benefit her development enormously. By seeking the ultimate answers to her questions, she fulfills her potential.

Fourth and Tenth Houses

Fourth house North Node, tenth house South Node: Your child wants to be the center of everyone's attention all the time. She eventually has to learn that she must shine on her own merits, in her own eyes, before she can expect others to perceive her in that light. As she matures, her challenge is to balance the needs of her family with the needs of her own career and to appreciate what she has. In other lives, she may have been in the limelight or in a position of power and she may have ignored her responsibilities to her family.

Tenth house North Node, fourth house South Node: Your child enjoys her home and her family so much she may never want to leave. It's easiest for her to settle into the familiarity of her family and their beliefs than it is to strike out on her own and discover what *she* believes. But this is the route to her fulfillment and the sooner she learn to think for herself, the more rapidly she evolves.

Fifth and Eleventh Houses

Fifth house North Node, eleventh house South Node: The challenge for this child lies in realizing she's the mistress of her own fate. The opinions of her friends are important to her, but she can't allow their opinions to subsume her own. She must learn to channel her energy into a creative passion, whether it's an art or the raising of her own children, and to trust her intuition. In other lives, she relied too heavily on her friends to answer her needs.

Eleventh house North Node, fifth house South Node: Your child finds her greatest fulfillment through friends and group associations. Through her association with them, she is able to clarify her own identity. Her challenge is to overcome the seductive voice of ego and pride. In other lives, her creative urges consumed her, possibly to the exclusion of her obligations to others.

Sixth and Twelfth Houses

Sixth House North Node, twelfth house South Node: One way or another, this child must learn to "trust the process" of whatever she's doing, rather than fretting over it.

She tends to get stuck in the past—past slights, past emotional injuries, past memories. This may weaken her general health. Once she realizes optimism and a positive outlook are her ticket to fulfillment, she's a tireless worker.

Twelfth house North Node, sixth house South Node: The challenge is to develop discrimination about what is important. Being critical of others and nitpicky about details only adds to her inner frustration. She needs to vent her anger and frustration; otherwise she internalizes it and it may create health problems. When your child learns to go with the flow, her world literally opens up. In other lives, she tended to compartmentalize everything and fretted about petty details.

Nodal Axis: The Signs

Aries/Libra: "Me versus everyone else": That's the challenge with this nodal axis. Is your child going to develop herself first or is she going to fulfill her commitments to others? With a North Node in Aries, the answer is that she's too selfish; a North Node in Libra says she's not being selfish enough.

Taurus/Scorpio: This lesson can be a tough one because it deals with values—your child's values versus other people's values. You, as the parent, are definitely included in the "other" category. A Taurus Node is a message to you to chill out; your child needs to find her values, at her own pace. She won't be rushed. A Scorpio North Node means hold onto your hat; it's going to be a roller coaster ride.

Gemini/Sagittarius: Your child explodes to life with a single burning issue: What's it going to be this time? The intellectually restless life of the scholar or the wild, primal life of the nomad? The dichotomy probably isn't that extreme, but the struggle can be. A Gemini North Node is a clear message that your child's fulfillment lies in communicating whatever she learns. A Sagittarius North Node says that her quest involves a search for the deepest truths.

Cancer/Capricorn: Home? Career? Or both? It isn't quite that simple, given the inherent qualities of the two signs, but home and career are a good place to start. North Node in Cancer says that your child needs to lighten up on herself and that she feels she can do this with her family. She fulfills her path through nurturing, whether it's children, artistic creations, or animals. The North Node in Capricorn points to her fulfillment through structure, rules, and parameters.

Leo/Aquarius: Is she going to put herself or others first? This axis bears some similarity to that of Aries/Libra, except that Leo thrives on applause and adulation for itself while Aquarius embraces humanity. Regardless of where the North Node is, your child's fulfillment ultimately lies in finding the right balance between the two.

17

Mix & Match

Your usually buoyant Leo daughter, a twenty-year-old honor student at a prestigious university, comes home at Christmas, bummed out and depressed. She won't discuss it, and you, of course, fear the worst. She's pregnant. On drugs. In the midst of a breakdown.

Over the Christmas break, you gradually piece together the truth, which turns out to be simple: She flunked a midterm. No big deal, you tell her. She'll study harder next semester and raise her grade. But to a Leo with a Virgo Moon, flunking a midterm is the equivalent of failing at life. Her Leo Sun seeks to shine in everything she does and her Virgo Moon demands that she do it perfectly.

Most young children have nothing to hide. They show who they are at a very young age. One Capricorn might be a stickler for rules, another couldn't care less. One Scorpio may be hung up on the meaning of the universe, but another would rather set the Guinness record for beer drinking in the Florida Keys.

One of the ingredients that makes these types so different is their Sun/Moon combinations. Ego versus emotion. The external versus the internal. Yang versus yin. Polar opposites.

In a relationship between parent and child, the Sun/Moon combinations are particularly important. If, for example, your daughter's Moon is in Aquarius and your Sun sign is Aquarius, then you probably communicate well. You have an instinctive understanding of your daughter's emotions and she understands your basic approach to life. This doesn't mean things between you will always go smoothly, but it indicates that you should be able to work out your differences more easily.

Your child's Sun and Moon signs, as well as their positions in the houses, can provide valuable insight about your child's experience of you and your spouse as parents. Astrologer Steven Arroyo, writing in *Astrology, Karma & Transformation,* says: "It seems to me that the Sun and Moon positions and especially their aspects usually symbolize one's inner experience of the parents, what the parents as a couple represented to the person, whether they seemed to the person to have a positive relationship with each other, and how the person felt in relation to them as individuals."

In the combination sections that follow, each Moon sign is described alone, then in combination with the various signs. To summarize, the Moon symbolizes: your child's emotions; her mother or the nurturing parent; her core beliefs about herself; what makes her feel secure; her early childhood and unconscious influences; her intuition; possible past life patterns; her immediate personal environment and home; and your child's "heart's desire," as Grant Lewi put it.

The Sun/Moon combinations are like primary parts of a complex puzzle. Some combinations work better than others, but all reveal intrinsic qualities that your child's soul chose for this particular life.

18

Aries Moon

Fearless, impulsive, reckless. Yes, all those adjectives fit. But there are many other adjectives that might describe this child equally well.

When he's in the mood, he's a leader and an expert on just about everything. Go ahead and ask him what he knows; he would love to tell you. When he's not in the mood to lead or to talk, he's busy doing, moving, being. At the heart of all this busyness lies a fear of stillness. If he stops, the little world he has built might collapse like the house of sticks that one of the three little piggies built. If he stops, he might have to think about what he has been doing or wants to do. He might have to mull stuff over. He would rather act, innovate, implement, command, know it all without having to think.

This Moon child's security lies in doing. For him, living is something to be accomplished; it's a work in progress. Anything less is . . . well, boring. His heart's desire is to embrace all of experience, as fast and passionately as he can, and to do it *this instant.*

He's got a short fuse. Anger is how he deals with conflict or obstacles. He should learn to control his temper and, instead of exploding, pause to ask himself why he's so angry. If he's encouraged to explore and talk about his emotions, he saves himself much aggravation later in life.

With a Moon in Aries, his mother is the type who encourages his independence. She does it without thinking about it, really, because she's busy doing her own thing. She may feel some resentment and anger at times about her parental role. But she herself is very self-reliant and independent and tackles obstacles head-on.

Aries Moon and . . .

Sun in Aries: Your child was born independent. He knows his own mind well and speaks it at every opportunity. This may be embarrassing for you at times because this double Aries doesn't recognize social timing, particularly when he's young. Overall, his inner and outer lives work in unison.

His impatience is often extreme and propels him forward, often quite recklessly. He's completely fearless, partly because he doesn't take the time to reflect on his actions or desires. He simply acts. His sharp intellect allows him to grasp complex concepts so quickly that he feels frustrated when other people just don't get it. If he learns to cultivate an interest in others that's as sincere as his interest in himself, the world opens to him.

His temper is legendary before he even gets out of diapers. Once he learns to talk, his anger can shoot out of him, causing him to say things he really doesn't mean. The good news is that he rarely holds a grudge.

He sees his parents as independent, self-reliant people. He feels they're so busy at times with their own lives that they don't pay as much attention to him as he'd like. Conversely, that's not so bad when he's in his teens and hungering to be out on his own.

Sun in Taurus: She's maddeningly stubborn at times, especially when she's convinced she's right, which is most of the time. If you push her too far, she explodes. Her show of temper never lasts long; once she gets out whatever is bothering her, it all blows over. Then she's loving and affectionate again, all charm.

She's a contradiction, even to herself. She thinks one thing, feels its opposite, and can't reconcile the two. A part of her wants to dominate people and situations, but another part of her just wants to be left alone. The key to resolving this conflict between her head and her heart lies in emotional detachment and the cultivation of patience.

Her inner experience of her parents is basically good. Mom tends to be explosive sometimes, but it takes dad a lot to get angry and that somehow balances everything.

She has her cosmic moments, which become more frequent with age. If she can find her natural rhythm and pace, she can be downright psychic.

Sun in Gemini: If you argue with this child, you're sure to lose. He's quick and agile with words, and while he's talking, everything he says makes sense. But later, when you mull over what he said, you wonder how you were so easily sucked into his logic.

He's passionate and shrewd, with a selfish streak that may deepen as he matures. This isn't necessarily bad; it depends on how he uses it. He's incredibly restless, sometimes annoyingly so, and it runs throughout everything he does, says, and thinks. The development of a single passion or interest tempers this restlessness and benefits him through his life.

At one time or another, he develops an interest in the invisible world, in the subtle energies that power and govern it. If you can show him how to use his dreams and the synchronicities in his life for clues to those powers and how to harness them, he then draws on his full potential.

Sun in Cancer: Her compassion and deep intuition are her most valuable assets. They allow her to peer inside other people, past the superficial masks to the core of who they are. She won't violate anyone's privacy intentionally, but sometimes she can't help blurting out what she sees in you and others.

Her home is her base of operations, and within its walls, she's a veritable hell on wheels, investigating everything, poking around, relentlessly curious. Never come up against her when the issue concerns memory; her memory is nearly impeccable.

Even though Cancer's water and the fire of Aries don't mix on an elemental level, both signs are cardinal and therefore lean toward action, initiation, innovation. This combination can be quite psychic, if the ability is nurtured and allowed to flourish.

Sun in Leo: He's all fire, this one, passionate and eager to embrace experience. His personality is magnetic and powerful, possessed of a kind of radiance that acts like a human magnet. Other people enjoy being around him because he makes them feel so good.

As a parent, his egocentric behavior is hard to take at times; everything seems to revolve around *his* friends, *his* conflicts, *his* concerns. But his loyalty, spontaneous affection, and unconditional love go a long toward mitigating whatever irritation you feel.

Besides, he's fun so much of the time, filled with ideas about interesting things to do and places to explore. So let loose, become a kid, and see the world as he does, even if it's just for an hour.

It's likely that he sees his parents as veritable dynamos whose relationship may be somewhat explosive at times. But at least the disagreements are all out in the open, which is where they belong for this Sun/Moon combination.

Sun in Virgo: Even at a young age, she's a whirlwind of questions. If your answers aren't detailed enough to satisfy her, she keeps at you. She's impatient to *know*. She's big on talking; it's how she sorts out what she thinks and feels.

Sometimes you probably wish she would just get on with it and act on her ideas. As her parent, you should urge her to do exactly that. Her instincts are sound, and the more she acts on them, the deeper she trusts them.

When she comes up against something that really bothers her, she may seem emotionally cold. But it's not that at all; she's just detaching from the situation so she can scrutinize it more clearly. This is when a little encouragement from you would permit her to really open up about what she feels.

Sun in Libra: Beneath his bravado, he's a real softy who likes harmony and time alone. His fascination with what other people consider the weird and the strange may lead him down unconventional paths and attract unconventional people into his life.

This child has an abundance of initiative and charm. But it vanishes like last summer's tan when other people demand that he conform to the kind of individual they think he should be. His challenge is that the Libra in him reaches out for companionship and the Aries in him jealously guards his independence.

When your child learns to draw on his natural intuitive ability and to listen to it, he finds just the right balance between his own needs and those of others.

Sun in Scorpio: This child seems to come in with a chip on her shoulder. Like the neighborhood bully, she's always ready for a fight and usually finds one. It's hard to say what pushes her buttons; it might be something as small as another kid playing with her toys without asking. Or it might be something much deeper. Whatever the truth, she won't bother explaining it to you. She just reacts.

The breakthrough comes when your child learns to turn her attention away from her own dramas, concerns, and opinions. Once she does this, light steals in and illuminates the real reason for her anger. Then she can marshal her considerable energy and magnetism to make a real difference in the world.

Her experience of her parents is likely to go through profound shifts in perception. At times, they seem to support her, to give her exactly what she needs. Other times, they miss the mark entirely.

Sun in Sagittarius: Forget the cooing baby who sleeps through the night from his sixth week of life. This child barely needs to sleep. Right from the start, he's a powerhouse of energy. What he lacks in diplomacy is compensated for in his blunt honesty. You may not like what he has to say, but time and again his words hit one of your private truths.

He may be fascinated by ghost stories and tales of lost civilizations. He likes foreign travel, especially to spots that wouldn't interest most kids his age—Stonehenge, for instance, or Mayan ruins. In his eagerness to dig up answers, he can be careless, maybe even reckless, but somehow he usually manages to land on his feet. Life with this child is challenging, but never boring.

One of his parents may not be around very much, perhaps because of career obligations, and the other parent is wrapped up in his or her own affairs. But this gives him the space he needs to develop his independence.

Sun in Capricorn: Earth and fire never mix. Earth, in fact, can suffocate fire, an appropriate metaphor for the challenge in this combination. Even so, the combination has a lot going for it. Both signs are cardinal, so your child's emotions and her ego work in unison when it comes to setting off across the back yard in a covered wagon. The structures and rules her ego constructs often direct and channel her enormous emotional energy. In a sense, Aries provides the fuel for the rocket that Capricorn builds.

What this means for you, as a parent, is that your child responds to rules, but not to coercion. She can be cajoled, but not tricked. If you do outsmart her, especially on an issue about which she feels strongly, it only happens once.

Sun in Aquarius: Arrogance is this child's middle name. He thinks he knows more than everyone else and doesn't hesitate to say his piece. Even when he's not right, he's rarely humble about the error. He's also brighter than other kids and has more foresight than many adults.

His intuition comes to him in brilliant flashes. When he acts on it, he gets to where he's meant to be. His instincts run through him like a high tension wire and his intellect races along, trying to keep up. When it does catch up, watch out. Ultimately, this child is a visionary.

Sun in Pisces: What the Aries/Aquarius combination conceptualizes intellectually, the Aries/Pisces combination can conceptualize psychically. Even though the combination lacks unity in its elements—fire and water—and in qualities—cardinal and mutable—one provides what the other lacks.

Your child's emotional energy drives her to explore realms and countries of the spirit that you can't even imagine. It won't happen overnight, but you'll notice gradual changes in her moods, the things she talks about, the questions she asks. At some level, she knows the answers lie inside her, but she needs guidance in uncovering them.

This child may report at breakfast that she left her body last night and went to a beautiful hillside where she talked to your dead father. Or she may announce that you'd better get your tires checked because you're going to have a flat—and you don't and, sure enough, your tire blows.

So listen hard when she shares her experiences with you. There's a truth for you in her stories.

19

Taurus Moon

Think of a little Mick Jagger, running around with his guitar, in his eccentric clothes, singing about how he can't get no satisfaction. Then think of Jagger the multimillionaire, the shrewd entertainer who managed to tap into the collective psyche of an entire generation of Boomers and is now tapping into the collective psyches of the Boomers' kids. That's one kind of Taurus Moon. Katherine Hepburn is another kind.

Graceful, earthy icon versus brilliant hedonist. Perhaps that's the real contradiction with this Moon child. Regardless of where your child falls within these two extremes, several things are certain. She likes pleasant surroundings, she enjoys what money can buy, and her intuitive sense is highly developed.

Her ideal is a place with fascinating art on the walls, a lush garden where she can putter and watch her summer vegetables grow, and music piped through every room. She wants a fabulous kitchen, where she can eat gourmet foods that she may or may not cook herself, and she wants people and animals that she loves around her. She wants Eden, she wants paradise.

She views her mother as solid, generous, nurturing, a real grassroots kind of woman who provides her with exactly the right amount of love and security. Mom is always there for her and she passes this kind of mothering on to her own kids.

This child's security lies in creating security and serenity for herself and those dearest to her. As for her heart's desire, well, that's all part of what she needs to discover.

Taurus Moon and . . .

Sun in Aries: She's industrious, a hard worker. When she wants something badly enough, she's the type who sets up a lemonade stand at the end of your driveway so she can earn money for that new toy she wants.

She seems to have been born with a strong sense of her own worth. She may occasionally blow her own horn, but she really prefers to keep her accomplishments to herself. Even though she doesn't lack for friends, she may be more of a loner that other kids her age. In a group, she goes along with whatever the agenda is unless she disagrees with it. Then she won't be a part of it; she digs in her heels and refuses to budge. This stubborn streak grounds her and slows down all that Aries Sun impatience. It also enables her to channel her energy into worthwhile projects and goals.

Her biggest challenge is learning to be in charge without trying to dominate everyone around her. This pattern may well be one that prevails between her parents. To modify it in her own life, mom and dad need to become aware of the patterns that exist in their own relationship.

Sun in Taurus: This child isn't just stubborn; he's intractable. You can't convince him of anything unless he's open to changing his mind.

He enjoys pleasant, aesthetic surroundings, the frills and pleasures that money buys. He likes collecting things—toy cars, building blocks, shells, whatever strikes his fancy. Later on, this may translate into more expensive and grander collections—of art, books, rare cars, something that holds it value. These things represent his security.

His insight is usually highly developed, so that he doesn't have to ask a lot of questions to make up his mind about an issue. He may not act very quickly, but his measured, dilatory pace works wells for him. In fact, his emotions and his ego function smoothly together. If he's artistically or musically inclined, which he probably is, this combination allows him to work from truly inspired depths.

He sees his parents as loving people who provide him with the emotional support and grounding that he needs.

Sun in Gemini: This child has an abundance of friends. Her quick wit and solid loyalty to the people she loves endears her to others. She's congenial in a group unless she's pushed to do something with which she doesn't agree. Then she spells out what's bothering her and you can either change your mind or count her out.

Even though earth and air aren't the most compatible elements, the combination stabilizes Gemini's restlessness and adds spark and speed to the emotions of the Taurus Moon. She loves books and learning, but not just for the sake of information. Always, she's seeking the deeper connections, the thread that connects one seemingly disparate piece with a greater whole.

She usually enjoys nurturing younger kids and may babysit to make extra money. As she matures, this nurturing aspect of her personality may prompt her to financially help out friends or family members in need. She can't stand to see people or animals suffering.

Sun in Cancer: He's sensitive and intuitive. At the deep core of himself, he knows who he is and what he wants. But he sometimes gets distracted by the business of living and forgets that he knows.

His aesthetic sense shows in his immediate surroundings, like in his room or play area, which he considers to be his private space. Don't enter without knocking; he's very proprietary about his space. As he gets older, this extends to his apartment, home, and personal belongings.

His imagination is quite fertile and original and he applies it in unique ways to his life. This is the sort of child who may spend hours by himself, writing stories and illustrating them.

His inner experience of his parents is good. He feels deep, psychic ties to both of them and to the traditions they believe in.

Sun in Leo: From the time she's old enough to get around, she has her particular way of doing things. If that way isn't followed, you hear about it. Remember, both Taurus and Leo are fixed signs. That means this child is very slow about changing her routines, opinions, and beliefs.

Most of the time, she's a joy to be around, filled with life and fun, eager to embrace whatever comes her way. The Leo in her has a dramatic flair; she loves to show off, to have an audience. But the Taurus in her grimaces at the scrutiny and is usually happier behind the scenes.

This is a child for whom balance is vital. Let her take acting and dancing lessons, indulge her in riding lessons, karate, baseball. But feed her Taurus soul with books, delicious food, camping trips. Then leave the decision about who she wants to be entirely up to her.

Sun in Virgo: He likes attractive surroundings, he's tidy, he thinks deeply about things. He's the four-year-old kid with the furrowed brow, a fretter at his worst, a thinker at his best.

This child is practical. If he's required to do something, he wants to know what purpose it serves. He needs to see, feel, and touch the results of his efforts. For a time, when he's very young, he may appear to be taking everything you tell him as gospel. But a part of him, even then, is turning it around slowly, scrutinizing it from every angle. He's careful, this one. How could he be otherwise with this earth pairing?

He has a rather wry sense of humor when he wants to. And when he's feeling good, he's flexible and cooperative and willing to go along with whatever the agenda is. But if pushed too far, he cuts you off cold.

He experiences his parents as practical people with a flair for drama. Maybe the dramas occur between mom and dad, in their relationship; maybe they're carried out between him and the people who come and go through his life. However they show up, this child learns to speak his mind even when his opinion may not be to anyone else's liking.

Sun in Libra: This combination is usually artistic. Sometimes the artistry occurs within the realm of human relationships, which are this child's work-in-progress. Other times, it shows up in the cultural arts, with a penchant for music or language or art.

As a youngster, she has an aesthetic eye for color, texture, shape. She has opinions on how you decorate her room, knows what kinds of clothes look good on her, has her tastes, her preferences. She won't argue with you about any of it, but she may well charm you into her way of thinking. That's how she works best. Her personal charm is legendary before she hits kindergarten.

She brings grace and harmony into her family. Her experience of her parents is likely to be positive. Mom and dad seem to have a harmonious relationship, and if they don't, she doesn't know about it.

Sun in Scorpio: This little soul searcher thinks in large terms even when he's young. He's the kid who wants to turn your home into a haunted house for Halloween and to charge admission! He can be an outright opportunist when it suits him, but he is so charming that you don't realize he has taken you in until after the fact.

As a youngster, he may exhibit a deep interest in things that go bump in the night. This interest often matures into a fascination with metaphysical topics and into considerable psychic talent. The challenge for a parent is to ground the child in reality so that his forays into the mystical and strange don't consume him.

Since this child tends to be so much of an opportunist, it's important that he learn right and wrong at a young age. Encourage him to open up and talk about his feelings with you and other people he trusts.

Sun in Sagittarius: Her infinite reservoirs of energy are apparent from the moment she's born. She probably doesn't require the amount of sleep that other kids her age require. This means you can forget about naps during the toddler stage. She would rather explore her environment. This penchant for exploration is also evident when she travels. In foreign countries, she wants to see and do everything as soon as she arrives.

If her artistic or musical talents are nurtured and allowed to flourish, they remain with her throughout her life. They are her refuge, uniquely hers. She may also excel in sports, and she benefits generally from all kinds of physical exercise.

Her idealism may bring surprises into your home—stray animals, lonely kids, community projects that you end up supervising. This is all part of her fiery enthusiasm for whatever she undertakes and her earthy compassion for all living things.

Your child's temper is most evident when she believes that one of her ideals or principles has been violated. If she's allowed to vent her anger, it blows over quickly. She doesn't hold grudges, but she doesn't forget such slights, either. Ultimately, she follows her own path toward truth.

Sun in Capricorn: As a double earth sign, his emotions and his ego work in harmony. He often seems stronger than he really is, but it gives him a certain charm and charisma that works well in groups, where other kids look to him to define the rules and direct the action.

He likes the luxuries that money can buy, but he is equally at home camping out in the wilderness. He needs the solace of nature just as deeply as he needs social contacts. In fact, the earlier he learns to balance the two, the happier he is. If he goes to extremes in one direction or another, he ends up blinded by materialism or living as a discontented hermit.

When this child has an interest in deeper spiritual mysteries, it's likely to show up through organized religion or some other structured venue. He's at his best when he's able to integrate his spirituality with his practicality.

Sun in Aquarius: She goes to great lengths to avoid dissension and argument. It's not that she's a born peacemaker, only that she deplores disharmony and believes that everyone has the right to live the way they see fit.

She doesn't recognize racial, religious, or cultural boundaries. Status doesn't impress her. In fact, the only criteria she has about people is that they interest her. If they don't, she can't be bothered. This may lead other kids to think of her as a snob, but hey, they'll get over it.

Her cosmic interests are likely to be broad and profound, even before she really understands what any of it is about. This combination indicates sound intuition and the ability to perceive the underlying order of seemingly random events. She's the type who would tell you what was *really* going on in your life the day your car blew a tire on the interstate—a type of insight you may find unnerving.

Sun in Pisces: He's so sensitive that his feelings are easily hurt. But this same sensitivity also extends to other people, giving him great empathy and compassion. He's the kind of child who hurts when you hurt, even if he doesn't understand why you hurt. He's a psychic sponge.

Art and music figure prominently in your child's life, whether he has these abilities or not. He's well mannered, with an innate consideration for others. In his heart, though, he feels inadequate in some way and really blooms when he's complimented for a job well done or when his uniqueness is acknowledged by the people he loves.

Over all, this combination results in a sweetheart of a child who, despite streaks of utter stubbornness, is a true joy to the family lucky enough to have him.

20

Gemini Moon

Okay, got it, over and out. That's how life is with this Moon child. As a parent, you live in *his* fast lane, adjusting yourself to *his* pace, *his* needs, his intellectual whims, *his* dramas. He's not selfish, exactly; he's just consumed by his need to know and to know it now.

Whether his immediate passion is German shepherds or the riddle of life on other planets, his questions burn at the center of his being until they are answered. His need to know drives him forward throughout his life, and you, as his parent, are jerked along in the slipstream.

Your child has respite periods, for sure, times when he burns out and has to step back to reflect, to project, to breathe. This is when he reads, watches movies, travels, or somehow distracts himself from the essential journey. But he always returns to the Gemini fold—to discover, to uncover, to ferret out, and then to communicate.

He isn't particularly emotional. He may not even be demonstrative. His love and his hugs come through on an intellectual level. For a parent, significant other, or a close friend, this may not be easy to accept. But accept you must, because he isn't going to change.

This child's security is found in the mental quest, whatever it is, whatever shape it takes. His heart's desire is to communicate, somehow, some way, what he learns.

He's apt to view his mother as an interesting person, bookish but fun, always on the move, intellectually stimulating. His mother can be nurturing when the situation calls for it, but she can also be too busy and caught up in her own things at times.

Gemini Moon and . . .

Sun in Aries: He probably learns to speak long before he begins to crawl because his need to express himself is one of the strongest thrusts in his personality. You won't ever have to wonder what's going on with this child. He tells you flat out, then goes on to dissect and discuss every little thing that's been bothering him today and last week.

His facility with the spoken word can dazzle you. But at times, as a parent, you probably wish he would just be quiet for five minutes so you can mull over what he has said. When he's angry, his tongue is sharp enough to pierce even the toughest shells.

He can be quite a gossip, too, buzzing about the latest arguments and dissension in the neighborhood. It's annoying now, but it could pay off professionally later on; it's a great placement for a gossip columnist or a broadcaster on tabloid TV. Encourage him to channel his talents into something constructive, then there's no telling what heights he may attain.

He experiences his parents as impatient, sometimes short-tempered, but always eager to talk with him, to communicate.

Sun in Taurus: From her earliest years, this child is adventurous and nomadic, a free spirit imbued with deep restlessness. Turn your attention away from her for a few moments and she takes off down the street.

159

As she matures, it's easy for her to find fault in others, but she's not nearly as sanguine about her own faults. Despite this, she's popular and well liked, although at some point this critical streak will need to be tempered. She's bright, eager to learn, and is especially passionate about subjects that interest her. Education and learning in general ground her and keep her mind busy.

She loves to travel and the destination isn't as important as the journey itself. Whether it's a camping trip in a park close to home or a vacation in some far-flung corner of the world, this child's nomadic spirit moves her forward constantly.

She experiences her parents as bright, articulate people who introduce her to the world of ideas and beauty. There's open discussion in the home, and sometimes it's louder and more heated than she likes, but they make her feel secure and loved.

Sun in Gemini: Remember the little girl in the movie *Matilda*? She was reading before she could crawl, and by the time she was four, she had found her way to the library, where she devoured every book in the children's section. Chances are she was a double Gemini.

Your child is an early reader and probably talks early as well. Her restless intellect devours information, seeking to combine this bit with that bit to find the common thread. She sometimes lives so much in her own head, she may seem emotionally aloof to others. When she's not reading or talking or socializing, her concentration is scattered. If she cultivates the ability to concentrate, there's little that she can't achieve.

She's a nervous, high-strung child, one of those kids who plays until she literally drops from exhaustion. It's important for her general health that she get adequate sleep and that she has a balanced diet. This is true for all kids, of course, but it's a must for this double whirlwind of energy.

She experiences her parents, particularly her mother, as bright, articulate people. Even though they may seem emotionally remote at times, they nurture her mind and intellectual abilities.

Sun in Cancer: If this child tells you that he dreamed the walls in your house caught on fire, then definitely have the wiring checked in your house. He is often clairvoyant and the first inklings of it may come to him in dreams or in a daydream state.

He's impressionable and sensitive, particularly when he's young. He wants so much to be liked that he can be too compliant at times, only to resent it later on. He's so social and usually such fun to be around that he has no lack of friends. But his mood can change suddenly, unexpectedly, and you never know for sure what triggered it. Just remember that the same duality which applies to the Gemini Sun also applies to the Moon and can be even more pronounced.

Cancer's usual yearnings for home and hearth are at odds with this Moon's unsettled nature. He would rather be out and about than stay at home. For him, security lies in understanding something completely. Yet, as this child grows up, he's the one who comes home every vacation and brings you the world at Christmas.

He experiences his parents as nurturers, and intellectually curious people.

Sun in Leo: Boredom is her worst enemy. This might be said of any child with a Gemini Moon, but when you toss in all that leonine energy, boredom must be avoided at any cost.

Her magnetism, which is part bravado and part dramatic flair, is hard to resist, even for her closest friends and the people who know her best. She's fascinating to be around, often daring and seemingly courageous, even when that isn't how she feels inside at all. At times like this, she's a lot like the lion in the *Wizard of Oz*; behind her mask of brave talk she's riddled with insecurities.

Her fickle affections are an intricate part of her growth process. She's always seeking excitement, change, an elusive, unattainable *something* that she can't even define.

She experiences her parents as bold, dramatic people who always speak their minds.

Sun in Virgo: Since both Gemini and Virgo are ruled by Mercury, this child is high strung and very mental. His mind works analytically, critically, forever picking away at little details and trying to connect them to something larger and greater.

He's an adaptable child, who readily adjusts himself to whatever changes come up during the family vacation or in living in general. He has no shortage of friends and they're likely to be as bright and eager to learn as he is. When one of these friends hurts him, however, he turns his detached, critical eye on their faults, picks them apart in his head, and dismisses them from his life.

Your child is a true workaholic. Give him a project and he goes at it with such focused purpose that he won't do anything else until it's done. The challenge is to achieve balance in his life, to play just as hard as he works, to allow his intuition the same freedom as his critical left brain.

He experiences his parents as very mental people, intellectuals who may be workaholics.

Sun in Libra: Even when she's very young, she's terrific company. She's witty, has a graceful manner and way of speaking, and she loves to talk about everything. She learns quickly, and even though she isn't likely to delve into any area in depth, she grasps the essentials and is able to communicate them.

She's popular throughout her life, partly because of her charm but also because she avoids arguments and dissension. As a double air sign, her talents find their best expression through the arts and communication. She connects with people primarily on a mental level, but you never sense an emotional detachment, as with a double Gemini. It's not that she feels things more deeply than any other Moon sign, but that she gives the impression she does.

She exhibits a wonderful finesse in everything she does and brings a particular kind of beauty to her family. Her parents, in turn, instill her with self-confidence and self-reliance.

Sun in Scorpio: His penchant for secrecy and privacy is at odds with the Moon's need to talk and communicate. One way around this is that he may talk avidly about other people's lives or be may be a marvelous storyteller, weaving fantastic tales on the spur of the moment.

He's fairly easy to get along with. The adaptability of his Gemini Moon blows apart some of Scorpio's fixed and rigid ways of doing things. He may stand on principle now and then just to show you he's no pushover, but basically he's willing to go along with the agenda.

Thanks to Scorpio's intensity, he gives the impression that he always knows what he's doing and why. The truth, though, is that he's often racked with indecision. If he can learn to act on his first instincts, which are quite sound, then he won't miss out on the many opportunities that are sure to come his way. This combination tends to be lucky, and sometimes it's so lucky that your child doesn't have to work very hard for what he achieves.

Sun in Sagittarius: These polar opposites tend to work very well together. Your child's expansive personality attracts friends the way a lake attracts ducks. They love her wit, her adventurous spirit, her capacity for joy.

Even when she gets into trouble, she's able to talk and charm her way out of it. You can't stay angry with her for very long. She is definitely an opportunist and is not beneath taking advantage of everything that comes her way.

She isn't dishonest, exactly, but she is able to justify most of her actions in some way. For this reason, it's important that she learn right from wrong at an early age.

Another important characteristic of this combination is travel. For this child, it isn't just a need, it's an itch that never goes away. When she's on the road, she opens fully to the vast experience of life.

She experiences her parents as people who are willing to defend what they believe.

Sun in Capricorn: On the surface, this combination wouldn't seem to work very well. But the airy, adaptable qualities of the Moon loosen up Capricorn's love affair with rules and restrictions. In return, earthy Capricorn provides a structure for the Gemini energy. The result is a child who expresses himself well and easily and does so with a certain flair that seizes other people's attention.

His inventiveness is usually motivated by need and practicality, rather than by a passionate creative spirit. Just the same, whatever he produces in this manner is impressive, because he does it with such seriousness. His earnest approach to life is one of the things you notice first about him. It confers a kind of authority that other kids either like or shy away from.

He often takes himself much too seriously and needs to lighten up on himself. Otherwise, he comes across as pompous, which only turns other kids off. He's very bright but may be mentally lazy at times because things come to him so easily. Imagine what wonders he might achieve if he brings his full power to bear on his ambitions.

He experiences his parents as being somewhat heavy on rules, but they always support his interests and goals.

Sun in Aquarius: She's a little bundle of contradictions. Even though she's exceedingly bright, she flits from one subject or friend to another, as if possessed by an odd form of wanderlust. She has a natural ease and facility with language, yet she is easily bored when pursuing any one single course of expression. She has artistic talent, but she can't seem to settle down enough to do much with it.

This tendency is mitigated somewhat as she gets older and realizes that the real world requires her to focus her energy in some way. It's best if she learns this lesson at a young age, then she's able to use her tremendous foresight and intelligence for personal and societal transformation.

Sun in Pisces: The challenge with this combination is decisiveness and security, both of which must be culti-vated. This child is often so adaptable that her own needs are swallowed by other people's needs. Her easygoing manner is actually the mask that covers her inability to make decisions. For her, it's often easier to just go along with the crowd.

Thanks to the duality inherent in both Pisces and Gem-ini, this child's inner conflict centers on the tug of war be-tween her heart and her mind. When up against people who are stronger or more opinionated than she is, all her insecurities come to roost and the war between head and heart is escalated.

She needs constant reassurance of her inner worth. When she comes to realize that other people can't give it to her, that it's something she must cultivate on her own, her life becomes much easier.

21

Cancer Moon

If you mistake what she needs, then you aren't paying attention. This Moon child, more than any other, needs the emotional security of her home, roots, and mother. She needs love and affection from everyone in her family. If she gets it, then she, in turn, is better able to nurture others.

A lot goes on beneath the surface with this child. She lives within a sea of emotions, of feelings and intuition. She senses what is invisible to the rest of us, feels what other people feel, and connects with them at that level. Feelings are her domain and her venue for creative expression.

She shares many of the attributes of the Cancer Sun, but in a larger, deeper sense. Intuition can easily develop into psychic or even visionary ability, particularly where her family is concerned. Remember the little kid in *The Shining*? That's how psychic this child can be.

Generations ago, this Moon child probably had an easier time of it. Home was where you had lived all your life, in a neighborhood where you had grown up with the same children and families. Gender roles were clearly defined.

In today's world, all that has changed, which makes this child's need for home and roots even more important.

The challenge for this child is to learn not to brood over every injury or slight, whether real or imagined. She should be encouraged to attend to her own needs as readily as she does to the needs of others. This will prevent her from having to fill a psychological void later in her life.

For these kids, nurturing from mom can go one of several ways—too little, too much, or just enough. For mom, the challenge is to find the right balance.

Cancer Moon and . . .

Sun in Aries: If you ever have any doubt about the challenge inherent in this combination, light a match and pour water over the flame. It hisses, sputters, and smokes before it goes out. While Cancer doesn't really extinguish all that Aries fire, it does temper her reckless, impulsive side.

It frustrates her when she's young because it seems that the things she imagines doing either never get off the ground or don't take off the way she expects. As a result, she may later channel her energy into a creative pursuit, where she feels she has more control over the outcome. Art, drama, music, even a grassroots business may interest her. With the Aries drive behind her, she usually excels at whatever she puts her mind to.

Her intuitive ability gives her great insight into other people and into the underlying meaning behind events. She also has a dramatic flair. The combination would help her succeed in acting, where she would be able to project herself into the character she plays.

She appears to be adventurous, a fearless risktaker. But within, she's astonished at the things she does and always wonders if she's really up to the challenge. If you can teach her at a young age that she's definitely equipped to meet the challenge, it bolsters her self-confidence and a belief in her own abilities.

Sun in Taurus: Taurus in any shape or form always brings stubbornness to the child's personality. In this combination, the Cancer Moon helps disguise the stubbornness.

On the surface, he appears to be diplomatic and agreeable, but within he may be seething and feeling resentful. You won't ever know the full truth because he refuses to confront any emotional issue head on. Instead, he moves forever to either side of the issue, perhaps hoping the problem will go away on its own.

He needs to learn what he really believes in the deepest part of himself and to take a stand on issues about which he feels passionate. Instead of trying to please everyone, he would be better off learning to please himself first. Part of this learning process involves trusting and acting on his highly developed intuition.

He experiences his parents as grounded, nurturing people.

Sun in Gemini: With this combination, your child thrives on anything that feeds her mind and yet absorbs it all through her intuition. Her intuition, in fact, bolsters her memory, perhaps by creating vivid mental pictures about events and people.

She's social and has many different types of friends. But she may be somewhat high strung and benefits from time alone or with just her family. She may go through periods where she's perfectly content to spend all her free time with her family, especially if she has brothers or sisters. When something is amiss at home, she feels it first. It's as if she reads the subtle emotional vibrations the way a blind person reads braille.

As she matures, this talent translates into an ability to read people quickly and accurately, either in a one-on-one situation or in a crowd. The talent can also be turned to writing psychological fiction with insight into what makes the characters click.

Sun in Cancer: A double whammy. All of the Cancerian sensitivity comes to roost with this combination. He's so sensitive that his feelings are easily hurt, and when he's hurt, he withdraws to lick his wounds.

When he's young, his wounds are numerous: an unreturned hug, a raised voice, a scolding, a friend who doesn't reciprocate his affection. Over time, any rebuff, real or imagined, is met with withdrawal. Withdrawal eventually spells loneliness. His shell, like that of the crab that symbolizes the sign, can become either his armor or his albatross. If he retreats too far, other children may find him too remote to bother with, so the sooner he toughens up, the better off he'll be.

Considerable intuition accompanies this combination. If he can learn to trust his impressions enough to act on them, then he saves himself time, heartache, and aggravation down the road.

He may experience his parents as over-protective.

Sun in Leo: She's first and foremost a realist with highly developed instincts. In the practical world, this means she's the type who writes and directs a play with her friends, then invites the neighborhood and charges admission. And because she has integrity, she divides the profits with everyone in the play.

She has a kind of universal appeal that draws people to her in droves. Her intuitive talent allows her to divine what other people need and want, and she provides it instinctively, thus making others feel good about themselves. She is always loving and affectionate and asks only for the same in return.

Her talents can be manifested in any number of areas: business, drama, the arts. Whatever she selects, she can have the whole tidy package, family and fame and the achievement of her heart's desire.

Sun in Virgo: There's a nervous, catlike fastidiousness about this combination that can show up in a preoccupation with details. Shyness and a certain reticence are part of this child's makeup, too. It's not that he's a shrinking violet; he's simply reluctant to let people too close too quickly.

His mind is sharp and very busy, always figuring, learning, absorbing, picking things apart and putting them back together again. He does this on an intuitive level also, where the process isn't quite as clear-cut. The differences between these two processes may sometimes confuse him, particularly when his head screams one thing and his gut screams something else.

The challenge with this combination, for both you and your child, is to convince him it's okay if he lightens up on himself and everyone else. He has a sharp mind and an intuition so rich that if he can find a way to bridge the two, he'll have it made.

Sun in Libra: She's great with people of all ages, able to feel her way intuitively and diplomatically through whatever labyrinths they erect. She's something of a chameleon, too, when it comes to others. Part of the reason for this is that she wants so much to be liked that she will become, in effect, whatever you want her to be.

This type of practice eventually results in an identity crisis in which she doesn't really know who she is. When that happens, she turns to her family or to friends who are like family who will allow her intuition to lead her back to herself. If she doesn't find herself on this first quest, the same patterns in relationships tend to repeat themselves unless she gets the point.

And the point is actually simple. She needs to know who she is and what makes her tick, apply that to her relationships, and then turn her knowledge outward, beyond herself. Then she's ready to take on the world.

Sun in Scorpio: He has the soul of a poet, the uncanny perceptions of a psychic, and the penetrating, often suspicious mind of a secret agent. In fact, everything important about this child happens beneath the surface. Most of the time you won't be privy to it unless you have established a solid communication between yourselves. Even then, you're working against Scorpio's secrecy and Cancer's deft evasion of emotional sore spots.

By the time he's old enough to think for himself, he has an opinion on just about everything. Why is the sky blue? Why does John Doe down the block act like such a jerk? Your kid will be glad to tell you why. To him, it's become a fact, the truth. But the real reason he'll argue about it all night is to win his point, not to convince you that he's right.

This child loves to win and that sentiment by itself may take him farther than even he imagines.

Sun in Sagittarius: The world literally lies at this child's feet. But first, she has to make choices. She has to discover who she is within the immediate scheme of things—her family, her circle of friends, her school. Is she a braggart? If she a homebody? Is she a student or a teacher? If she's a seeker, what kind of seeker is she? And just what does she want to be when she grows up?

Her abilities are vast, her intuition is sharp. In the best of circumstances, she can use both in some visionary capacity. It's likely that she is or will be interested in some facet of metaphysics or in the investigation of deeper mysteries.

Her optimism is one of her greatest assets. Sometimes, though, it can carry her too far too quickly because she doesn't pause to gather all the facts. Once she learns to get to the core of an issue before she acts, she can accomplish virtually anything.

Sun in Capricorn: Even as a little kid, he's very serious and somewhat secretive. He may spend hours alone in his room, building an elaborate structure out of building blocks that holds meaning only to him. Or he may lock himself in the basement with his chemistry set and attempt to rearrange the molecular structure of a rock.

This same penchant for secrecy also applies to his feelings. If he's hurt or depressed, he usually keeps it to himself. He dislikes dissension and goes out of his way to avoid it. He needs to loosen up, to get out of his own head, to reach out to friends his own age. Once he does this and learns to act on his deep insight into other people, his life becomes infinitely easier.

With a bit of guidance, he enjoys setting goals and achieving them. At first these should be short-term goals, so that he sees the tangible results within a period of days or weeks. Once he gets the hang of it, though, goal setting feeds the Capricorn need for structure.

Sun in Aquarius: She's idiosyncratic about most everything she does and some people even think she's a bit of an eccentric. But everyone loves her anyway because she's so uniquely and completely herself. Besides, she has a way of putting others at ease.

She can be secretive about her feelings, unwilling to discuss them even with people to whom she's closest. In her heart, she's a true romantic, the kind of child who wants every story to have a happy ending. Divorce or a sudden move deeply disturbs her equilibrium. Even when she understands a situation intellectually, she is fundamentally a creature who *feels*.

Sun in Pisces: His emotions run through him like an underground river. When he's moody, you may not have a clue about what's really bothering him. If you prod, he may or may not tell you, depending on how badly he needs someone else's input.

His sensitivity to the people around him sometimes borders on clairvoyance; at the very least, it's a heightened sixth sense that guides him through the complex maze of human emotions. His compassion and kindness are genuine. He's a good listener, especially for others who need someone to listen to them.

His capacity for self-sacrifice is admirable, but unless he does it without expecting gratitude or compensation, it may make him bitter. His greatest challenge is to control his emotions so they don't sweep him away.

22

Leo Moon

Make no mistake about it: This Moon child is king of the jungle—or at least he thinks he is. He's flamboyant and dramatic, warm and generous, and somewhat self-centered. He is usually affectionate and demonstrative and needs a lot of both shown to him in return.

A child with a Leo Moon can be difficult to live with because he needs to be the center of attention. If he has brothers or sisters, they learn early on that he must have center stage. He's better off as an only child who has exclusive rights to his parents' attention.

When he feels he isn't getting enough attention, he creates situations or acts in a way that gets him that attention. As a youngster, this means he may do things consciously that force you to pay attention to him—throw a temper tantrum, talk nonstop, run away from you at the mall, show off in some way. As he gets older, this need for attention may take more subtle forms—a chronic health problem, a string of failed relationships, a succession of jobs that he hates. In each instance, there's a repetitive pattern that shrieks for attention.

Despite his bravado and apparent self-assurance, he should be encouraged to believe completely in himself and his abilities. He should be applauded for jobs well done, appreciated for what he is. Once he has this kind of encouragement, he doesn't need to brag or show off or always be the center of attention.

His mother is like royalty, a woman who enjoys the attention of others and who caters to her "court" with flair and drama. The problem arises when she's so consumed by her own needs that she neglects her child's needs. Then the child may still be throwing temper tantrums at thirty years old. His mother, however, encourages pride and style in her children and a grand dignity that nothing can squelch.

This Moon child enjoys other kids, takes them under his wing, into the folds of his protection. And when he has a family of his own, this love of children becomes one of his greatest assets. He can achieve nearly anything he desires, particularly if he brings concentration and focus to his fierce passion.

Leo Moon and . . .

Sun in Aries: He's an adventurous little devil who wants to run the show and also star in it. He doesn't care what the show is, as long as it involves an audience that applauds him.

He has a clear idea of who he is, but he doesn't like to mull it over. He would rather act it out. He needs to be constantly on the move, involved, doing, pressing forward. In this way, he tests his own parameters, learns his limits, and further defines who he is.

He has many friends, who are as loyal to him as he is to them. His warmhearted, magnanimous nature reaches out to others, especially to those in need, to provide comfort, shelter, food, whatever is required. With this in mind, never take him to the local animal shelter unless you're ready to adopt several pets!

Sun in Taurus: Once she makes up her mind about anything, that's it. Nothing shakes her from her position. This double-fixed combination makes her intractably stubborn and strong willed. But it also gives her sound instincts that guide her and alert her to the truth about people and situations.

She may be short on tact, but her direct manner cuts right to the heart of any issue. Once her friends realize that she tells the truth as she sees it and acts on that truth, they respect her.

Her Taurus Sun hungers for peaceful harmony and more solitude, while her Leo Moon enjoys noise, people, activity. This tug of war can create conflict for her until she learns that the secret to this combination lies in learning to balance the needs of her ego with those of her heart.

Sun in Gemini: He's sharp, shrewd, witty, and fun. Other kids love to be around him because he comes up with such outlandish things to do and makes it all seem so adventurous!

His love of learning doesn't necessarily make him a diligent student. Thanks to his considerable intellect and his deep belief in his own ability, he gets by just fine without having to apply himself. This changes as he gets older and uncovers his true passions.

Other people will always play a vital role in his life. He's too social to ever become a proverbial hermit and he deeply needs the love and appreciation of others. He may drive you nuts during his teenage and college years, when he has a new love weekly. But sooner or later, he discovers that his own capacity for love and generosity draws his soulmate into his life for keeps.

Sun in Cancer: Sugar and spice and everything nice: Isn't that how the nursery rhyme goes? On the surface, this child seems to fit the ticket.

She goes along with whatever the agenda is, her nature so cooperative and agreeable that she's every mother's dream. Then that curve ball whips out of left field and you realize the truth. She has her own agenda and somehow has engineered circumstances so that everyone has done things her way, after all. She's not manipulative, at least not consciously. She's simply an individualist who brings you around to her way of thinking through the art of compromise—your compromise.

She enjoys her numerous friends and enjoys them best when they're at her house or in her backyard. Her home is her showcase, and this is true whether she's five or forty-five. She has a lot of pride in her family, whom she considers to be almost an extension of herself. She's at her best when she uses her innate intuition combined with her passion.

Sun in Leo: This is another double whammy. He's a cyclone of energy, action, and ambition. Forget introspection or retrospection for this child. He doesn't look back or inward. He simply barrels forward, fueled by his passion of the moment.

When he's young, his friends and family are his world. He would rather spend time with them than be alone. Even though he has a high opinion of himself, solitude doesn't suit him; it doesn't offer that essential, immediate feedback that he needs. Although he's generous with other people, there's an emotionally detached quality about him that may baffle the people closest to him. The truth is that he's an incurable romantic and in his journey through his teens, he'll fall in love dozens of times.

Once he's out on his own, your child probably finds his niche quicker than most. Even if he doesn't have clearly defined goals, he somehow lands in the right place at the right time. And because he wants to be the one giving the orders rather than taking them, his ambition usually takes him right to the top of whatever profession he chooses.

For this combination, the child perceives his parents as dynamic people. Sometimes, they may be so dynamic that he feels he has to compete with them.

Sun in Virgo: She's a little drone with a huge heart and a soul filled with compassion. She feels bound by duty at every turn, and yet her need for attention distracts her. She's a conscientious student who can spend much of her time alone, working out intricate details in her head. Then along comes that Leo Moon, demanding that she get out and play, socialize, have fun.

She can be detached when she needs to protect herself emotionally. This may come in handy later in life, allowing her to scrutinize a situation or an individual with a left-brain sharpness. But if, when she's young, she's applauded for her efforts and encouraged to follow her dream, she won't need that emotional detachment. She won't crave attention. She'll know her own worth.

She perceives her parents as flamboyant people, who still get the job done on time, perfect to the letter.

Sun in Libra: Poetry, music, and romance breathe in his soul, and one way or another, they define who he is. As young as two or three, he stands apart from other children his age. It might be the celestial look in his eyes. Or the peacefulness that he emanates. Or it might be the incredible miniature drawings that he sketches on his bedroom walls or the way he plays that keyboard you bought him at Christmas. His talent, whatever it is, is sure to be impressive.

He can be temperamental at times and he may not fully outgrow it. But as he gets older, his little shows of temper and frustration ride tandem with his idealism. He wants everything to be harmonious and beautiful, whether it's his relationships or his artistic endeavors or both.

The challenge with this combination is that he must cultivate a belief in his own power—and claim it.

Sun in Scorpio: This double-fixed combination lends itself to a string of dramatic adjectives: magnetic, charismatic, romantic, idealistic, judgmental, sensationalistic. All are true, but not all of the time.

In the ordinary world of daily life, this child is strong willed and stubborn. Part of her wants to be secretive about what she does; the other part of her wants everyone to know it and to applaud her. This conflict is likely to be fundamental to her life. How she deals with it will test her character again and again. The house placements of the Sun and Moon indicate the areas of her life where this conflict will manifest most strongly.

Once she learns the true power of her emotions and how to use them to alter her reality, she can accomplish virtually anything. But the lesson itself may be difficult for her to learn because she's distracted by her opinions, her fixed attitudes, and that fundamental conflict between her inner life and her ego.

Sun in Sagittarius: At his best, this child's life is based on the highest integrity. He's like the gents of old, whose word was their bond. At his worst, however, he's a braggart who stretches the truth whenever it suits him.

Most children with this combination fall between the two extremes. In daily life, he's fun to be with, asks endless strings of questions that don't deserve glib answers, and seems to have been born with a clear distinction between right and wrong. This isn't to say that he never breaks rules; on the contrary, he tests your limits all the time. But you'll never have to dig the truth out of him or play elaborate word games to discover what he's thinking. He just tells you flat out.

He has a vivid imagination, vivid dreams, a vivid inner life that he's aware of but doesn't analyze too much. And that's fine. The fodder is there regardless and he can use it to create the kind of life for himself that he desires.

Sun in Capricorn: At two, she's an authoritarian who makes sure the family pets follow the rules. Cats: Use the litter boxes. Dogs: Bark to go outside. Like that. At ten, she's explaining the rules of the games to her friends and she's toeing the line herself, adhering to whatever parameters have been established at home. At fifteen . . . , well, you get the picture. But what's not so obvious is that, in doing her thing with rules, she's on center stage, in the limelight, and loving every minute of it.

She's materialistic. She likes nice things. She deserves nice things. She likes to look nice. She probably has a certain style in the way she dresses, the way she combs and styles her hair. Even as a youngster, her control issues can be annoying because she's usually certain that she is right.

There's no doubt that she'll get whatever she wants. But she may not get it in the way that she hopes. She must learn that the only authority that matters is the authority she exerts over herself. If she opens herself to love—thereby risking that she might get hurt—her life soars.

Sun in Aquarius: You won't always understand him. But you will always admire his flair, his intellect, his imagination. This is the kid who can sit, spellbound, through a Broadway musical or act like an adult in a restaurant at the tender age of five. This is also a kid who can break all the rules just because a rebellious mood is upon him.

He seeks the new, the different, and he seeks them in dramatic, often public ways. The big question for him revolves around which part of him will be in the limelight—his head or his heart? His intellect or his emotions?

The persona that is already visible or the one he keeps locked up in a closet in his imagination?

Only he knows. And he's probably not telling.

Sun in Pisces: She's a gem in the rough, the best parts of her hidden away.

At times, she seems like the most self-assured child in the world. At other times, she's shy and reticent and you are her shield. She's a dichotomy to herself and to the people who know her. The conflict between her ego and her emotions is constant. That Leo Moon wants and needs attention; that Pisces Sun prefers to keep to herself, in the shadows.

Her intuition is well developed, but may remain dormant for much of her life because she's hardly aware of it. Sometimes, circumstances help her develop an awareness of her own wisdom and then everything changes for her. She becomes more focused and centered, able to draw on her intuition for guidance.

Her compassion often finds expression in the arts, in caring for animals or people, or in her own children. Once she uncovers the vastness of her potential, the roughness wears away and the gem that she is begins to shine.

23

Virgo Moon

She's as finicky as a cat, picky about everything, but usually the very height of discretion. She's also a tireless worker, whose little mind races along, chewing at every small detail. She's often consumed by her own journey, replete with its dramas, its highs and lows, its failures and triumphs.

She likes working with her hands and may become quite good at it. Some of these pursuits might include: planning and landscaping a garden, sculpturing with clay, painting, making dollhouses. Metaphysics is usually of interest to this child. As she matures, she may develop excellent clairvoyant abilities or a talent to pick up impressions from objects that she touches.

Her quick, agile mind enjoys language, the way words are put together, the sheer beauty of expressing a thought in just the right way. This can give her great talent in writing.

This Moon child likes order. Contrary to popular belief, this doesn't necessarily mean she's a neat freak; it may be that she simply needs her personal areas arranged in a way that makes sense to her. Clutter may or may not bother

her. She's always willing to help in whatever way she can. She should learn to do this, however, only because she wants to and not just because it's expected of her.

She's compassionate without sentimentality. She's also very self-critical at times, believing that she isn't as good at something or as popular as the next kid. In many instances, this can turn into blistering critiques of other people. It arises, in part, from her desire for perfection. She should strive to pay less attention to the abstract mental idea of perfection and more attention to the intuitive flow of her own perceptions. She sometimes has a "prove-it-to-me" attitude, particularly when it involves something that's new to her. But once you prove it to her satisfaction, she rarely questions it again.

Her mother probably works outside the home, in some capacity that requires her to work long hours. Her mother may be picky and detailed about certain facets of their home life, but she is generally a sincere woman who seeks the best for her child.

This child's security comes from helping others help themselves, which in turn deepens her understanding of herself. She's a sweetheart of a child with a heart large enough to contain the world.

Virgo Moon and . . .

Sun in Aries: He's one of those kids who alternates between frenetic social activity and down time, where he reads and studies like some little scholar. He's mentally restless, an eager, avid student. When he's young, he's easily distracted by sports, friends, and excitement. As he matures, his study skills support and enhance his analytical, · curious intellect.

He's a discriminating kid, whose abundant energy should be bolstered through education, books, art, sports, and his other interests and passions. At times, particularly when he's younger, he tends to start things that he doesn't finish. This is just a phase, his way of defining what interests him—and what doesn't.

The challenge for this child is that his Aries Sun wants to play and socialize and his Virgo Moon wants to read, study, and analyze. Even though he enjoys his friends and tends to be popular, he finds fault with them. They somehow never quite measure up to his standards of perfection. Then again, he has the same problem with himself. This child benefits from encouragement and recognition for his abilities. The sooner he develops self-confidence and a belief in himself, the easier his life will be.

Sun in Taurus: She's a real pleasure, blessed with charm, grace, and an ineffable beauty in her demeanor. Her independent streak is a mile wide and may rear up when she's told to do something that she doesn't want to do. She's apt to infuriate you with her stubbornness at times like this. And when her stubbornness erupts in a rare show of temper, just get out of her way. But beneath all that is a little kid who wants to please you, so be patient with her.

Her friends aren't necessarily numerous. But the friends she has will be around for the long haul and are as loyal to her as she is to them. She is attracted to artistic types, probably because she has an abundance of creative talent herself. This can show up in the arts or in science; in either case, she works harder at her passion than most kids her age.

She's capable of scathing criticism about petty things that she blurts out, tact forgotten. Directed in another way, however, this ability for discernment is one of her greatest strengths.

With some early guidance and encouragement to follow her dream, her avocation can become her vocation.

Given her natural propensity as a tireless worker, she can achieve whatever she desires.

Sun in Gemini: Dramatic flair, very bright, an abundance of nervous energy: These are the most obvious traits of this combination. Under the surface, however, this child is a tumultuous river of emotions and thoughts, capable of intellectual achievements if he can stick with something long enough. And that's the core of his challenge, really, to find his all-consuming passion, that one shining gem that he pursues throughout his life.

He's so adaptable that he never lacks for friends or social activities. He does well with change, too, even dramatic changes like a move or a new school. His gregarious personality can be misleading because he goes through periods when he's anything but sociable. At times like this, his discriminating intellect turns in on itself, picking apart every little flaw or failure, real or imagined, that he has ever experienced. He needs lots of positive reinforcement and expressions of love to counteract his natural tendency toward self-criticism.

His buoyant, intellectual curiosity never falters or slows down. In college, he probably changes majors several times, but by his junior year he should have a clear idea of what he wants to do. With this Moon combination, it is likely he'll decide to attend graduate school.

Sun in Cancer: She's a virtual powerhouse of intuitive drive and intellectual discrimination and something of a dichotomy even to herself.

By the time she's out of diapers, her intuition gives her deep insight into others. This is a child who knows when you're feeling blue and gives you a hug just to show you she's on your side. Her discriminating intellect allows her to approach people on their level, according to what they need. As a youngster, this may make her seem too willing to compromise when it comes to friends. But as she gets older, this trait is precisely what allows her to achieve and succeed.

Her sensitivity is acute, but not so much that it debilitates or paralyzes her. If anything, her sensitivity makes her unsure of herself at times and when she falters, she criticizes herself for it and vows to do better next time. Eventually, she feels comfortable enough with herself to stop gnawing at the petty details that undermine her self-confidence.

Sun in Leo: His flamboyance and bravado are usually at odds with his shyer Virgo Moon. But earthy, adaptable Virgo helps channel that flamboyance in constructive and creative ways. He's good with words, both spoken and written, and pity the adult who takes him on about any issue about which he feels passionate.

Both the boys and girls with this Moon combination are demonstrative kids who show and need a lot of affection. But they are too outspoken for their own good and should learn tact while they're still young. It's fine to speak your mind and make your opinions known; it's how you do it that makes the difference.

Despite his bravado, he wants to please you and his friends. He wants to be liked. Once he learns the difference between bravado and expressing his opinions, his charm takes him nearly as far as he can imagine.

Sun in Virgo: She's mentally quick, loyal and loving, a perfectionist in most things. She is often critical of others in a kind of nitpicky way, but is never more critical of others than she is of herself.

She has plenty of nervous energy and is able to hum along for hours at a breakneck pace until exhaustion finally catches up with her. When this nervous energy is channeled into doing something she really loves, there's no limit to what she might achieve. She enjoys learning, is probably an early reader, particularly if given the opportunity, and may have writing and artistic ability. Whatever she undertakes is marked by attention to detail and a painstaking need for perfection.

When she's emotionally upset, her health problems are likely to show up as digestive problems—colic as a baby, stomachaches, and perhaps a sensitivity to certain foods, when she's older. If she internalizes disharmony in her family environment or at school, she's more disposed to health problems. She might even believe she's at fault.

Like all kids, she needs parental acknowledgment of her uniqueness. But for a double Virgo, a solid belief in herself and her abilities is vital to her well-being and happiness.

Sun in Libra: He's resilient, artistic, and well balanced. This balance is often evident in an argument, when it's tough to find flaws in his thinking. This can be disconcerting to a parent who is trying to make a point and suddenly sees things from the child's point of view. As one wise man said, "Children are just small people with the same feelings and thoughts that adults have." His words certainly describe this Moon/Sun combination.

When this child's reasonable arguments fall on deaf ears, he reacts in one of several ways. He backs off, genuinely puzzled by the lack of openness to his arguments; he blows up, thus clearing the air; or he goes about his business and does what he wants, in secret, without hurting or bothering anyone else.

He should be encouraged to develop his artistic abilities and to rely on his intuition, which always provides him with valuable insight into other people.

Sun in Scorpio: In many ways, this child is inscrutable to others, even to the people who love and know her best. She possesses a kind of magnetism that you can't quite put your finger on. Even when she's young, she's private and secretive about her actions and her thoughts. You can't second guess her.

She's individualistic in the way she expresses her talents; she copies no one. She tends to be very loyal to her family and close friends, but the terms of that loyalty are well defined: "Don't talk about me with other people." If a friend violates that single rule, she cuts them out of her life completely. Her emotions are black and white, either/or, a fulcrum of extremes. You can't change that about her, so just accept it.

Her ambition develops as she matures. She wants very much to make herself known and recognized and chances are good that she'll succeed.

Sun in Sagittarius: Get out of his way and let him do what he does best: make connections between little details and the big picture. He's the kid who starts out selling a unique homemade brand of lemonade, then sells franchises to his friends.

He's a champion of the underdog and passionately defends his beliefs and his principles. To sway him to your way of thinking isn't an easy task and won't be accomplished through threats or force. Always take the quiet, gently persuasive route with this child; appeal to his logic.

Earthy Virgo constantly reminds fiery Sagittarius to slow down and get grounded. But because both signs are mutable, the mix of earth and fire works surprisingly well in this combination.

Sun in Capricorn: She's eminently practical, this one. Given a task, she always finds the most efficient way to do it. She needs to feel useful, so even at a young age she's a willing and eager helper.

She's even-tempered most of the time, but she can be stubborn about doing things *your* way unless you can convince her your way is the most practical. Praise is important to her, especially at a young age, when it helps bolster her self-esteem. She tends naturally to feel shy and reticent in new situations, so the sooner she develops self-confidence, the better off she'll be.

Her emotional nature is high strung at times, a result of Virgo's need for perfection. By channeling this emotional energy into practical pursuits that produce tangible results, there's little that she can't accomplish. She's conventional in most respects, with a need for rules and parameters. She should be encouraged to nurture her creativity, whatever form it takes.

Sun in Aquarius: He's a whiz with words, either written or spoken. In an argument, he talks circles around you and you probably give in because at the time everything he says makes sense. To win an argument with this child, you have to match his facility with language and appeal to his reason. Dictatorial tactics and dogma won't work.

He takes himself way too seriously, getting caught up in his own thoughts and concerns to the exclusion of other people. Teach him to lighten up on himself, to enjoy each day as if comes, to live more fully in the immediate present. One of the toughest lessons for this child is to realize that the people he loves and who love him won't always agree with his opinions and ideas. If he takes offense at this, it may isolate him from others. Love must be large enough to accommodate many diverse opinions.

He's an innovative, creative child who may be light years ahead of his peers intellectually. But emotionally, he needs reassurance that your love is unconditional.

Sun in Pisces: There's no fooling this child. Once she realizes other people exist in the world besides mom and dad, she relies on her formidable intuition to make her own decisions about them and their place in her life.

As she matures, her intuitive abilities meld beautifully with Virgo's logic and reason and allow her to make instantaneous judgments about people. Once she decides someone is worth her time and efforts, she's loyal to that person forever. She overlooks and forgives the individual's weaknesses and foibles and her tolerance prompts the person to do the same for her.

Since both the Sun and Moon are in mutable signs, she adapts well to change. If she does feel uneasy in new situations, her innate humor rescues her and the unease rarely lasts long.

She perceives her parents in uneven ways, seeing one parent as the tireless worker and the other as a romantic, dreamy sort. But her inner experience of the two is that they function well as a couple.

You won't have to reprimand this child repeatedly. She seems to be born with a strong sense of right and wrong.

24

Libra Moon

Imagine a little Mel Gibson, with that winning smile and all that charm, the diplomat of the tot lot. This kid is sociable, enjoys beauty in all its diverse forms, and wants very much to be liked by everyone. He's eager to please, and even if he disagrees with you, he probably won't show it for fear he'll lose your approval.

One of the hardest lessons for this Moon child is learning how to say no. He wants so very much to be liked and has such little tolerance for disharmony that he often compromises his own needs. As a parent, your most profound gift to this child is to encourage his independence and self-reliance at a young age. It will prevent him from becoming overly dependent on his mate later in life.

His aesthetic soul gravitates toward music, the arts, writing, poetry. He may have talent in these areas and, with the proper encouragement, may develop them. His sense of security is found in harmony; the more harmonious his life, the happier he is. His emotional well-being, in fact, depends on it.

The mother in this child's life seems to be of two types. The first type may be artistically inclined, a lover of the arts, a woman with enough love in her heart to see her child through all challenges of childhood. The other type may be similar in temperament, except that she's emotionally starved and seeks to satisfy that hunger through her child. Through her, the child learns to keep peace at any price.

Thanks to the poise inherent to the Libra Moon, it's an excellent position for diplomats and dancers. The careers of Henry Kissinger and Rudolf Nureyev are two outstanding examples of the heights that can be attained by a child with this Moon.

Libra Moon and . . .

Sun in Aries: One day he's ready to take on the world, to go into battle, to fight for what he believes. The next morning, however, he feels like hanging out at home, reading and listening to music or playing with his friends. Sometimes, he feels like doing both simultaneously. And that's where the challenge lies for this combination.

Emotionally, he seeks harmony and peace and the company of friends. But his vitality thrives on action and doing, on leading the neighborhood kids into their next adventure, whatever it may be. Emotionally, he's a dreamer, a romantic, a kid whose imagination soars. But the Aries part of him demands that he act on those dreams.

This essential conflict becomes more pronounced as he gets older. As a teen and perhaps well into his twenties, he's more interested in romance than in school or work. He may flit from one romantic drama to the next, the Aries part of him thriving on the emotional action. Much of his creative energy is dissipated in this way.

If, however, he can learn from a young age to channel this energy into art or theater or some other creative pursuit, he may save himself a lot of heartache later in life.

Shakespearean drama, after all, is better left on the page or the screen.

Sun in Taurus: Venus rules both the Sun and the Moon in this combination and that means only one thing: plenty of charm. This child can charm her way out of virtually anything and does it because it's her fundamental nature to do so.

From her first cry to her last, her emotions run through her like some endless river, dominating everything. Relationships are of paramount importance to her. From her earliest friendships in preschool to all the romantic relationships she forges later in life, she's always seeking the ideal. The ideal friend. The ideal lover. The ideal spouse.

More than anything else, she must learn to believe in herself, to believe that she's complete without someone else. Complete without that special friend, without that lover, that spouse. The earlier she learns this, the happier she will be.

Sun in Gemini: His energy, ideals and innate restlessness may drive you nuts at times. But he keeps you physically active and mentally sharp and brings experiences into your life that are beyond your usual element. And he's never boring or dull—not to his family or his friends or even his casual acquaintances.

Friends, in fact, flock to his doorstep. Other kids enjoy his company because he's so interesting and accommodating. When a disagreement breaks out in the ranks, he's right there, the mediator. When someone has a question about how something works, he knows and can explain it better than any grown-up.

He loves to travel, to see and absorb new cultures and ideas. If he can't do that, then he sates his curiosity vicariously, through books and people who have been where he wants to go. This child may stray from what you, as a parent, consider conventional. But if you respect his ideas and beliefs, he will respect yours.

Sun in Cancer: She's a homebody who enjoys the company of her numerous friends, so you can expect your place to be the center of the action. To a large extent, her early years are a process of defining who she is through her family and social circles. This is true of all young kids, but it's especially true for this water and air combination.

She's an excellent observer and has a keen eye for detail. Her ironclad memory provides her with a rich album of mental photographs that she carries with her throughout her life. At fifty, she can easily recall an experience that happened when she was five.

She can be quite intuitive, particularly in an environment where intuition is allowed to flourish and develop. Her flashes of intuition generally concern her immediate family and, later, her own children. Emotionally, she can be quite fickle and, at times, somewhat insensitive to other people's feelings. But generally, she's a sweetheart of a child who needs to learn to temper her trust of others, but not to squelch it altogether.

Sun in Leo: Astrologer Grant Lewi called this combination the position of Narcissus, who fell in love with his own image. In a child, this self-love is expressed as tremendous self-confidence and a tendency to do everything in a grand, sweeping manner. This is the kid who doesn't just set up a lemonade stand; he gets his buddies together and they stage entertainment to lure customers!

Despite his self-confidence, he seeks the approval of others. He needs to know that you, his parent, accept him as he is and that you approve of what he does. When you don't approve, he's crushed. Later in life, this tendency may cause him considerable anguish in his romantic relationships.

His instincts are good. He knows intuitively how to win people over, and as he matures, this ability and his personal appearance prove to be among his greatest assets.

He needs to learn that he has the power to achieve whatever he can imagine and that he doesn't need everyone's approval to do it.

Sun in Virgo: She's a loner who enjoys her own company and chafes at rules and regulations. Her mind is active, restless, and hungry for knowledge and information. She's undoubtedly a good student and may excel in a creative endeavor, especially if the talent is nurtured. In music or art, her intuition allows her to delve deeply into uncharted realms so that what she produces is highly original.

Her poise and diplomacy attract many friends, but she always reserves part of herself for herself. She possesses an innate understanding of the self's "sacred space" and respects the same in others. Her compassion, however, runs deep and true and she's always willing to lend her own strength to someone in need.

Sun in Libra: He's all air, a daydreamer, a romantic, a kid with his head so far in the clouds that from time to time you have to remind him to float back to earth. He's the type of kid who may have imaginary playmates, exceptionally vivid dreams, and an almost ethereal quality to his personality.

He prospers in a loving, harmonious environment in which his flights of fancy and his vivid dreams are recognized as significant and important. He's deeply affectionate with the people he loves and wants so much to be liked for who and what he is that he can be quite gullible at times.

As he gets older, his imagination and his mystical nature may take him into realms where you can't follow. But as long as you're open to his beliefs, even if they differ radically from yours, his loyalty and love never wane.

Sun in Scorpio: Her primary lessons in life concern emotions. She feels everything so deeply that a sharp word or a reprimand can send her into a blue funk for hours. By the same token, a word of encouragement bolsters her self-esteem and propels her to work at her full potential.

She reads other people well and can, at a glance, understand the dynamics of any group, whether it's a gathering of her peers or her family or even a group of strangers. She's a loyal friend, but she expects that same kind of loyalty from others. If a friend gossips about her or betrays her in some way, she cuts the person off cold and never looks back.

Her bluntness can be disconcerting to people who aren't prepared for it. She needs to learn that not everyone's emotions run as close to the surface as hers do. And yet, her intense emotions are the very thing that make her different from the pack. They are the vehicle through which she explores her world.

Sun in Sagittarius: He's a whirlwind of energy, a dancing sunbeam of grandiose plans and ideas that may be brilliant but that need to be grounded before they find expression in the real world. The fire part of him needs action; the air part of him needs intellectual stimulation. If he can find a way to wed the two, there's nothing that he can't achieve.

He likes his creature comforts—his water bed, his pets, good food, the love and communion of his family. But part of him hungers for adventure and experience, and it's this insatiable need that eventually takes him a long way from home.

Quite early in life, he probably develops his own sort of philosophy, bits of wisdom pieced together from things he has heard and read. His philosophy changes and deepens over the years, paralleling his own experiences. But always, there's a metaphysical bent to his beliefs. Given the right conditions and commitment, he may burgeon into a true mystic.

Sun in Capricorn: The beat of a different drummer leads this child. Sometimes she seems to be off in her own world, oblivious to the real world of school, friends, and family fun. Other times, she's right there, on top of things, her presence so immediate that you forget she's not always like that. This is part of the dichotomy of the earth and air combination, two cardinal signs that function in very different ways.

Her Libra Moon gives her an innate appreciation for the arts and makes her so sociable that she never lacks for friends. Her Capricorn Sun drives her to action, to achieve, and awakens her competitive spirit. As she gets older, other people may find her somewhat eccentric, which probably won't bother her in the least. As long as her early childhood is secure and loving, *she* doesn't feel eccentric or strange.

Her magnetism and her commitment to whatever or whoever she loves can propel her to the very heights of achievement.

Sun in Aquarius: He's a loving, romantic kid, with a heart large enough to accommodate just about anyone. In fact, that creates his primary challenges in life: how to say no, how to back off, how to maintain his own space.

His idealism and his romantic notions about other people often blind him to their faults. This is fine unless the truth emerges, then his disappointment is acute. This process is how he learns discrimination in his affections. The sooner he learns it, the happier he'll be.

He won't ever lack for friends. But if he can channel some of his social energy into a creative pursuit about which he feels passionate, he really begins to shine. If something doesn't work or click for him immediately, he may lose interest and nothing will come of his passion. But with early encouragement to persevere and to follow his dream, whatever it is, he achieves what he sets out to do.

Sun in Pisces: Her intuition is so finely hewn that most of the time she functions from deeply unconscious levels of her personality. She's the type of child who may spontaneously talk about her "other life" or her "other family." Or she may have unusually vivid dreams that prove to be precognitive or psychic in some way. With encouragement and balance, this natural ability can blossom and expand.

All types of art and creative pursuits interest her, perhaps because their inspiration rises from the places where she feels most comfortable. She's at her best when she's loose, unfettered, not bound by rules and regulations. This is when her creativity and intuition really surge.

Her main challenge in life is to allow herself this free, intuitive flow of emotion and unconscious *knowing*. If she gets blocked in this respect, it can affect her health and her well-being.

25

Scorpio Moon

Think of a miniature Liz Taylor or James Dean, intense and magnetic, secretive and complex. This child is probably one of the most interesting of the zodiac, but also one of the most difficult to understand.

Even as a youngster, her emotional life is so layered that she's an enigma to the people who love her and know her best. Quite often, she's a puzzle even to herself. She doesn't understand her own moods, and if she lacks for attention from her family and friends, she may feel isolated and lonely. She tends to brood and sulk about hurts inflicted by other people or things that have happened to her.

Encourage her to talk about her feelings and to release the past so that she can live more fully in the moment. If she learns to do this when she's young, she'll save herself a lot of heartbreak later in life.

This child possesses excellent insight into other people's motives and emotions. Her compassion is genuine and she may be the one in whom other neighborhood children confide. Her intuition is highly developed and can be manifested as hunches, impulses, or full-blown psychic impressions.

At its highest level, a child with a Scorpio Moon has the capacity for deep and long-reaching transformation and healing, both of self and others. But she may also have an obsessive facet to her personality, a need to control and manipulate others and, in some cases, a need to get even with people who have hurt her. This often rises from early childhood trauma and loss, a sense of being abandoned, or difficult family relations. It can be mitigated to a large degree by parental nurturing and by giving your child a loving, caring environment in early childhood.

Any child, male or female, with a Scorpio Moon will have intense sexual feelings and experiences. By being open and honest about sexuality and creating a loving and secure environment in early childhood, the obvious pitfalls in adolescence can be avoided. But if sexuality is approached as something bad or sinful and if harsh restrictions are placed on dating and curfews, the child will rebel in a big way.

The mother or the early home life is likely to be difficult, a severe challenge on some level. Even when the extremes don't apply, the child may sense resentment from mom; she isn't, in fact, all she's cracked up to be. She may be so centered in her own intense emotions that she isn't much of a nurturer. She may love her child deeply, but she somehow misses the point of nurturing.

Scorpio Moon and . . .

Sun in Aries: Boredom isn't something you'll ever experience with this child. He's all about action, aggression, and an unflinching belief in his own worth and abilities. This can try your patience, especially when you, as a parent, want him to do something your way and he insists his way is better.

Remember: Scorpio is a fixed sign and this kid has fixed ideas, even as a youngster, about how things should be. If you attempt to force him to see or do things your way, you probably won't get very far. Better to work with him and attempt to understand the inner code by which he lives. There are hidden recesses in this child you'll never know about, secret, sacred places in his soul that he never talks about. The earlier you, as a parent, realize this, the smoother your relationship will be.

He can be generous to a fault at times, giving away the last of his lunch money to a classmate in need. But he can spot a user or a phony a mile away and is rarely conned into anything. This is an excellent Moon for artists, musicians, actors, writers, anyone in the creative arts. He has the ability to manifest whatever he desires.

Sun in Taurus: Forget "time out" when this child is a toddler. She's headstrong, fiercely independent, and has quite a temper when she's backed into a corner. Establish the rules and parameters early on and make it clear that she forfeits privileges and pleasures when she breaks those rules. It will enable both of you to get through the toddler years much more easily.

A certain amount of possessiveness accompanies this combination. If she's an only child, she will want you exclusively to herself. If she has brothers or sisters, she won't readily share her things with them. Cooperation and a sense of giving is something she needs to learn early on.

She's intuitive, but this is apt to be manifested in vastly different ways throughout her life. In childhood, her dreams might be particularly vivid and telling. In adolescence, her intuitiveness may show up in an artistic or acting ability. As an adult, the trait may be realized through an astonishing perspicacity about people.

Sun in Gemini: This combination is a tough one simply because the two signs are at such opposite ends of the spectrum. Gemini is mutable air, intellectually hungry; Scorpio is fixed water, intensely emotional and intuitive.

If your child can get the two to work together, his charisma and flexibility enable him to achieve just about anything he wants. But if the two are forever working counterpoint to each other, much of his energy is squandered on emotional excess and intellectual drifting.

This combination produces an abundance of creative ability, which must be encouraged and nurtured for it to develop fully. This talent, however it's expressed, is vital to his happiness. It becomes something that is uniquely and completely his, a sanctuary in which he replenishes himself.

Sun in Cancer: At its best, this pairing of water signs makes her passionate and charismatic, the kind of child other kids look up to for her strength, clarity, and compassion. At its worst, this pairing can make her obsessive about the things and people she holds dearest. At times like this, she withdraws into her protective and very secretive shell and builds walls around her little private world to keep out the larger world.

As a youngster, her friendships go through many changes and transformations. It takes other kids a long time to get to know her; she has to be sure first that they are worthy of her time. Once a friend has been accepted into her private world, he or she is expected to be discrete and loyal, to never gossip or talk about her behind her back. Her requirements for friendship and, later on, for love, are always strict.

Her sense of security is always found first in her home and family. But as she matures, romance and relationships awaken her Scorpio side and she flits from one intense affair to another. These sexual adventures are endemic to most of the Scorpio combinations, but with Cancer, there's always this underlying need to create her own family.

Sun in Leo: This combination can read like a Shakespearean play, something with big themes, big emotions, big dramas. This child is a bundle of contradictions: flamboyant yet secretive, public but private, a crowd pleaser who needs periodic bouts of solitude. He brings his considerable magnetism and power to bear on all his relationships and it starts before he even speaks.

In some respects, it's easier to describe this child in terms of what he is not. He isn't an infant who sleeps through the night from six weeks of age onward. He isn't a toddler who is easily placated by a bottle or a thumb to suck on. He isn't a kid who accepts everything you tell him as gospel. He needs to *experience* and he'll do it with or without parental blessing.

This combination usually indicates a temper. It ranges from the sort of tantrum a two-year-old can throw to a full-blown teenage shouting match. If you attempt to squelch his temper or forbid him from expressing it, he can erupt into an explosion that purges or the anger can turn inward and may eventually affect him physically. Best to understand what triggers it and encourage him to channel it into all that he is equipped to achieve.

Sun in Virgo: She can be the very paragon of decorum when it suits her, one of those perfectly behaved kids who makes other parents notice her. She can also be a little devil of a thing, moody, sullen, a pouter.

Her intellect is as sharp as glass, discerning and focused. When she doesn't understand something, she questions and pesters you for answers, digging ever deeper until your patience snaps or she gets it. But it's her emotions that actually seize her intellect, that drive it. She has to *feel* something before she understands it, has to understand it in her bones, at an instinctive gut level. Then it becomes part of who she is, as intimate to her as her blood.

Sometimes, she argues because she doesn't understand why you can't see things her way. She needs to learn it's okay to have differing beliefs and opinions; not everyone has to think and believe as she does. This tends to be more of an issue when she's older, but it impacts on her friendships and concerns when she's younger, too.

She should be encouraged to act on her intuition without scrutinizing every little detail that occurs to her. Then there's no limit to what she can attain.

Sun in Libra: Never lie to this child or toss out clichés just to answer his questions. He will recognize the lie and won't accept the cliché. He may think less of you for it, too. If you don't know how to truthfully answer one of his questions, then tell him so. Offer an opinion, a comparison, a parable, but don't be glib just because he's a child.

He's something of a rebel, one of those kids who challenges the established way of doing things. If you can't give him honest answers and guidelines, he'll go elsewhere to find what he needs. He's a social creature who bounces his ideas and emotions off his friends. Sometimes he does this just to see their reactions, playing devil's advocate; other times he needs to know what his peers think, how his thoughts and feeling fit or don't fit with theirs.

One thing is certain: he needs love and open expressions of that love. With this kid, regular hugs and appreciation of him as he is can soften problems considerably.

Sun in Scorpio: Her intensity is a force to be reckoned with. In some ways, she's like nature herself, a primal cyclone of energy that can't be contained or conquered or restrained. Other times, she's the very essence of water, fluid and free flowing, healer and transformer, a creature so evolved, so far beyond your capacity to grasp, that she seems only marginally human.

There's no middle ground for this child. She wants to control and dominate everything and everyone she touches. Quite often she succeeds through whatever means she can. As she matures, she may use sex or money or metaphysics or just power for the sake of power. Her childhood is likely to be tumultuous.

Balance is important for this child. She must learn to appreciate simplicity and trust her intuition. Then she finds the power and the humility to achieve her heart's desire.

Sun in Sagittarius: He's blunt, independent, and wants to go his own way, free of restrictions and rules. From his earliest years, he has a good idea about what he wants and pursues it with a kind of relentless ardor.

This child's temper can be fierce and unforgiving. Unless he learns to control it when he's young, it will create problems for him as an adult. When his temper is combined with Scorpio's sting, get out of his way. He has an exceedingly long memory for slights and injuries and tends to hold grudges against people who cross him.

At an unevolved level, this combination can result in a zealot who believes his way is the only way. At its most evolved, the combination brings excellent intuition and penetrating insight into the nature of reality.

Sun in Capricorn: This child is responsible, hardworking, and opinionated. Her opinions are a combination of fact and supposition and she clings to them despite evidence that she might be wrong. This tendency never really disappears; it goes underground, where she silently judges and dissects other people's viewpoints and beliefs. She needs to learn tolerance of other people's viewpoints.

In her friendships, she's unflaggingly loyal and won't hesitate to help a close friend in need. And yet there's an emotional detachment about her that can be disconcerting because it seems so much at odds with her willingness to help. This is merely how she controls her intense emotions and channels them into her various projects and goals.

Even as a young child, she's well organized and goal oriented. Give her a task and she does it well. Her creative urges are usually strong and she achieves just about everything she sets out to do.

Sun in Aquarius: He's born with a well-developed sense of his own worth and not much is likely to change in that department even as he gets older. His primary interest is in himself. He is the Sun around which other people revolve like planets. He radiates a certain charisma that attracts other children, especially kids who aren't as self-assured.

As he matures, evidence of his personal power is apparent to the adults in his life. It's as if he has tapped into something larger than himself that speaks to other people. Fame often accompanies this combination, but it seems to come through the power of his personality rather than through the works that he produces. His challenge is to move away from his all-consuming interest in himself and to build a foundation in his life that doesn't rest solely on his personal charisma.

Sun in Pisces: She has imaginary playmates, lucid dreams, an intense inner life. It's as if she's hooked into a cosmic pipeline that feeds her all sorts of psychic tidbits, which she then absorbs and uses in unusual and original ways. She's the sort of kid who may suddenly announce one day that, in her other life, she was a servant or a princess or something in between.

As a young child, she may exhibit an unusual interest in death, life after death, destiny and free will, all the "cosmic biggies." If she's discouraged from talking or thinking about such things, she'll merely keep them to herself. It's her nature to mull over these kinds of issues. These interests can also show up in her artistic creations, whether these are derived through art, writing, music, or acting.

She has a wonderful sense of humor, a rollicking feel for the absurd that often rescues her when she's feeling blue. Overall, she's a bright, perceptive child whose company is genuinely enjoyed by everyone who knows her.

26

Sagittarius Moon

Oprah Winfrey, Neil Armstrong, Yoko Ono, Al Pacino: This kid is rarely what you expect when you're expecting. From early on, his independence and his difference from his peers is evident in the way he conducts himself.

Even as a toddler he's eager to explore his world and to taste everything in it. In fact, he may never go through the crawling stage because it won't get him where he wants to go quickly enough. One day he'll simply start walking, and from that point forward, his hunger for travel and exploration will never cease.

His mind is sharp, penetrating, capable of understanding broad, sweeping concepts that would make another child dizzy with frustration. But forget nuances. He doesn't have the patience or the temperament for endless details; he jumps right to the chase.

Despite this dislike for details, he's usually a good student, easily absorbing information and somehow balancing schoolwork with some type of involvement in sports. He needs physical exercise the way other children need eight hours of sleep a night.

Spirituality, education, travel, and philosophy form the cornerstones of his interests, but they come into play at different junctures in his life. Children with this Moon sign often have a genuine affinity with animals, an almost telepathic link that enables them to work with and understand animals in ways that other kids do not. Sometimes, this empathy with animals is the child's route to spiritual awareness.

Their sense of security lies in finding the answers to their burning questions. When this child doesn't understand something that's important to him, he becomes fretful and tough to live with.

Any combination with Sagittarius tends to prolong physical youthfulness, so that this child will always look younger than he is.

This child's mother is a teacher in the truest sense of the word. She's forever imparting her wisdom, helping with schoolwork. She may have deep spiritual beliefs that she passes on to her child. She's a stickler for honesty.

Sagittarius Moon and . . .

Sun in Aries: Double fire signs always mean an abundance of energy, action, motion. She keeps you running from the day you bring her home as an infant to the day she leaves home as a grownup and you probably thrive on the constant activity.

She never has problems launching projects, whether it's getting the neighborhood kids together for a party or starting a pet food drive for the local animal shelter. But she may have trouble finishing what she starts simply because she isn't good with details. She's a tad too blunt at times, even with the people she's closest to, but that's her scrupulous honesty. You never have to doubt her word.

She should be made aware that at times she isn't considerate of other people's feelings and needs. Part of the lack is that people get lost in her love for ideas.

Sun in Taurus: This combination is that of a born story-teller, a kid who loves to hear stories, tell them, write them, and think about them. In some respects, this child sees his own life as a story. As soon as he can talk, you hear about his imaginary friends and playmates. He'll probably be an early reader.

He has a well-developed sense of his own beliefs and moral code. He can always see your viewpoint, but if he doesn't agree with it, he tells you. To him, there are few gray areas. Either something is right or it's wrong; it can't be both.

When he combines his love of learning with his love of travel, he may find himself in some far-flung corner of the world on an archaeological dig or on some spiritual quest. This child rarely does anything halfway.

His inner experience of his parents may be conflicted. As a young child, one parent may be away from home frequently, which can lead to a yearning for a deeper relationship with that parent.

Sun in Gemini: These polar opposites are something of a conundrum and yet work amazingly well together. This is the child who may come to breakfast one morning with tales about the places she has traveled in her sleep. Rather than dismissing these stories as the products of an overactive imagination, listen closely. You may find that your little cherub is an astral traveler, who leaves her body at night to explore invisible realms.

She's a trivia expert, her restless little mind absorbing facts at an often alarming rate. The problem is that she always thinks she's right, even if she's not. This tendency can trip her up later in life unless it's nipped when she's young. Despite this tendency, she's much loved by her friends.

There's nothing mean in her personality, nothing cruel, and this extends to her relationships with animals as well as people. She maintains an elusive quality throughout her life, due as much to her mental agility as to her need for freedom. But at the heart of it, she needs love and appreciation as much as any child, and when she gets it, her life is complete.

Sun in Cancer: The contradictions in his personality are probably evident from a young age. He enjoys his home and his family, but given the opportunity for a sleep over or a camping trip with a friend, he seizes it. He wants roots, a sense of belonging, and yet a part of him hungers for places he has never seen, for experiences he hasn't had and for ideas he hasn't thought. His inner needs push him out into the world, away from all that is secure and safe.

He's well liked by his peers. His fairness, his practical idealism, and his sense of adventure inspire them. He has a certain preternatural grasp of situations and people. His insight is often piercing and the urge to blurt out what he perceives nearly always wins out. He should learn to take a deep breath before he speaks, to consider the very real possibility that what he's about to say may hurt the other person. It would behoove him to learn basic tact.

He won't need constant reprimands to stay on course. His feelings are so easily hurt that sometimes all it takes to express your displeasure is a cross look. He isn't the type who holds grudges; he forgives and forgets. The exception is dishonesty. He won't tolerate it, and if you try it on him, he'll make himself scarce very quickly.

Sun in Leo: This is the kid who runs toward experience with her arms thrown out to embrace it. Her appeal is immediate, charismatic, sweeping. She's dramatic and restless and often brilliant. The challenge for her is to learn to channel that energy so that she doesn't burn out at the age of ten.

She's undoubtedly an early reader and may be an early candidate for a gifted program as well. A profound curiosity compels her to take on challenges—a book that's a bit too complex for her age level, a movie with large themes, a trip with the soccer team to a foreign country, an audition for a starring role in a school play. She's courageous and charming and uses both traits to their fullest.

The odd and wonderful thing about this child is also a contradiction: She should learn restraint and yet, if she does, who does she become?

Sun in Virgo: Earth and fire don't mix well, but the double whammy of mutable signs helps to compensate. He readily adapts to change—a move, a new school, a new circle of friends. But once he has made the change, he tends to pick things apart, to examine every little detail, to track his own progress across this new and different continent.

This can be his downfall, for sure, because emotionally he really is more concerned about the big picture, the big questions. It's just that his ego demands a petty accounting and he has to bow to it when the urge is strong enough.

Take him traveling when he's young. Have adventures. Sate his appetite for the unusual and the exotic so that, as he matures, he can focus more on what he wants to do with his life and what he wants to become. He has the mind, energy, and emotional makeup for success at whatever he pursues. All he has to do is focus, believe in himself, and go for it.

Sun in Libra: She may drive you crazy with her questions: why this, why that, what's this mean, why did you act like that? These questions are never frivolous; she *really* needs to know. And once she knows, she processes the information in a way you may not understand, but in a way you have to respect if you want to know her at all.

She's social; expect a lot of kids to traipse through your living room and your backyard. And they come, these kids, from diverse backgrounds, with creeds that are different from hers, from cultures that bear little resemblance to her own. Her education and her hunger for travel actually begin in her own neighborhood.

She's impulsive about most things, and even though it may make you crazy, it's really just fine for her. Her impulses rise from the deeply intuitive parts of her personality. Trouble for her happens when those impulses are squelched, when that inner voice is silenced. Even if her path differs from the norm, respect it. Give her the freedom to pursue it, trusting that you, as a parent, have instilled in her the guidelines that she needs to make her journey fruitful and productive.

Sun in Scorpio: Quite bluntly, there are times when he is Mr. Obnoxious, a know-it-all with a hotline to some greater intelligence. But then there are the times when his idealism and compassion make you proud to be his parent. After all, water and fire are forever at odds, and his ego's fixed ideas about things don't seem to mesh with what his heart is telling him.

A part of him worries about the homeless, the starving, the injured. Another part of him couldn't care less as long as those dire happenings don't touch his life. Until these two extremes meld together for him, he's at war with himself.

Quite often, this child finds a cause or a creative pursuit or a passion that resolves this dichotomy. He finds it faster and at a younger age with guidance and advice from an adult who understands his conflict and who provides guidelines and advice with more than just words.

Sun in Sagittarius: There's no dichotomy or contradiction in this child. She is who she is. And what you get may well be a reflection of some unexpressed portion of your own personality.

This may be true for most parents and their children, but with this child the message is clear: Get with the agenda, folks. She's on a fast track toward the exotic, the strange, the unusual. She's busy finding the big picture and you're still back there in the dust somewhere, trying to connect the dots. Forget the dots. Let her sweep you up. Let *her* show *you* Europe or Tahiti on *her* terms.

Accept that you won't ever be able to interfere with her path. You can provide guidance, the wisdom of your own experience, parameters that work for you. But you will never be able to force this child to do something that runs contrary to her nature.

Sun in Capricorn: He's a doer, a thinker, a tireless worker, a diligent student, an avid Type A before he's out of diapers. He's going to run you ragged in his first three months of life. But he also opens possibilities, vistas, unimagined worlds of mind and heart that take you by surprise.

Animals are important to him; he feels a deep kinship with them. He's likely to have pets throughout his life that are like members of the family. Whether he lives in the country or the city or somewhere in between, expect him to bring home strays. His compassion runs as deep as his need for comfortable surroundings.

Most of all, this child should learn to relax. The sooner he learns that diversions are fun, the happier he is. If you can teach him to meditate before he's ten, great. Get him into a yoga class for kids and into acting or the arts or into some kind of team sport.

Remember Drew Barrymore in *The Firestarter*? Once she learned to fling her telekinetic energy into a tub of water, she had better control over her ability. This child must learn the same kind of control in his life. As soon as he does, he can apply his enormous energy toward fulfilling his potential.

Sun in Aquarius: A cliché presented as the ultimate truth simply won't work for this child. She's an independent thinker and something of a visionary. She *feels* the future in her bones, *feels* it when she wakes in the morning, *feels* it crowding around her when she goes to bed at night.

And whatever she feels must be incorporated somehow into who she is.

She enjoys group activities, particularly when the activity involves something that interests her. She learns best through groups and independent travel, an apparent contradiction with which she's quite comfortable. It's almost as if the group infuses her with the energy she needs to head out on her own.

She's honest and forthright and will never compromise her principles just to please someone else. This is especially true if she's artistic; this child won't produce for a particular market, but she will follow her own vision, which may well be right in step with the times.

Sun in Pisces: Part of him is always elsewhere, journeying through realms of the imagination and countries of the mind where others can't follow. Even when he's very young, he thinks in broad, visionary terms.

This propensity can work against him in school, where teachers may peg him as a daydreamer. Education is vital to his fulfillment; he needs the mental discipline to express his visionary qualities and make them comprehensible to others. His artistic abilities may be extraordinary and can find expression through the visual arts. To whatever career he ultimately chooses, he brings spiritual or prophetic vision.

If he spreads himself too thinly, his magnificent vision and abilities are scattered to the wind.

27

Capricorn Moon

She's shy and reserved much of the time and not particularly comfortable around kids her own age. But inwardly she's a powerhouse of ambition, self-discipline, and drive. Imagine, if you will, such diverse Capricorn Moon people as Lucille Ball, Cher, Adolf Hitler, and the Dalai Lama. What a lineup.

This child is a tireless worker. Give her a task and she tackles it with the same seriousness that she brings to her schoolwork or the care of her pets. She likes feeling useful and needs the sense of accomplishment that she gets from a task completed well.

If she gets an allowance, chances are she always saves part of it, stashing it away in a drawer and saving it for something she really wants or as a hedge against leaner years! Security is a big issue for her—security concerning her family, then her education, then her finances and profession, then her spouse and children, and security in old age.

It's one security issue after another throughout her life unless she learns to trust the flow of her own feelings and intuition. This isn't something that can be taught.

As a parent, you can make her aware of the nudges she gets from her own soul or higher mind. Make her aware of synchronicities, of how seemingly random events aren't random at all, but hint at some underlying order in her life that will guide her if she pays attention. She'll listen to you because she respects you and because your family is tightly knit.

When she's older, her ambition and drive are likely to carry her to the top of her profession. Her challenge is to take her low periods lightly, as transitory events that she passes through on her way to where she wants to be.

This child's mother either has her own career or she should have one. Her business skills are impressive. She may not be a nurturer in the classic sense of the word, but she will exceed even her own limits to provide for her child.

Capricorn Moon and . . .

Sun in Aries: He not only initiates things, he completes them! He needs to be recognized for what he does, whether it's cleaning out the garage or rounding up the stray cats in the neighborhood. In fact, he hungers for recognition—first from his family, later from his friends. And when he's an adult, he hungers for recognition in his profession. This kid wants fame.

At times, the degree of his self-control is astonishing. He seems to know exactly what he wants, where he's going, and how he's going to get there. Then suddenly he's just a kid again, on his way out the door to go play with his friends. He's got a temper, but that earth Moon keeps it in check most of the time.

As a parent, you and your child have a good relationship. You're close, you're honest with each other. But as he gets older, he needs to fly alone for awhile, to find himself separate from his parents and the rest of his family.

Once he does this, nothing stops him from achieving his goal.

Sun in Taurus: Once again, this kid's a little charmer. But in this case, all that charm hides a core of self-confidence that serves her throughout her life.

She's a leader, a realist, and she likes her creature comforts. Her room may be uniquely decorated in some way, with collections of shells or rocks or something else that holds personal meaning. She likes nice clothes, and as she gets older, she develops her own style, a unique presence.

This style eventually may include a kind of prescience about people, what makes them tick, what they think, how they feel. This insight allows her to put her finger on the public pulse and to use that to further her own ambitions once she's out on her own.

Her greatest challenge is to understand that material comfort and achievements are only part of the big picture and don't mean anything if she loses sight of her soul.

Sun in Gemini: Why, why, why: That's what you hear all the time from this child. Why can't he go to the movies with his friends? Why is the Moon so yellow? Why did the family cat kill that bird? If you answer his questions fully and honestly or admit it when you don't know the answer, your relationship with this child will always be sound.

Most of the time he's fun and sociable and can be so easy to get along with that other people think he's a pushover. But inside this genial exterior lies a tough core. This is the child who knows what he wants to do with his life and begins doing it before he goes into kindergarten.

He realizes that he needs to understand people to achieve his agenda, whatever it is, and so he becomes an astute observer of his friends, his teachers, his family. He seeks to understand their motives, their fears and triumphs, and the secrets in the darker places in their hearts. Once he has assimilated this knowledge and has tucked it away in some corner of his restless mind, he sets out to make his mark on the world. It's likely that he will succeed in doing exactly that.

Sun in Cancer: These two work smoothly together, compatible in elements, both in cardinal signs. She's intuitive but rational, painfully sensitive but tough, prescient but grounded.

She feels most secure within the embrace of her own family, but to fulfill herself she must be encouraged to step beyond the familiar boundaries of family and hometown. Take her camping for a couple of weeks during the summer; awaken her passion for the unknown.

She'll complain about how uncomfortable and miserable she is, what with the hard ground and the sleeping bag and the bugs. She won't be crazy about having to trek *way across* the campground to use the restroom. But she eventually realizes that the trip broke her habitual perception of things and allowed her to see herself in a new, better way. And that's the greatest gift a parent can give this child; make her aware that there isn't just one route to the fulfillment of her potential.

Sun in Leo: This powerful pairing is filled with passion and links up with ambition rather early in life. You may never fully understand what makes this kid tick, but you nonetheless are swept away by his ability.

And yet, he's still a child who needs you and your guidance and the wisdom of your particular experience. His challenge is to remain self-confident but without pride and arrogance; to understand that he doesn't always have to be the center of attention for assurance that other people love him. He needs to develop his intuition and listen to it. He must learn to love others as much as he loves himself.

Sun in Virgo: Double earth, double grounding. With this pair, it's almost as if the soul were saying, "Get your head out of those clouds; get real." And real she is, from her tummy upsets and bumps and bruises as a kid to her sharp mind and ambitions as an adult.

Early on, she learns how to persuade people to her way of thinking. She does it through a combination of charm and kindness. She's always aware of the other person's feelings and won't willfully hurt anyone.

She's got the gift of gab, but is she never a braggart or boisterous about her opinions. Her challenge is to not lose sight of the big picture through her minute attention to detail.

Sun in Libra: Sometimes he's the very essence of a great kid, courteous and sociable, able to hold his own in the company of adults. Other times, he's arrogant, selfish, and quietly challenges everything you say. Between these two extremes lies the balance that he truly seeks within himself.

His need to be liked by others actually makes him quite popular with his peers because most of the time he bends over backward for other people. And yet, there's a part of him that craves solitude, periods when he refreshes himself with books, nature walks, music, and the refinement of his own personality.

This child is complex, often torn between a need to make his mark in the world and his desire to simply go on his merry way through life.

Sun in Scorpio: There are things about her other people simply never know or touch. She has a deep core of privacy and a rich inner life from which her intuition springs. Once she makes up her mind about something, her opinion is pretty much set for life.

Her early years are vital to her later understanding about the choices she makes, who she is, and what she hopes to accomplish. Remember: A Scorpio is never passive about anything and a Capricorn always has a sense about where she's going. Put them together and you have a dynamo of power.

Sun in Sagittarius: He's always headed in many directions, each of which is important to him because it expresses part of who he is. Soccer, school, travel, dates, animals, friends. Then, suddenly, something stops him—a cold, bad grades, problems with a friend—and he has to take an honest look at where he has been and where he's going.

When he stops like this, he doesn't consider the small, vital details of a situation. He immediately leaps to the big picture and tries to figure which big picture fits him best at this point in time. This is actually a powerful form of visualization because it focuses on the goal and not on the details of how the goal is to be attained. It's an effective way to achieve what he wants and a lesson that he carries with him through his life, even when he doesn't have a name for what he does.

Never diminish this child's ideals or the ways that he achieves these ideals. His innate sense of fairness and his sound intuition won't steer him wrong.

Sun in Capricorn: The preponderance of Saturn with this pairing makes for a serious, ambitious child. At times, he is so emotionally remote that other kids may feel put off. Most of his peers miss the point of his insistence on rules and structure and tradition; they think he's a stick in the mud, sort of odd.

What no one really understands is that he has come into life with an agenda, and one way or another, that agenda will be realized. He uses everything he possesses to get his way or to control situations and the lessons he learns while young are forever with him.

Sun in Aquarius: When she's young, she may seem divided within herself. One moment she's a total individualist, with a need for freedom from any restrictions. The next moment, she's completely conventional, willing to go along with whatever the family agenda is.

As she moves into her teens, these two extremes begin to merge. She learns how to use Aquarius's foresight and imagination with Capricorn's determination and grounding to make her way in the world. Whether she's an early achiever or comes into her own later on, she may do something unique that seizes the public's attention. As astrologer Grant Lewi pointed out, this Sun/Moon combination has produced many eminent Americans—Abraham Lincoln, Thomas Edison, and Charles Lindbergh.

In terms of how she interacts with people on a daily basis, this child creates her own opportunities, relies on facts and logic, and has a warm, generous aura about her. If you try to take advantage of her or get her to do something she objects to, she cuts you off cold.

Sun in Pisces: He's sensitive and perceptive, the sort of child who knows what you're feeling just by looking at you. His dreams may be unusually vivid, and if he's encouraged to remember them when he's young, they will deepen his understanding of himself and provide him with answers.

He may be quite secretive at times and won't divulge his plans or ambitions until they're fully formed in his own mind. He can be dramatic when it suits him, particularly when he wants to make a point, and he has a certain bluster that hides whatever unease he may feel.

He's kind but not sappy about it, and when he promises that he'll do something, he does it. His challenge is to maintain his course, whatever it is, without losing himself in the endless diversions that his Piscean Sun may toss his way.

28

Aquarius Moon

From the time he's very young, he shows a natural proclivity for gadgets, unusual colors and designs, and the newest toys. This later translates into avant garde interests—fads, belief systems, ideas—and a certain rebelliousness against the status quo. Not surprisingly, many sixties rebels had Aquarian Moons—Angela Davis, Jerry Rubin, and Timothy Leary.

Of all the air signs, Aquarius is the most mental and the most detached from their emotions. This child can rationalize virtually anything he feels. Intense emotions make him exceedingly uncomfortable, whether they are his own or someone else's. At times, he's so detached from what he feels that he comes across as utterly cold. When his emotions build to the breaking point, he becomes impulsive and may do something completely out of character and inexplicable, even to himself.

He dislikes feeling dependent on anyone and doesn't want other people to depend on him, either. As a result, he's the type who rarely hesitates to go off with friends and is more likely to play at someone else's house than at his own.

Great visionary traits accompany this Moon sign. If he's encouraged to develop his natural clairvoyance and precognitive hunches, he makes an excellent psychic. His vivid dreams may become a valuable resource in his life, if he's encouraged to pay attention to them.

His sense of security lies in his freedom and independence.

This child's mother is likely to be a thoroughly liberated woman with progressive ideas. She follows her own agenda and probably has unusual spiritual beliefs that she tries to communicate to her offspring. Or she may be so far *out there* that her children are incidental to her life.

Aquarian Moon and . . .

Sun in Aries: She has no problem with self-worth or self-confidence. In fact, at times she may be too arrogant and smug for her own good, an attitude that puts off potential friends and allies. Emotionally, she can be passionately demonstrative at times, filled with hugs and embraces for the people she loves. At other times, she couldn't care less about showing what she feels.

She's mentally quick and shrewd, with an interest in people that wins friends easily. She's very conscious of conventions, however, and is quick to tell you when you embarrass her. She should learn to care less about appearances, about how other people see her, and more about what she really wants and feels about her life.

Her passion for the things she enjoys can be easily translated into a profession when she's older. She has the drive and the vision to become just about anything she sets her sights on.

Sun in Taurus: He has a genuine interest in other people, so he never lacks for friends or allies. In fact, he won't make many enemies in his life. When he comes up against someone unpleasant, he won't be provoked into proving his point to anyone who wants to argue just for the sake of argument. He would rather not argue at all. His abundant charm is his greatest ally and he uses it freely to win you to his way of thinking. He's a manipulator in this sense, but never in a malign or hurtful way.

As a youngster, he's one of those genuinely happy kids with a bright, sunny disposition, a joy to be around. But don't ever mistakenly think you can force him to do something he objects to just because he's so easy going. You'll discover the true depth and innate stubbornness of his personality.

If he learns to trust his intuition at a young age, his course through life is practically unimpeded.

Sun in Gemini: Talk about energy. This double air combination keeps you running. As a toddler, she's into everything, eager to explore her world, to absorb everything about it. Once she learns to talk, she besieges you with questions, then brings her enormous insight to bear on whatever she learns.

At times, the future may seem as clear to her as the moment she's living. It's as if the veil that separates today from tomorrow is less dense for her. As she gets older, she may venture into mysticism, Eastern religions, the use of oracles, astrology, alchemy. Always, she seems to be following a thread that connects seemingly disparate pieces of some large, intricate puzzle.

It's likely that she won't follow the spiritual beliefs of her family. She finds her own path, her own beliefs, and eventually incorporates them into who she is and uses them to achieve whatever she desires.

Sun in Cancer: She's softer than many combinations with the Aquarian Moon, not as emotionally detached. Even when she's young, her mind is capable of grasping large concepts. When she learns, for instance, about the planets in our solar system, her hungry little mind immediately leaps to the possibility of life in other solar systems.

In a group of peers, she's not one to shrink to the back of the room and remain silent. She speaks her mind and does it magnetically, persuasively, the same way that she seizes opportunities. She has a wonderful talent for making other children feel important, which means she never lacks for friends.

There's something of the actress in this child and any kind of dramatic training would benefit her. She needs a creative outlet for her particular brand of energy, something that is uniquely hers. If she can't find it, she may create little dramas for the rest of her life, dramas in her relationships, with her health, with her profession

Once her ambition is awakened, there's no stopping her. The earlier she learns to stay grounded, the happier she will be.

Sun in Leo: He does things in a big way, with considerable force and imagination behind all of his actions. His imagination, in fact, is often so sweeping, so grand, that he's compelled to channel it into something tangible.

The fire in this combination adds passion and creativity to the emotions. Even when he's young, he wants very much to be recognized and acknowledged for his talents. If he isn't, he may go to great lengths to seize attention. As a toddler, this can mean temper tantrums. As a teen, it can mean outright anarchy. As an adult, it can mean unstable relationships.

So give him the attention he needs, acknowledge and praise him for his abilities. This early appreciation equips him to fulfill his vast potential.

Sun in Virgo: From her earliest years, her approach to most things in life is through her intellect. As a child, her intuition may not be as fully developed as some of the other combinations, but her mentality compensates for it.

Her curiosity is profound and opens doors she might not pass through otherwise.

Words come easily to her and it doesn't matter whether they're spoken or written; she's equally at home with both. Books are her venue to larger worlds and to deeper mysteries. As she gets older, her interest in alternative thought may be profound and it may change her life in dramatic ways.

As soon as she can express herself, she should be encouraged to talk about what she feels. To do this, she must feel secure enough within the embrace of her family to know it's okay to express the full range of her emotions without judgment or chastisement from others. By being fully aware of her emotions and her intuition, this child can accomplish whatever she sets out to do.

Sun in Libra: This double air combination is all about relationships and romance. When he's young, this means that he has an active imagination. He gets lost in his own fantasies and daydreams and may have an imaginary playmate as well. Half the time, you won't know what he's thinking because he hardly knows himself!

He has a streak of idealism that just won't quit. It isn't compassion, at least not in the way the word is normally understood. This is a sort of intellectual despair at the sight of a homeless person willing to work in exchange for food or at reading about the number of cats and dogs that are put to sleep each year because no one wants them. These tragedies affect him because they probably aren't a part of his immediate experience; they're eye openers.

His refinement and good taste carry him a long way and make turbulent periods like the teens go more smoothly for him than for most of his peers. It's important, though, that he find a singular passion when he's young, whether it's an artistic pursuit or a spiritual belief, that fires up his ambition.

Sun in Scorpio: For the most part, life is serious business for this child. He's a good student (because school is what you do when you're a kid); a solicitous sibling (because you're family); and a loyal friend (because you've earned his loyalty). He's also aware that his powerful personality intimidates some of his friends, but that's okay. They respect him because of it.

He needs to be admired and applauded for his accomplishments. But his instincts are so finely honed that he knows when he doesn't deserve applause; he knows when it's been an act. He sometimes feels that he can't really get away with anything because something in him rises up to scold him.

Much of the time, he can't adequately describe what he feels about anything. But his compassion is genuine and his imagination is incredibly rich and layered. The challenge is how to make real what he can imagine and how to find the one thing that brings him his deepest satisfaction and happiness.

Sun in Sagittarius: The good news is that you won't ever have to guess what she's thinking or feeling; she tells you straight out. She's sometimes so blunt and so seemingly oblivious to other people's feelings that she appalls herself. At moments like this, she just can't help saying whatever she says.

Her mind works in curious ways. One day, she's into toys, the next day she's into animals. One month she wants "cool" clothes, the next month she slops around in cutoffs and a T-shirt. But always, her head whirs away with ideas and concepts, both the broad and the specific, and she plots and plans to put these ideas into concrete form. Whether she succeeds or not depends on how secure she feels from her earliest years within the embrace of her family.

Sun in Capricorn: Whatever he does, he rises and falls on his own effort and merit. He rarely blames others for his misfortunes or attributes his success to others.

His friends and the groups to which he belongs (and there will be many) are important to him. At various times in his life, he defines himself by his social affiliations and takes what he learns and applies it to himself in the most intimate sense. He's strong, determined, and often brilliantly intuitive, at least when he allows himself to be.

His greatest challenge is to break free of the restrictions and limitations that others impose on him. He must find his own way in the world, must seek out his own belief systems. Once he does this, his true self shines through.

Sun in Aquarius: This double air, double fixed combination makes this child a true visionary and very individualistic. Has a deep need for freedom. Friends in the group he's a part of will always be vital to his well-being. By connecting with kids who share his interests and passions, he furthers his own development.

The challenge with this double whammy is to remain grounded. This child may spend a lot of time living in his head, so he needs to balance that with physical exercise and sports.

Sun in Pisces: The challenge for this child lies in finding the ideal balance between her humanitarian spirit and her propensity for sacrifice. Yes, animals in the local shelter are put down. Yes, it's tragic. But she can't save every one of them; she may not even be able to save a single one. So she decides she's going to change the system and do it single-handedly.

Her passion for causes is sometimes based on a visionary awareness, a true glimpse of how the future might be if things were different. If she's fortunate, if she allows her intuition to speak to her and if she listens to it, then she finds people of like mind who believe in the same causes she does. She faces the knowledge that change happens more quickly when a number of people work toward the same end. She can't do it all by herself.

She's endlessly persuasive and it doesn't matter if it's getting a toy that she wants or ending world hunger. Her vision may not be your vision. But if you respect her choices, then she'll respect yours.

29

Pisces Moon

This child is among the most sensitive in the zodiac. Her emotions connect her to the collective unconscious, allowing her to dip into the symbols and images that are common to all people. This can show up in her creative works, which often have a deeply spiritual or mystical flavor to them. Leonard da Vinci, Michelangelo, Paul Cezanne, and Elvis Presley all had Pisces Moons. So did Grace Kelly, Audrey Hepburn, and Helen Keller.

She's very compassionate, sometimes to a fault. When she's young, this compassion is most obvious in her concern for animals, particularly those that are hurt or sick. She may bring home ailing strays or even other kids whose family lives are in disarray or chaos.

This child is quite often an avid daydreamer, lost in the richness of her imagination and fantasy life. She probably has at least one imaginary playmate and definitely perceives dimensions of reality that escape the rest of us.

One nine-year-old girl with a Pisces Moon found that, when she touched the walls of an old fort in northern Florida, she could hear wailing. She sensed that the people who had been in this particular room of the fort had been hungry and had suffered terribly. This was later confirmed by a tour guide at the fort, who said that during the mid 1800s, Seminole Indians had been tortured in that room.

The challenge for this child is to be sufficiently nurtured during childhood so that she doesn't become an escapist as an adult. Elvis Presley's life is an excellent example of the kinds of addictions these kids can suffer. In an evolved soul, the Pisces Moon can result in a spiritual leader.

This child's mother comes in two distinct types. The first may be somewhat psychic, with such deep wells of compassion that she helps out people and animals in need. She may be torn between her head and her heart, so that concrete decisions are difficult to make. The other type of mother may be trying to fill an emotional void in her life through addiction to drugs, alcohol, or food. This type can be ill frequently, so that the child ends up taking care of her.

These are the extremes. In between is the mother who reflects traits of both types.

Pisces Moon and . . .

Sun in Aries: His moods are difficult to deal with. He tends to brood and sulk and always seems to be torn in at least two directions. His heart wants to do one thing, his head screams to do another.

Outwardly, he seems confident and even brash at times, but it's mainly bravado; inside, he's shy and retiring and prefers his solitude. His periods alone are actually vital for his well-being and the maintenance of his health. It's the way he recharges his energy and gets centered.

His imagination and creativity are probably his greatest assets, but to make full use of them, he must learn to concentrate and focus. If he's reading a book, for instance, or doing his homework, then he needs to focus only on that instead of letting his imagination run away with him. He's never too young to understand the importance of goals. In fact, once he successfully merges his reason with his imagination, true creative genius may result.

Sun in Taurus: Quite early in life, it's apparent that there are places inside this child you will never touch or see. She's private, with a genuine penchant for the mysterious, the unseen, the mystical. Given the opportunity, she's an early reader; books hold some of the secrets that fascinate her. She may also be intrigued by certain kinds of movies that show the mystical side of magic: *Aladdin* or *Fluke,* the story about a man who dies and comes back as a dog and looks for his former family.

She's impressionable and, despite the grounding influence of her earth Sun, can be taken in by a sob story. This tendency won't be as prevalent if she learns to follow her hunches because her first impressions about people and situations are usually accurate.

Her naturally sympathetic nature opens her to being imposed upon by others. She needs to become aware of this tendency in herself and to learn when to say no to people.

Sun in Gemini: Both Gemini and Pisces are represented by a pair of symbols, Gemini as the twins and Pisces as the two fish. When combined, this inherent duality becomes even more pronounced. Heart and mind wage constant battles, and it's difficult for this child to make a decision.

He functions best at an intuitive level, where the flow of his impressions are steady and usually are reliable. If he listens closely to these impressions, he rarely goes wrong. But when his intellect intercedes and insists on analyzing what he feels, he begins to doubt his instincts. Once that doubt is seeded, it grows like a weed and undermines the fundamental process he uses to navigate through life.

He should be encouraged to develop and direct his intuition into an area about which he feels passionate. This takes him out of himself, out of his blue and gloomy periods, and infuses him with self-confidence and self-worth.

Sun in Cancer: She's a loving, affectionate child, the family diplomat, who mediates disagreements and calms tempers. Her personality is so easygoing and pleasant that sometimes her family and friends mistakenly believe that's all she is.

Under the surface, however, lies a rich ocean of secrets and suspicions, thoughts and dreams, that no one knows about. She has many acquaintances, but because she doesn't trust other people easily, her true friends are few. But those she has are as loyal to her as she is to them.

Like all Pisces Moon combinations, her instincts are sound. A great deal of information comes to her through intuitive means and some of it may be precognitive: tomorrow's pop quiz in social studies, a problem with the family van, an upset with a friend. This valuable talent should be nurtured when she's still young and free of any preconceived notions about what it is or how it works.

Sun in Leo: He's a joy to be around, his personality constantly buzzing and humming with the business of life. Under his amiable exterior, however, lies a somber little kid who muses about issues larger than his experience can illuminate.

Even though a part of him is a daydreamer, his natural bent is toward action, movement, doing. He's not content to merely think about or imagine something; he must make it tangible and real. This is the kid, for instance, who decides his neighborhood needs bike paths, then organizes a drive to get it accomplished. He does it out of the community's need and not for personal gain or glory.

He needs an outlet for his energy, something that will lighten his mood when he's blue and that will lift his spirits when he's mulling over the travails of the world. Physical exercise and team sports would satisfy some of that need and a pursuit of art, music, or the dramatic arts would satisfy his creative urges

Sun in Virgo: This mutable combination works extremely well, thanks in large part to the mix of earth and water. This child is a good example of how reason and intuition function as a unit, one feeding the other, supplementing the other, confirming the other. It's as if the left and right hemispheres of the brain are perfectly in synch.

Her sense of responsibility and duty is well developed even at a young age. She does her share around the house, picks up her room and her toys, and pretty much does as she's told. She's a conscientious student, and this ideal melding of intellect and intuition allows her to achieve just about anything she wants in her life.

The challenge with this combination, though, is that her sympathy for others whose situation isn't as fortunate as her own affects her deeply. She wants to help others, and even when she's young, other kids come to her with their problems. Her creative urge is strong, and if she can channel her considerable gifts into writing or the arts, she may help those in need even more than she can imagine.

Sun in Libra: Like any combination with Libra, this child has a certain refinement and grace that he comes by naturally. He's far more layered than he appears even to the people who know him best.

His solitude is important to him, vital to his well-being. In his times alone, he draws on inner reserves of strength and fortitude that bolster his confidence and equanimity in the larger world. He needs his books and his music every bit as deeply as he needs his friends.

This child is fair and honest with other people and expects the same in return. He's not the revolutionary type you find with the Aquarian Moon; when he sees how something can be changed for the better, he works through the system to do it.

Sun in Scorpio: Water, water, water: Always keep that in mind with this combination. Everything for this child comes down to instinct, intuition, the unconscious, the psychic, the emotions. It's as if she breathes, fishlike, within the vast ocean of the unconscious.

The downside of this talent is that, unless it's creatively channeled, her imagination can literally run away with her. If she smells smoke in the middle of the night, then the house must be on fire. If she finds out she and her family are moving, then it has to be the absolute worse thing that's ever happened to her. If her dad is late picking her up from school, then it's because he's been in a car accident.

Even in an aware child, this kind of raw psychic talent needs grounding. Take her camping, teach her the sacredness of all life, allow her to nurture stray animals, appreciate her for who and what she is. Most of all, encourage her to express herself through art or writing. This kid has tales to tell.

Sun in Sagittarius: On the surface, these two wouldn't seem to work cooperatively. After all, no matter how you try, fire and water just don't see eye to eye. And yet, because both are mutable, a certain alchemy takes place. This child is adaptable and enjoys new situations, rising to meet whatever challenges are presented. He's quick and broad minded, with a sincere concern for people who don't have the advantages he does.

As a youngster, he's emotional. He goes along for days, a free spirit who loves his life and everything in it. Then, suddenly, something disrupts his illusions and he's an emotional mess. Crying jags. Lots of whines and he doesn't feel good. Maybe he stays home from school. Maybe he steals some solitary hours for himself. However it plays out, he vents his emotions, then snaps back to his buoyant Sagittarian self. He rarely holds a grudge, perhaps because his insight allows him to see the larger picture behind any disagreement or slight. His compassion extends to all people and creatures.

Sun in Capricorn: She's a genuine humanitarian with deep insight into people. She's serious about most things and somewhat secretive at times. This is the child who gives her lunch money to a kid who needs it more than she does, then suffers in silence when she's scolded for not having any lunch.

From the time she's old enough to talk and get around, she assumes her share of responsibility in the family. She brings this same sense of responsibility to her schoolwork, her friendships, and every other facet of her life. Her challenge, in fact, is that she may be too willing to assume responsibility. She must learn to balance her seriousness with a lighter touch and not to give in to periodic slumps. She has everything it takes to fulfill herself.

Sun in Aquarius: She's a thinker even before she knows the meaning of the word, with a kind of brooding awareness of the invisible realms of life. She's fascinated by stories about ghosts and otherworldly visitors, vampires and werewolves, aliens and other worlds.

When she's younger, she may have fears and nightmares surrounding these things. Never poke fun at these fears or dismiss them as nonsense. Encourage her to talk about them. For this child, talking about a fear banishes it.

She's private, sensitive, and her feelings are easily hurt. Deep introversion should be discouraged for this child simply because her imagination is already so active. She needs to share her visions and fears in a constructive, creative way. This combination can lead to genuine psychic ability in clairvoyance, precognition, or mediumship.

Sun in Pisces: The challenge for this child is overcoming ambivalence and learning to ground himself in the real world. His daydreams and fantasies are often more real to him than anything else and he retreats to this private place whenever the real world disappoints him.

Any Pisces Moon combination indicates heightened intuition, but with a double Pisces, it's so obvious it can't be ignored. He has a natural predilection for the weird and the strange, which are neither to him. He feels quite at home with things that go bump in the night. This can create problems for him when he comes up against mainstream thought and realizes that not everyone thinks as he does. But if he learns at a young age to trust his own perceptions and to communicate them to other people in a reasonable way, he won't feel as isolated as he might otherwise.

His creative urge is strong and developed, but he needs encouragement to make it shine. He needs to believe in himself and his own abilities.

30

Moon through the Houses

The house placement of your child's Moon reveals the area of her life in which her emotions and unconscious influences are most prevalent. It indicates the part of her life where her intuition will dominate.

The strongest placements are always in angular houses—the first, fourth, seventh and tenth. Interpret the house placement according to the *sign* of the Moon. If your child's Moon sign is in Cancer and it falls on the fourth house cusp or in that house, then you know she feels intimately connected to her home, her roots, and her mother. She is likely to be exceptionally intuitive and may live or wants to live near water when she's older. Use your own intuition in the interpretations.

First House: She's changeable, moody, and often inconsistent. She relates to herself on an emotional level, frustrated when she feels she isn't working to her full capacity and almost giddy with delight when she does.

If a friend needs support and understanding during a trying time, this child is right there, compassionate and willing to listen. But when she's on the outs with someone else, this house placement may cause temperamental outbursts and emotional explosions.

With the Moon in the first house, everything about her is colored by her emotions—her sense of style, her likes and dislikes, and her approach to school, family, friends, and, later on, lovers. She is often a psychic sponge, soaking up the moods of the people around her. For this reason, it's important that she associate with upbeat, positive people.

She should cultivate consistency in her behavior and learn to think before she blurts what she feels.

Second House: He's a collector, one of those kids who just has to have all the latest action toys or movie tie-in toys from fast food restaurants. Even if he plays with them only once, it's the act of possessing them that's important. This is where his sense of security . As he gets older, this possessiveness may extend to people—family, friends, lovers, a spouse, his own children.

He should strive not to attach too much importance to his belongings and to look, instead, at why he feels he has to own whatever he sees. An adult can help him gain some perspective on this issue. If he gets an allowance, he should be encouraged to save part of it for something that he really wants, rather than giving into the impulse to spend it all in one place. Throughout his life, his finances and possessions go through many fluctuations.

Third House: She's very attached to her brothers and sisters and to her own neighborhood. Even though her relationships with her siblings and neighborhood friends are emotional and changeable, she feels most secure when things between her and others are going well.

She's good with words, especially when she needs to express what she feels, and communicates from the deepest parts of herself. As she gets older, she should be aware that she may be clinging to outdated beliefs, vestiges of her childhood, and she should try to discover her own beliefs.

Fourth House: He's close to one of his parents and is very attached to his family. His emotional security comes from a tranquil family life, both when he's young and when he has his own home and family. He needs this security to be able to function at his full potential in the larger world. He enjoys collecting old things or objects that hold familial significance. His early childhood greatly influences his relationship with his own children

If the Moon is in a water sign, then he probably feels at his best and most creative when he's living near water. If the Moon is in a mutable sign, he may experience many changes in residence.

The Moon in the fourth house is very similar to a Moon in Cancer. It indicates deep psychic connections to the place of birth, to his own family, and to his mother. Family traditions and history may be of special importance.

Fifth House: She's honest and forthright about everything she feels. Sometimes, in fact, she's so fascinated by her own emotional life that she talks about it too much. Other times, she keeps it all bottled up inside.

She has strong opinions and is very definite about her likes and dislikes. Many of her friends are female, and among those she's closest to, there may be strong past-life ties. Even when she's young, she enjoys children. She may work part time as a baby sitter or in a day-care center or, later, may find herself teaching elementary school.

This Moon can be troublesome in the teen years, when emotions are already erratic. She may take risks in relationships and have many flings before she finally settles down.

Creative and intuitive urges are strong with this placement. Artistic and musical abilities tend to rise from the deep unconscious.

Sixth House: Her emotions have a direct impact on her health. A prolonged case of the blues, a falling out with a friend, an argument between her parents: Any of these events can make her sick.

Her dietary habits are crucial to her physical well-being. She isn't, however, just what she eats. Equally important is what she thinks about what she eats. If she adopts negative beliefs from the adults around her about food, diet, and the physical body generally, this, too, can affect her health.

Her work habits are generally efficient, but they are not always thorough unless she's doing something she loves. If she has any artistic inclinations, she's able to draw on the deeply intuitive parts of her personality for inspiration. She's quite intuitive overall, and given the chance, her intuition will guide her physical, mental, and spiritual self. This intuitive side will become very important once she's on her own, particularly in relation to her work.

Seventh House: Remember the song about the age of Aquarius and the Moon in the seventh house? Well, here it is. The emphasis is on relationships and the emotional support of friends. This child chooses his friends by what he feels about them and, to some extent, defines himself according to how his close friends see him.

A child with this Moon placement is often very intuitive about people. He may feel either an instant rapport with a stranger or an instant dislike. It's as if some part of his soul pierces the individual's appearance and goes straight to the truth of who the other person really is. There can be past-life ties with close friends and, later, with a significant other.

As an adult, he needs emotional support from his significant other or spouse. He may go into business with this person or meet the individual through work.

Eighth House: Her emotions are extremely powerful and dictate many of her actions. Yet, she may keep her feelings hidden from others and, sometimes, even from herself. Certain topics fascinate her that other children might find gloomy: death and dying, life after death, metaphysics, the occult.

Love is always important to this child, and as she matures, sex will be important to her too. Rather than fight her over the issue of sexuality, a parent's best course is to educate her. She should cultivate the development and attunement of her intuition, which is particularly strong with this Moon placement.

Through women, she inherits knowledge, power, resources, and sometimes money and possessions. The Moon here usually indicates fluctuations in her partner's resources and finances or with trusts, insurance, and inheritances.

Ninth House: From the time he's very young, he's a restless seeker, forever on the prowl for new experiences. This kid has a philosophical bent that becomes apparent around the ripe old age of five, when he's old enough to have his first few ideas about how the world works.

He's probably a natural-born traveler, with a special fondness for foreign countries and cultures. But even a trip to the next town is a treat for him. He simply enjoys seeing how other people live.

His intellect is deeply colored by his emotions. If he doesn't feel passionate about an idea, he won't bother. The Moon here indicates that his memory is excellent, a storehouse for all the emotional experiences he had in early childhood. The challenge is to make sure that the beliefs he holds as a child are positive, the kind that foster a belief in himself.

He benefits from higher education. Even though his interests may go through many changes and he will change majors the way other people change clothes, he shines when he finds his passion.

Tenth House: She enjoys having an audience and finds that she can be quite persuasive with large groups of people. She might, for instance, galvanize the neighborhood children or the kids in her class to undertake some kind of recycling project. Or she might start a drive for the humane society or the homeless in her area.

Her mother has an enormous influence on her values and her beliefs in herself. In fact, women through her life play an important role in who she is and who she becomes. She may change professions a number of times before she finds her true passion.

The Moon in the tenth is often indicative of the ability to affect mass thinking. It can also indicate fame.

Eleventh House: Groups are an important part of his life. From his preschool days to his old age, his group associations help define who he is.

His friendships, however, follow his moods. He blows hot and cold with people. One day he's eager to play with the kid down the street and the next day he doesn't care if he never sees him again. This comes across as a certain abruptness in manner, a coldness that may turn off other children.

As he matures, he should strive to examine his beliefs for outmoded ideas that he has carried with him since childhood. He must find his own beliefs, his own path, to fulfill his potential.

Twelfth House: Fantasies, daydreams, visions, secrets: They all accompany this Moon placement. She's a loner, who works best by herself, who is usually happiest by herself, and whose heart is really more *there* than *here.*

She's emotionally insecure much of the time, but not in the Woody Allen sense; this kid would never do well with a therapist. But she would excel at expressing her insecurities through some kind of artistic endeavor—photography, music, filmmaking, writing, anything behind the scenes. Her talent often borders on visionary simply because her intuition can be so sweeping. William Blake had a twelfth house Moon.

Her natural empathy for other people, especially

people in need or pain, expands her inner world and feeds her creative urge.

Part Three

Your Child's Ascendant

31

Who's Rising?

Birth Times

Your child's *date of birth* determines the signs of the Sun, Moon, and planets in her natal chart. But the *exact time* of her birth determines her ascendant, or the sign that was rising when she took her first breath. The rising sign sets up the astrological wheel according to the sign and degree on each house cusp, and this, in turn, indicates where the planets fall. In other words, the ascendant is the starting point. Without the exact birth time, the chart won't be accurate.

While gathering data for this book, I found that most mothers, even those who are now in their seventies, remembered the time of day their children were born—morning or afternoon, evening or night. Those with only one child often remembered the exact time. Mothers with several children sometimes took a few minutes to figure out which child was born when, but they usually knew. One mother of five gave me the exact time of birth for her oldest and youngest but had to look up the times on the birth certificates for the three in between.

Birth, marriage or divorce, and death are major events fixed in the here and now. We remember them in the same way that we remember what we were doing when we heard about JFK's assassination. For astrological purposes, the time of birth *has to be exact.* The answer, "around midnight," isn't close enough. A new planet rises about every two hours, so if your child's birth at 3:35 a.m. seemed like "around midnight" and the chart is cast for that time, nothing will be accurate. The time on the birth certificate is usually the accepted time for birth. But if the child was born in a foreign hospital or at home or in the back seat of a cab, the time on the birth certificate may not really be accurate, either.

A birth time on the precise hour is sometimes suspect because it's so exact. Some years ago, an astrologer asked if I was absolutely sure about my 3:00 p.m. birth time. I'm as sure as I can be, since that's what is listed on my birth certificate. I was born in Caracas, Venezuela, which is officially only half an hour behind Eastern Standard Time. But until the advent of computers, these calculations were done the old fashioned way, with calculators or fingers, and Caracas time was miscalculated. As a result, I've been told I'm a late Libra rising by some astrologers and an early Scorpio rising by others.

Once I learned astrology, the answer was obvious. My rising is Scorpio, but at a mere fifty minutes, so the margin for error was understandable.

It's possible to rectify a birth chart according to the dates of major events in a person's life. This system, though, breaks down when the child is relatively young and hasn't experienced any major events or traumas. Fortunately, most children born in the United States since the middle of the twentieth century have birth certificates that show the time of birth. Use this time unless you or your spouse actually looked at the clock as your child was born.

The Ascendant

Some astrologers place the importance of the ascendant third in line behind the Sun and the Moon. But the rising sign is as important as the Sun sign because it symbolizes how you appear to others and how you interact with the larger world. It also symbolizes your physical appearance, your overall physical health, and the energy you put out and receive.

The planet that rules the rising sign is considered to be the ruler of the chart. That planet's energy is every bit as important in your child's makeup as the energy of her Sun and Moon. If your child has a Gemini rising, for example, then Mercury is the ruler of her chart. Mercury's energy focuses on communication and the intellect, so that is how other people see her.

With a Gemini rising, Gemini rules the first house, Cancer rules the second, Leo rules the third, and so on around the horoscope circle, ending with Taurus as the ruler of the twelfth house. The rulers of each sign are listed in table 6.

Sometimes, a natal chart will have an "intercepted" sign, one that doesn't appear on a house cusp but that is wholly contained within a house. An example of this kind of chart is in figure 31-1. Here, Capricorn (♑) is rising and rules the first house. The second house cusp is Pisces (♓), instead of Aquarius (♒), which is contained within the first house. Whenever there's one intercepted sign, its opposite will also be intercepted or contained. In the example chart, this occurs with Leo contained entirely in the seventh house.

An interception means that the affairs of that first house are colored by both Capricorn and Aquarius. This individual is seen by others as a structured individual with Aquarian visionary qualities to her personality. She is multifaceted.

Table 6: Planetary Rulers

Aries	♈	ruled by Mars	♂
Taurus	♉	ruled by Venus	♀
Gemini	♊	ruled by Mercury	☿
Cancer	♋	ruled by the Moon	☽
Leo	♌	ruled by the Sun	☉
Virgo	♍	ruled by Mercury	☿
Libra	♎	ruled by Venus	♀
Scorpio	♏	ruled by Pluto	♇
Sagittarius	♐	ruled by Jupiter	♃
Capricorn	♑	ruled by Saturn	♄
Aquarius	♒	ruled by Uranus	♅
Pisces	♓	ruled by Neptune	♆

Other factors to be considered about the ascendant are the quality and element of the sign. In figure 31-1, with Capricorn rising, the quality is cardinal and the element is earth. This person has no problem initiating action (cardinal) but may be easily influenced, particularly with the Pisces Moon sitting in the first house. Capricorn's earth gives her a practical approach in her interaction with other people.

According to astrologer Jeanne Avery, author of *The Rising Sign: Your Astrological Mask* (Boston: Doubleday & Co., 1982), the ascendant also "indicates an individual's particular outlook on life. . . . The circumstances of birth, the environment, and the conditions of childhood determine our particular point of view. We are the sum total of

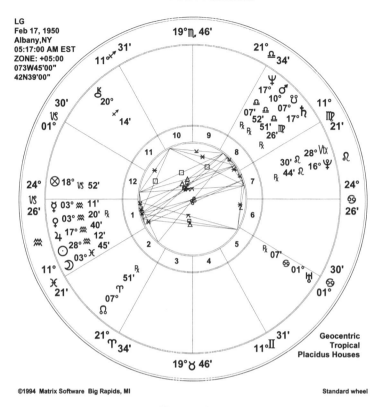

Figure 31-1

those conditions." And one of those conditions concerns the decisions we make about survival, says Avery.

The chart in figure 31-1, with that cluster of planets sitting in the first house, indicates that one of the individual's survival mechanisms is a focus on the self. "Me first," those planets say.

If the Sun sign and the ascendant are the same, then the individual is usually exactly what he appears to be. There won't be any conflict between the self that he is and the individual other people see. In this instance, the house position of the Sun will either be in the twelfth or in the first house, which have vastly different meanings (refer back to Sun through the houses).

In the chart in figure 6, the child's rising in Sagittarius (♐) and his Sun in Capricorn (☉15♑51) create a difficult combination. To others, he appears to be a freewheeling kid with a cheerful disposition. But his Sun in Capricorn in the first house of self says that he's actually ponderous and takes life and himself very seriously. Jupiter, which rules his chart because it rules Sagittarius, is the planet of expansiveness and luck. And yet Saturn, which rules Capricorn, is heavy-handed, a task master that insists on containing all that Sagittarian energy.

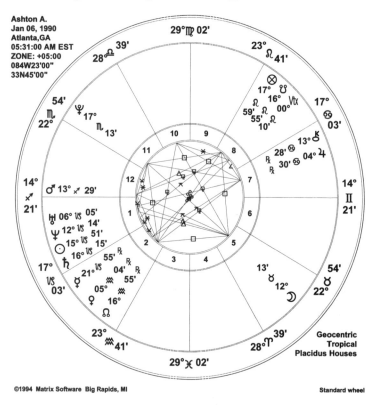

Ashton A.
Jan 06, 1990
Atlanta,GA
05:31:00 AM EST
ZONE: +05:00
084W23'00"
33N45'00"

Geocentric
Tropical
Placidus Houses

©1994 Matrix Software Big Rapids, MI   Standard wheel

Figure 31-2

Notice that Mars in Sagittarius (♂13♐29) sits almost on top of the rising in the twelfth house, within a one-degree conjunction of the ascendant. Any planet this close to one of the angular cusps should be treated with the same sort of respect accorded the ruler of the chart.

In this instance, Mars brings considerable dynamic energy to the rising. Since it's in the same mutable, fire sign as the ascendant, it indicates that the child is impulsive, quick-tempered, and accident prone.

The Gifted Child

One of the sure signs of a very bright child is evident in the chart in figure 31-3. This twenty-year-old film student has Scorpio rising at 10♏30 (ten degrees, thirty minutes), with Uranus in the first house at 12♏20. In other words, Uranus is conjunct the ascendant within two degrees.

This gives her a mind that is highly original, innovative, rebellious. She is capable of astonishing vision that is likely to be light years ahead of her time. *She isn't like her peers.*

Even though Pluto, as the ruler of Scorpio, dominates her chart, Uranus colors everything she is and everything she does. She also has the Moon in Taurus at a three-degree conjunction with the cusp of the seventh house and the Part of Fortune conjunct with her Midheaven, or the cusp of the tenth house. Since these conjunctions, like Uranus, fall at critical angles in the chart, they deserve special consideration.

That Moon makes it clear this kid is very stubborn where relationships are concerned. She wants to be surrounded by beauty, by fine things. The Part of Fortune means that luck and synchronicities are vital in her profession.

She was in a gifted program in the Palm Beach County, Florida, school system from the first grade onward. In high

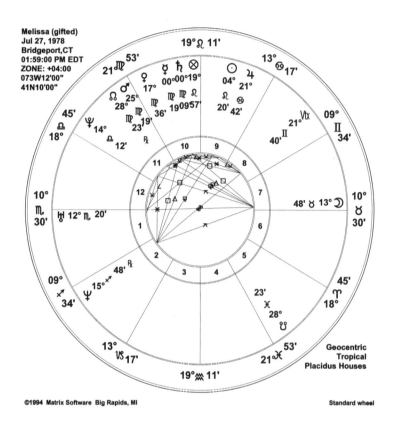

Melissa (gifted)
Jul 27, 1978
Bridgeport,CT
01:59:00 PM EDT
ZONE: +04:00
073W12'00"
41N10'00"

Geocentric
Tropical
Placidus Houses

©1994 Matrix Software Big Rapids, MI

Standard wheel

Figure 31-3

school, she was part of an accelerated program in which students could earn college credits, which enabled her to graduate more than a year ahead of her peers. Her I.Q. puts her in the top 1 percent of children her age.

The mere presence of Uranus conjunct the ascendant doesn't ensure that your child is gifted. But it's a *pattern* that may manifest in that way.

The Mask

The ascendant is often referred to as a person's mask because it's the image we project. Jean Avery compares it to the mask an actor wears when he's in uncertain situations. Astrologer Steven Forrest, writing in *The Inner Sky*, notes: ". . . [O]n the stage of the world, a person with no mask is mute, extraneous, and invisible. When, through a failure to create an effective first-house mask, we lack clarity about who we are, life feels out of control. And when life feels out of control, we get scared."

If your child's rising sign and Sun sign aren't compatible, it doesn't mean your child will fail at what he does or that his life is doomed to be plagued with tragedy. It only means that certain tensions will be created between how he sees himself and how other people see him. By developing self-awareness, he learns how to utilize his potential to its fullest.

The planet that rules the ascendant provides major clues to how your child may choose to fulfill his greatest potential. If, for instance, your child has Scorpio rising, then look to the house placement for Pluto, which rules Scorpio, to understand the area of his life that assumes significance.

Let's say the child's Pluto sits in the tenth house of professions and careers and has only positive aspects to it. This indicates that he will be able to fulfill his potential through his profession. He'll go through tremendous personal transformations related to his career, but the changes that lead to these upheavals will deepen his understanding of himself and expand his professional talents.

In the chart in figure 31-4, the child has Cancer rising in a late degree—28♋34—with a Sun in Scorpio in the fifth house. The Moon, which rules his rising, is in Capricorn in the sixth house. This says that his attachment to his home and family, to his roots, is expressed through the areas of health and work. His Capricorn Moon grounds the water elements of his Sun and rising. He and his mother share some sort of intuitive link through work.

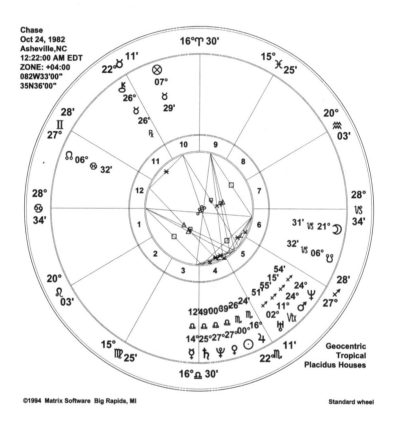

Figure 31-4

The shape of this child's chart, with all the planets falling within three houses, means the thrust of the child's life is very focused. Tremendous energy is being poured into the affairs of the fourth, fifth, and sixth houses. Mercury conjunct the fourth house cusp indicates that his home life is filled with talk, books, intellectual concerns.

Chase's mother, Carol Bowman, is a writer and came to that profession through him. When he was about four years old, he developed a sudden and unexpected aversion to loud noises. Rather than dismissing it or running off to a child psychologist, his mother attempted to get to the root of the fear. What evolved was an astonishing book, *Children's Past Lives.* Chase's life, in other words, seem to be following the blueprint of his chart; he found his path. And his mother, represented by the Capricorn Moon in the sixth house, also found her path. She is now a researcher of children's past lives.

In the next section, the description of each rising sign includes a look at the planet that rules the sign. When using this information with your child's natal chart, remember that any planet within three to five degrees on either side of the ascendant is as important as the ruling planet. It's a good idea to read that planet's description as well.

32

Aries Rising

With Aries on the rise in your child's chart, you may be gray before your time unless you learn that you can't watch him every second that he's awake. Besides, even beneath a watchful eye, this child's impetuous and impatient nature prompts him to take risks and to venture into places no other child would go.

He's a self-starter. You won't have to prod him into starting his homework or that science project that's due next week. But you may have to make sure that he finishes it. If he runs into a problem, if his homework or the project doesn't go exactly the way he wants, he may just walk away from it. It's important that he learns to finish what he starts, since this is one of the areas where Aries rising often falls short.

Long before he reaches his second birthday, his temper is legendary. If he doesn't get what he wants, he may throw a fit, and this can happen anywhere, he doesn't care. His needs are immediate and all consuming. No question that he needs discipline, but forget any heavy-handed stuff. What works best with this child is a clear understanding of parameters and boundaries. The word "no" isn't enough.

He has to realize that if he violates the boundaries you've set, he loses a privilege or a right: no more soccer, forget hockey camp this summer, good-bye to that new bike.

This child desperately needs physical activity to vent his energy or frustration. Team sports might provide such a vehicle or, as he gets older, he would benefit from regular workouts at the gym or from running. In lieu of either of those, he might try screaming into a pillow. Whatever he does, his anger shouldn't be allowed to build up inside him.

One thing this child does understand is immediate rewards for good behavior. Yes, it could be called bribery; but if it works, use it.

A child with Aries on the rise usually enjoys animals and the more, the merrier. He's as loving toward his pets, in fact, as he is toward everyone he likes. He's usually spontaneously affectionate, eager to hug and be hugged. As he matures, this manifests as very physical love relationships.

Physically, the Aries rising child may have a flushed complexion, particularly when he exerts himself. Since Aries rules the head, there is often some sort of scar or mark on the face or around the head. It's not unusual for the hair, regardless of its color, to have a tinge of red to it.

This child is an innovator and can't understand why others don't think and move as quickly as he does. His impatience can be his undoing.

The sign opposite Aries, forming an axis to it, is Libra. As an ascendant/descendant axis, it indicates that your child needs to learn cooperation with others. He should consider other people's feelings when he speaks or makes a decision.

This child fights for what he believes, and often, he fights very hard. For this reason, he should explore his beliefs as he gets older and define what he believes. Once he does, he can become a force for transformation and sweeping change.

Mars, Ruler of Aries

What are the first images that come to mind with this planet? Fire. Energy. Aggression. Sexuality. The god of war. Temper. In astrology, Mars represents the energy your child possesses and expends, his ability to assert his individuality, his physical vitality and sexual drive, and the way he tackles obstacles in his life.

When this energy is properly channeled, great achievements can result and physical stamina and productivity are increased. If the energy is misused, it's often expressed violently, in a fit of rage or even cruelty. Powerful stuff, for sure.

As your child enters his teens, Mars and the sex drive becomes more of an issue. Mars in a fire sign in the eighth house can indicate a lustful appetite for sex. It doesn't mean your son or daughter will be parents at the age of sixteen, but it's more worrisome than Mars in a fire sign in the third house of communication.

The house in which Mars falls in your child's chart tells you how the energy is likely to be manifested, which areas will be the most active for him, and which ones may be difficult in terms of other people. Apply the description of Mars to the meaning of the particular house in which Mars is placed.

When Mars hits one of the angular houses or an angular cusp, its capacity for positive or negative use is magnified, often dramatically. Refer to the chart for Ashton in figure 31-2. His Mars in Sagittarius, conjunct the ascendant, not only makes him accident prone, but it makes him impulsive and impatient as well. It energizes his personality, so that to other people he seems to be a veritable powerhouse.

There are different takes on his Mars in the twelfth house. One astrologer might interpret it in terms that would read like the plot of an espionage novel: that he should watch his back because his secret enemies will always be ready to do him in. But another astrologer might interpret it to mean that he can become a terrific force in charity work or behind the scenes or even in some aspect of public life because the Mars is conjunct the ascendant. Again, it's only a *pattern* and how it is manifested depends on the child's free will.

Such diverse personalities as Mick Jagger and Arthur Conan Doyle had Mars in the twelfth. For the first, Mars was the driving force behind his success; for the other, Mars illuminated what was hidden, secret.

Refer to the chart in figure 31-3 for Melissa. Her Mars lies in the eleventh house of friends, in Virgo. This means that a lot of her energy goes into cultivating friendships and group associations and into achieving her goals and dreams. She expends a lot of mental energy with her friends, exchanging ideas and beliefs.

The sign Mars is in describes the way your child expresses his energy. The house placement indicates the area of his life where this energy is expressed.

If, for example, your child has Mars in Taurus in the seventh house, then he faces obstacles in partnerships with a relentless, plodding steadiness. He doesn't give up easily. He may not give up at all. His challenge is compromise.

33

Taurus Rising

This child is the tortoise of the zodiac. She doesn't like to be hurried and approaches everything she does in a slow, steady manner. She is stubborn, with fixed opinions about many things, and is slow to change her mind once she's convinced she's right.

Her calm exterior calms the people around her. Other kids may mistakenly believe she's always this calm, this poised and balanced, only to find that, when she's backed into a corner, she has an explosive temper.

The child with this sign rising enjoys the good things in life—delicious food, pleasant and aesthetic surroundings, fine music, a garden bursting with flowers. She's something of a romantic, too. She may enjoy poetry, love stories, adventure tales. She has a mystical edge, which may not be readily apparent to the people who know her best. She's quite private about these issues, preferring to explore them alone.

She's usually liberal with her physical affections—hugs for mom and dad, brothers and sisters, the family pets, and even hugs for people she doesn't see that often. She needs physical touch, and as she gets older, this need can be briefly sated through sex. But really, the core of it extends well beyond sex. It's the sensation and grounding of physical intimacy that seize her.

Physically, she's usually vigorous and healthy and may have broad shoulders and a thick neck. Her forehead is often broad. Her face is nice looking, pleasing, and she usually has large, round eyes. She needs physical exercise to balance her slower metabolism and her love for good food.

Her talents range from music and the arts, to doing things with her hands. She's not an innovator like Aries, but she can certainly seize on Aries's ideas and carry them through to the end, long after Aries rising has lost interest. Tenacity is her middle name.

The Taurus/Scorpio axis indicates that, to fulfill herself, she should deepen her psychic awareness and develop an intense passion in something. This intensity in others often disturbs her precisely because it's something she lacks.

Venus, Ruler of Taurus

Love, of course, that's what Venus is about. But until love enters the picture, Venus symbolizes how your child gets along with others, particularly her friends, the depth and quality of her affections, and her creative urges and expression. It tells you a great deal about the friendships she cultivates and why she attracts certain people.

Venus has a lot to do with sensual pleasures and yet it also indicates the kinds of values your child holds. Is she petty or magnanimous with others? Stingy or generous? Duplicitous or honest? Does her need for sensual pleasures overshadow everything else?

In the chart in figure 33-1, the Taurus rising is in an early five degrees. Venus in Aquarius occupies the eleventh house with the South Node in Pisces. This indicates

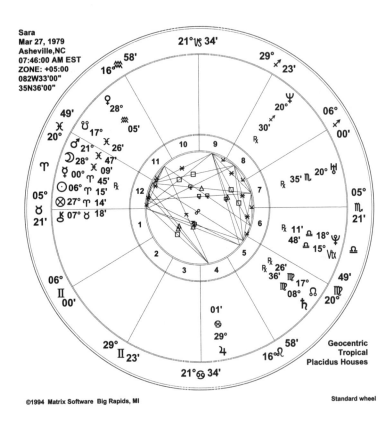

Sara
Mar 27, 1979
Asheville, NC
07:46:00 AM EST
ZONE: +05:00
082W33'00"
35N36'00"

Geocentric
Tropical
Placidus Houses

©1994 Matrix Software Big Rapids, MI

Standard wheel

Figure 33-1

that Sara is an attractive young woman, who finds her greatest pleasure through her friends. She enjoys original thinkers who may be a tad eccentric and very creative. Her friends will always be important to her.

If her friends make too many demands on her, Sara withdraws. She needs her freedom. At times like this she feels lonely and isolated. She's at her best when she's part of a group, sharing her beliefs or creative urges with people she likes.

If Venus sits on the cusp of an angular house or within one of the angular houses, pay special attention to the affairs of that house.

34

Gemini Rising

Boredom is this child's nemesis and he knows it as well as you do. As a result, he makes sure that he is rarely bored. He eagerly strives to entertain—through his quick wit, his mental gymnastics, his capacity for sheer fun. And when all of that fails, well, so be it. He rides out the blues with a sort of resigned attitude that makes you want to scream.

It's in these blue funks that a child with Gemini rising may find that writing or communicating somehow with people he trusts helps him to define who he is and where he's going. He's not stuck in the past; his problem is that he yearns for the future he can only now envision. He always figures the future is going to be better than where he is now, clearer and more beautiful than his present. By learning to express his desires and his disappointments, whatever they are, he is better able to fulfill his tremendous potential.

The duality associated with this sign is readily apparent to others. One day, he's all fun and bubbly, curious and adventurous, the very paragon of a great personality. The next day, all that stuff is gone and in its place is a morose little kid stuck in the mud of his own confusion. The good news is that the blue moods rarely last long.

This child needs positive reinforcement as he's growing up; the more he gets as a kid, the happier he'll be as an adult. With Gemini rising, Sagittarius rules the cusp of the seventh house, unless there are intercepted houses in the chart. Jupiter rules Sagittarius, so this is one of the luckiest positions for romantic and business partnerships.

He loves to travel and the travel may start rather early in his life. Education and learning will always be important areas for him as well and, with Aquarius on the cusp of his ninth house, ruled by Uranus, he may well attract fame in his life.

Physically, the Gemini rising child is usually slender, with widely set eyes. He moves and speaks quickly. He does everything quickly. He may not be all that interested in food, except as fuel for his ever-moving, restless body.

His talents are often multifaceted, with great facility in speech and writing or in communicating through the dramatic arts. Audrey Hepburn had Gemini rising. So does Phyllis Diller. Among writers with a Gemini rising were Arthur Conan Doyle, John Steinbeck, and Jack London.

Mercury, Ruler of Gemini

Mercury rules the central nervous system, communication, and the reasoning, left brain. It concerns physical movement and travel of the routine, daily variety. It represents brothers and sisters, the capacity for and ease with language. After the Moon, it's the fastest moving planet, so it's always in the same sign as the Sun or in the sign immediately before or after.

If Mercury and the Sun lie in an exact conjunction, Mercury's energy can be subsumed by the energy of the

Sun. In astrology, this is called *combust*. In the ordinary world, it's known as burnout. What it means for a child is that his mind never rests; it's constantly chewing away at various things, trying to analyze and dissect in order to understand. It means the child needs periodic respites from anything that's left brain. Take him camping. Take him to the ocean. Buy him a dog. Distract him.

Mercury isn't just concerned about communication. As the ruler of a chart, it compels a child to explore whatever captures his interest and curiosity. But he explores it mentally and intellectually and can also explore with his hands. These kids are often impressive little painters or sculptors. Some of them like mechanical devices. Many enjoy the physical sciences.

Mercury as the chart ruler can indicate a love for books, for stories, even for mythological tales. Once this child's mind is blown open by learning, the learning never stops.

With Gemini rising, Mercury's sign tells you a great deal about how your child communicates and how his mind is wired. The house placement should give you some idea of what your child thinks and talks about, although this is probably obvious from the time your child is young.

If, for instance, Mercury is conjunct the ascendant or falls within the first house, your child is very impatient, curious and restless, and he talks to everyone. He needs to discuss and exchange ideas with his peers; it's how he learns about the world when he's young.

With Mercury in the twelfth house, there's a tendency to keep his thoughts secret. He has a private fantasy world and enjoys anything that is hidden and metaphysical. As with any other planet that rules an ascendant, pay special attention to Mercury when it hits an angular house.

35

Cancer Rising

Whereas Gemini rising enjoys talking about ideas, the domain of Cancer rising is feelings. This child can be as changeable as the Gemini twins, but she's far more moody. Some days, she wakes up ready to take on everything and everyone at once, eager to cram as much as possible into the day. But several hours later her mood has plummeted and she's beyond consolation. Welcome to the world of Cancer rising.

As a water, cardinal sign, this child is all about emotion. She's fluid, she's tidal, she's a vast sea of intuitive energy. Quite often, this rising sign, like Scorpio rising, absorbs other people's moods and energy, so it's important that she have positive, upbeat friends. Her magnetic and nurturing personality, however, may attract some people who are anything but upbeat. This is an area where parental guidance is vital.

The crab symbol for Cancer can be most revealing for this child. If you, as a parent, are ever puzzled by your Cancer rising child, head for the beach and observe a crab. Watch how it moves, how it attacks its prey, how it takes refuge, how it navigates a change in the tides. Granted, a human being is more complex than a crab, but the intrinsic qualities of a child with Cancer rising are evident in the creature it's named after.

If you want to know what this child feels, you may have to gently prod her, get her to confide in you. She has vivid, often prescient dreams, and if she starts talking about them, listen closely, because the dreams will tell you what's going on inside of her.

Physically, this child is among the easiest of the zodiac to identify. Her face is usually quite round, the shape of a full Moon. Her eyes are like liquid. Just peering into those eyes, you know she can be easily wounded. Her body tends toward plumpness.

This can be a very psychic rising, particularly if her early environment nurtures her natural ability. Sometimes, she has an attachment to objects that hold a nostalgic meaning for her—family heirlooms, for instance, or dusty family photo albums. She may be a collector, a clutter freak whose closet is filled with stuff she never plays with but that makes her feel secure.

Moon, Ruler of Cancer

So you think you've got a handle on this child? Guess again. With the Moon as the ruler of her chart, your knowledge of her will come only from the heart, the unconscious, the intuitive connection the two of you have.

The Moon symbolizes your child's *emotional patterns,* habits, the attitudes she holds on a deeply unconscious level. These kinds of attitudes are usually formed in early childhood. Even though we don't have to be held hostage to them, we often are. And because many of our early attitudes are formed by the mother as the nurturing parent, the house placement of the Moon describes the child's relationship with her mother.

Is the mother a workaholic? Look for a Moon in the sixth house. Is she a stay-at-home mom? Look for a Moon in the fourth. Is she a mom on the professional fast track? Look for a Moon in the tenth house.

The Moon's sign describes how your child expresses her emotions. It does best in the water signs because water is associated with emotions and intuition. But every sign has benefits and strengths. The challenge for a parent in this case is to guide your child so that she capitalizes on her strengths rather than her weaknesses.

If the Moon and the Sun are in the same sign, then your child's emotions and her conscious mind work in unison. If they aren't in the same sign, the child may feel conflicted, her heart wanting to do one thing and her mind, another.

Astrologer Jean Avery suggests in *Rising Sign: Your Astrological Mask* that one way to understand the child with Cancer rising is to understand Neptune, the esoteric ruler of Cancer. "Neptune is the planet of vision, idealism, inspiration. This child can be inspired through his ideals to productive action. . . . It is essential that his imagination be given an outlet."

Look at Chase's chart in figure 31-4. His Neptune (Ψ) is in Sagittarius in the fifth house. At its highest levels, Neptune rules poetry and music. Chase, in fact, is a musician who has played professionally. Mars (σ) is conjunct Neptune in the fifth, so a lot of energy goes into his music and he feels passionate about it.

36

Leo Rising

This kid is a powerhouse of energy, dramatic and proud, a true leader. Wherever he goes, wherever he is, other kids generally notice him. He possesses such magnetism at times that he literally dominates a room just by his presence.

Drama, in fact, is at the core of this child's personality. From his earliest years onward, he needs a creative outlet for this dramatic energy, and the obvious outlet is acting. But he may benefit equally from any artistic training. Such diverse personalities as Marilyn Monroe, chess champion Bobby Fischer, and Ernest Hemingway all had Leo rising.

As a youngster, he needs praise and recognition for who he is and for his accomplishments. If he doesn't get it, if he is bombarded with criticism instead, his ego doesn't get the nourishment it needs. This can lead to the less-evolved aspects of Leo rising, which is excessive pride and arrogance.

These kids are inherently kind and never forget a person who is kind to them. As a fixed fire sign, they can be incredibly stubborn, especially when they know they're right.

Integrity is important to them—other people's integrity and their own.

He loves bold, bright colors and his personal style is reflected in his personal surroundings and in the clothes he wears. Physically, this child usually has striking eyes and luxuriant hair. Tall or short, slender or plump, he has a regal bearing that is apparent in his every movement.

Sun, Ruler of Leo

The Sun in your child's chart represents his behavior patterns, personality, and physical vitality and health. It also describes the kinds of activities he enjoys, his capacity for independence, and how he relates to others.

For a child with Leo rising, the house placement of the Sun describes the area of life where he best expresses his intrinsic nature. Aspects to the Sun describe whether this expression occurs easily or with difficulty.

In the chart in figure 36-1 (Jenny), Leo rises at 23 degrees and 56 minutes. The Sun in Virgo occupies the first house, an excellent position for a Leo rising. It gives Jenny good physical health and a magnetic personality. Her will is strong and well developed. Given this Sun position, it isn't surprising that she's been involved in physical activities like karate and ballet.

The only planet in the chart that is conjunct one of the angles is Pluto (♀) on the cusp of the fourth house. This two-degree conjunction indicates that some event is likely to transform her childhood. In Jenny's case, it was the divorce of her parents when she was six.

The chart in figure 36-2 also shows a Leo rising. Kate's Sun in Aquarius lies in the sixth house of health and work. It means she brings considerable vision and foresight to her work. With Mercury (☿) at a three-degree conjunction

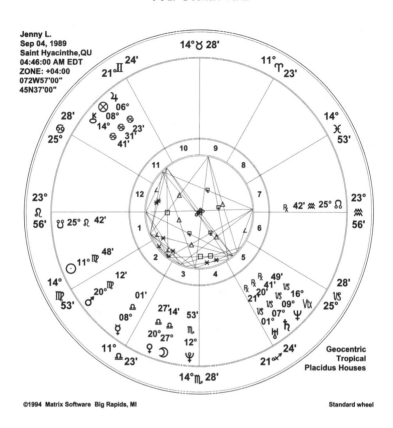

Jenny L.
Sep 04, 1989
Saint Hyacinthe,QU
04:46:00 AM EDT
ZONE: +04:00
072W57'00"
45N37'00"

Geocentric
Tropical
Placidus Houses

©1994 Matrix Software Big Rapids, MI   Standard wheel

Figure 36-1

with the Sun, her work is intellectual and involves some facet of communication.

She has two planets conjunct critical angles. Jupiter (♃) is within a four-degree conjunction of the Midheaven and is the highest planet in the chart. Jupiter rules the higher mind, foreign travel, higher education, the law, and publishing. Given the Sun/Mercury conjunction in the sixth, she would excel in any ninth-house pursuit. Pluto (♇) is within a one-degree conjunction of the rising. This is an extremely powerful position for Pluto. It brings intensity and

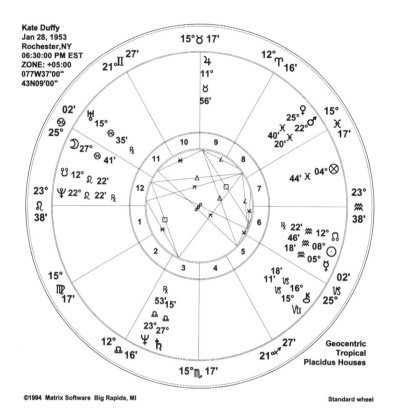

Kate Duffy
Jan 28, 1953
Rochester, NY
06:30:00 PM EST
ZONE: +05:00
077W37'00"
43N09'00"

Geocentric
Tropical
Placidus Houses

©1994 Matrix Software Big Rapids, MI

Standard wheel

Figure 36-2

magnetism to her personality. Her emotions are a power-ful force in her life, capable of transforming everything about which she feels passionate. Issues of power and con-trol often enter into this Pluto placement, which may cre-ate problems. But if Pluto's energy is properly channeled, this position can bring about momentous change that ex-ceeds her own expectations and goals.

This woman certainly fulfilled the prevalent career patterns in her natal chart: She's an editor at a New York publishing house.

37

Virgo Rising

She has a discerning mind, capable of handling all the picky details that no one else wants to deal with. She likes order in her environment and tends to be more fussy about tidiness than Virgo Sun. She detests clutter and goes to great lengths to have a niche and drawer for everything.

Although Virgo is a Mercury-ruled, mutable air sign, just like Gemini, the two risings are manifested in very different ways. Whereas a Gemini rising does everything quickly, the speed of this ascendant is evident most strongly in the speed that her thoughts move, like lightning. Not much escapes this child's attention. If you're not feeling up to par one morning and try to hide it, she notices it anyway and asks about it. If you make changes in your bedroom, even small changes, she immediately notices them and comments on them.

She brings this same discernment to her schoolwork and friendships. Ask her how one of her friends smiles and she won't just describe it, she'll show you, right down to the dimple in the corner of the friend's mouth. She should learn to see the larger picture as well, something she learns from Pisces, her polar opposite. It goes back to the adage about the forest and the trees. Virgo can see the trees but has trouble seeing the entire forest; Pisces is great at the big picture but not so good with the nitpicky details.

She's an excellent reader and was probably an early reader as well. Information is often a Virgo rising's life blood, but too much information may make it difficult for her to form her own opinions about things. Encourage originality in her thinking; once she realizes it's okay to have opinions of her own, she can excel at creative thought.

Physically, a Virgo rising can be slender; all that Mercurial energy keeps their metabolism buzzing. Many have compelling eyes and enviable complexions. Most are meticulously groomed.

She tends to be critical of others, but never more critical than she is of herself. This may be a defense mechanism that she developed in early childhood, but she needs to move beyond it and keep her criticism of others to herself.

Once she finds her passion in life, she works at it tirelessly, seeking to perfect her talent and abilities. Then she's able to successfully merge her intuition and her reasoning mind.

Mercury, Ruler of Virgo

See the description of Mercury under Gemini rising.

38

Libra Rising

He's quite the charmer and is so agreeable most of the time that he seems too good to be true. He does his homework when you ask him to, pitches in with chores, and pulls his share of the weight in the family. He seeks balance in everything he does, cringes at disharmony and disagreements, and doesn't like to see anything ugly or unpleasant.

He may be so agreeable, however, that he doesn't learn to stand up for himself, or he compromises too much just to keep peace. He must learn that it's okay to have his own opinions and it's okay to be selfish. He shouldn't try to cover ugliness with something more pleasing; he should acknowledge it, then move on.

This child enjoys music, art, books, good food, nice clothes—that is, the finer things in life. He has no particular fondness for solitude. He would rather be with his family or friends. His primary thrusts in life are relationships and fair play. Quite often, kids with this rising sign are drawn instinctively to the arts, theater, music, and dance. They can also be attracted to color, perfumes, design, architecture, and politics. Given a fertile environment, this child's sense of fair play may show up as an inordinate interest in national news. Liz Taylor, a Libra ascendant, began as an actress, has her own perfume line, and is also politically active, notably in raising money for AIDS, a charitable work that fits with her Pisces Sun.

Physically, this child is usually attractive. He's soft spoken, with an aesthetic aura about him that other people always notice. If his home life is unusually disruptive, then he may be a quiet, retiring child who, deep inside, figures he's somehow at fault for all the strife. This is precisely the kind of setting that makes it difficult for a Libra child to assert himself as he gets older.

Venus, Ruler of Libra

See the Venus description under Taurus Rising.

39

Scorpio Rising

Right from the start, she's intense, private, emotional. Just when you're beginning to understand her, she does something that throws your neat perceptions into total disarray. Get used to it. With this child, you and your spouse must draw heavily on your own intuitive skills to even scratch the surface of her personality.

She tends to see things in black and white, even when she's young. For her, something is either right or it's wrong. The problem is that her sense of right and wrong may not be everyone's and she often tries to bludgeon people with her point of view. She needs to learn to compromise or at least to keep her opinions to herself, and the younger she learns it, the easier her life will be.

Regardless of her physical build, her eyes have a piercing gaze and seem to instantly assess people and situations. She relies on her first impressions, and if she deems you unworthy of her attention, that's it. She writes you off. But if she likes and trusts you, she immediately shows a warm, affectionate side.

Her early childhood has a deep impact on the rest of her life. If she's made to feel secure and loved, then she carries these emotions into her adult life. If she doesn't feel loved as a kid, this can translate later on into a vindictive, selfish, and totally ego-centered personality.

As a fixed water sign, this child is one of the most intuitive of the zodiac. Her innate power comes from the depth of her emotions, and it's this power that she will wield for good or bad as she gets older. When used for good, this energy is profoundly spiritual and transformative.

Pluto, Ruler of Scorpio

When you say the word "Pluto," you either think of Goofy's dog or of the mythological god of the underworld. The first symbolizes the kind of humor you sometimes need to navigate this planetary energy successfully, and the second, of course, is what Pluto is about.

This planet is the most distant in our solar system, and yet its power is considerable. Pluto is about transformation and regeneration, destruction and power. It describes how your child uses power, how she deals with power that comes to her, and tells you something about her quest for deeper truths. Badly aspected, it indicates power struggles your child may have with other people. Well aspected, Pluto gives your child the ability and stamina to get through difficult times. It also gives her ambition and drive, expressed through the area indicated by house placement.

Since its discovery in 1930, Pluto has passed through only five signs and entered its sixth, Sagittarius, at the tail end of 1995. Since it takes 248 years to go through the zodiac, its sign affects generations of people. The sign is important in your child's chart if it hits one of the four critical angles. Otherwise, its house placement is more personally significant.

The house placement describes the area of your child's life where her greatest change and development will occur. In the charts in figures 36-1 and 36-2, Pluto conjuncts the ascendant and IC (cusp of the fourth house) respectively.

40

Sagittarius Rising

If you attempt to pen this child in, to impose harsh restrictions on how he lives his life, you'll regret it. For him, freedom isn't just an abstract concept; it's a burning need. He seeks it the way a hungry stray seeks food.

He enjoys sports, an excellent way to burn off some of that Sagittarian energy. He also loves being outdoors, where nature feeds the essential part of him that is either religious or philosophical. Even if he is traditionally religious, his spiritual nature expands far beyond a church. In a sunrise, he sees the face of All That Is; in the crashing of a wave on a beach, he sees the pattern of his life. There's a mystic in this kid.

Travel is one of the pursuits that wakes him up inside. The exposure to other people, particularly foreigners and their cultures, brings out his curiosity and passion to *know*, to understand. He integrates these travel experiences into the intimate circuitry of who he is, thus expanding his world.

He's blunt, there's no way around it. When he has something to say, he says it straight out and that's that.

Only after the fact does he realize that maybe his bluntness hurt the other person's feelings. Well, get over it. He's not going to change. What you see is pretty much what you get.

Profound humanity usually accompanies this rising sign. It extends to people, animals, even plants. He has an instinctive understanding that all of life is connected. Expect this child to bring home stray cats that need a home, injured birds that need nurturing, even plants that have wilted in the heat.

Physically, this child may have an angular face and body. Everything about him is animated—his movements, the way he talks and dresses. He looks youthful and may retain that youthfulness throughout his life.

The challenge with this rising is to think before he speaks and to realize that not everyone believes as he believes. This rising, however, is one of the luckiest in the zodiac because it's ruled by Jupiter, known in astrology as the "benefic" planet.

Jupiter, ruler of Sagittarius

It seems only appropriate that, as the largest of the planets in our solar system, Jupiter's significance in astrology concerns expansion. It's considered a lucky planet, like Venus, and it denotes areas in life where your child finds prosperity and is protected.

It is one of the slower moving planets and remains in a sign for about a year. Its sign is significant primarily if the planet hits one of the critical angles and describes the way your child seeks to expand his life. If Jupiter falls in Libra, for instance, then your child seeks to expand through relationships, the arts, and other Libran affairs. If Jupiter falls in Cancer, then your child expands himself through his family, his ability to nurture, and other Cancerian pursuits.

The house placement of Jupiter describes the specific area in which your child finds luck and prosperity and the way he seeks to expand himself and his world. The ninth house Jupiter in the chart in figure 33-2 suggests expansion and luck through law, higher education, publishing, foreign travel and cultures, and spiritual issues.

In the chart in figure 36-2, Jupiter in Cancer lies in the eleventh house. This suggests that Jenny will always be lucky with friendships. As she gets older, opportunities will come to her through her friends, many of whom may be socially prominent people.

41

Capricorn Rising

This child is often perplexing. The very nature of this ascendant tends to hide much of what she's really feeling. She takes on responsibility readily, without argument, but does so because she feels she must.

From her earliest years, she seems older than she actually is. She may associate with older children and adults and do so on an equal footing. She's conscientious and pays attention to rules and parameters that exist in society, in her school, in her home. If she's supposed to wear a helmet when she rides her bike, she does it. If she's supposed to wear shoes when she goes outside, she does it.

She wants to achieve something in the world, to make a contribution. She needs encouragement, however, to find her strengths and to nurture them. At times, she seems abrupt or remote with her friends, cutting them off cold. It's nothing personal. She just doesn't feel like being with any of her friends just then.

Her parents are important to her, especially her father. There's some evidence, gleaned primarily through hypnotic regression, that children with this rising feel a deep reluctance to be born. As Avery also notes in *Rising Sign: Your Astrological Mask*, "The resistance to birth is so strong that many individuals with this ascendant recall a feeling of digging in the heels until fatigue set in. The reality of having no way out and no choice in the matter forced him to give in and be born. This extreme dread of life seems primarily concerned with the feeling of not being wanted."

This sense of being unwanted may be why her security lies in controlling her immediate environment and assuming responsibility so readily. Perhaps a part of her feels that, if she assumes burdens, she makes herself indispensable.

Physically, this child may have heavy eyelids and a pursed mouth. She nearly always looks and acts older than she is.

The antidote to the problems she may experience center on love. First, she must learn to love herself. Once she does, it's easier for her to love others.

Saturn, Ruler of Capricorn

This planet used to have a bad reputation among astrologers. It was seen as malefic, symbolic of the "karma" brought into the present life, and taught harsh, often brutal lessons. But its meaning has changed over the years.

It's still seen as the planet of "karma," but in the sense that it represents what the soul came in to do. It describes the parameters in your child's life, the boundaries and rules, and the lessons she must learn to further her development. Saturn is, most of all, about learning discipline.

It takes Saturn two and a half years to go through one sign. Its sign describes how your child will learn the discipline she needs. If Saturn is in Aquarius, for instance, then she will learn through her intellect. The house placement, however, describes the area of her life where her boundaries will be the most strict and where she must learn discipline.

In other words, if Saturn in Capricorn appears in her tenth house of profession and careers, then chances are very high that she will be a tireless worker who sticks to the rules of her profession. She may not achieve her potential until after the age of forty, because Saturn sometimes delays the fulfillment.

In the chart in figure 41-1, Capricorn is on the rise and there are four planets in that sign in the twelfth house. This

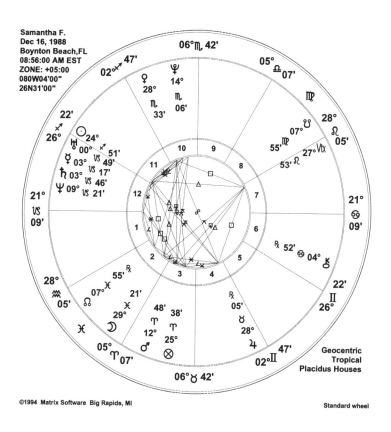

Figure 41-1

cluster of four or more planets is known as a *stellium*, and it indicates an intense focus on the personal unconscious. Saturn, the ruler of the ascendant, falls in the twelfth house, too. This suggests a deep insecurity rooted somewhere in early childhood. She's very conscious of rules and follows them to the letter. By doing so, she feels safer, as if the rules somehow protect her.

Interestingly, her Moon is in Pisces in the second house of finances and her Sun in Sagittarius lies in the eleventh house of friends and ambitions. Earth, water, and fire. These three elements may work counterpoint to each other at times. Her fiery Sun thirsts for travel and adventure and new horizons; her earth rising imposes discipline and restrictions; her watery Moon connects her to much deeper mysteries and makes her very emotional, something her Capricorn rising objects to.

42

Aquarius Rising

He's mentally sharp and quick, open and curious about new ideas, and tends to be a nonconformist in every sense of the word. This child is unique, a true individual, and this is apparent from the time he's very young.

As a fixed air sign, however, it's difficult to change his opinion on anything once he has made up his mind. There's a certain emotional detachment that accompanies this rising, perhaps because Aquarius is more comfortable in the mental realm.

His interests range from science and math to books and theater and art. As he becomes aware of the larger world, his humanitarian traits may begin to emerge. He hates to see anyone in pain, whether it's the homeless man on the corner or a stray dog in the neighborhood. He may have an early interest in metaphysical topics.

Aquarians are the joiners of the zodiac. This character-istic becomes obvious once they start school, when they sign up for every available club and activity.

Physically, a child with this rising sign can be slender or heavy, tall or short, but his body is usually nicely propor-tioned and he has good coordination.

There's a lot of the rebel in this child. The way this rebellion is expressed depends on the house placement of Uranus, the ruling planet.

Uranus, Ruler of Aquarius

This planet is all about freedom and the unconventional. It seeks to destroy the rules and parameters and the rigid systems that Saturn erects in our lives. Then it replaces these with new systems that allow us greater room for growth. Its energy acts suddenly and unexpectedly.

Uranus takes 84 years to travel around the zodiac and spends about seven years in each sign. As one of the slower moving planets, its sign is less important personally than its house placement. The house placement describes the area of your child's life where he will seek his greatest expression of freedom. When it hits one of the angular cusps, its importance in the chart is even more significant.

If, for instance, Uranus falls on the Midheaven, or the cusp, of the tenth house, then it's likely your child will experience sudden and unexpected career changes. He will do something brilliant that suddenly propels him into the spotlight. This may be his fifteen minutes of fame or it may be long lasting. It depends on how he deals with the Uranian energy.

If Uranus hits the cusp of the fourth house—the IC—then it's likely you and your family make numerous moves. Your home is highly unusual in some way and may have a lot of electronic devices or be decorated in an eccentric manner.

If Uranus falls on the seventh house cusp, then the child is attracted to people who are highly unusual in some way. Later in life, the spouse or significant other will be unusual also.

43

Pisces Rising

He's a dreamer. Never mistake that about him. There are depths to this child that are so layered, so complex, that even he doesn't realize they exist. At times, his eyes glaze over and his attention is diverted elsewhere—not at the TV, even if it's on, not at the book that's open in his lap. He's looking within, at the movies that run through his mind. Or he's navigating the tides of his emotions.

There seem to be two ways this rising evolves. In the first, the child strives to be accepted and loved by being mom's or dad's little angel. He's cooperative and agreeable and others erroneously believe he's capable of doing nothing wrong. After all, just look at him, that ethereal face, those liquid eyes, that sheer physical presence: How can this child be anything but exceptional?

The illusion, in this instance, belongs to others who choose to see this child as a paragon of perfection, rather than as the little human being that he is. He needs your love and guidance even when he doesn't act as you think he should.

In the second scenario, the child with this ascendant follows the flow of who he is. When he's sad or ecstatic or just mediocre, it shows.

In either case, this child is likely to be quite intuitive and, in some cases, psychic. He's also artistic—theater, photography, painting or sculpture, writing, you name it, he has the seed. The problem rises when he isn't sure which seed to cultivate. Help him find his greatest strengths and this child flourishes beyond anyone's imagination.

More than any other rising sign, this child has the innate ability to make real what he desires. But first, he has to know what he wants. Second, he must learn how to fine-tune his psychic ability so that he opens a clear channel between his conscious and unconscious minds. Once he can do this, despite acclimation to a society that generally discourages psychic ability, he understands the true power of his gift and fulfills his greatest potential.

Neptune, Ruler of Pisces

Neptune governs everything from the basest escapism to the most evolved spirituality. It rules glamour, the arts, film, dance, spiritualism, mediumship, and clairvoyance. In many ways, Neptune belongs to the world of dreams, that country of the inner mind that is often vague and misty to the conscious mind.

Neptune, like Pluto, literally strolls through the zodiac, and you won't see its entire passage in your lifetime. It spends about fourteen years in each sign, which makes its house placement more important than its sign in the individual natal chart. The house placement indicates the area of your child's life where he may experience illusion or spiritual heights, confusion or mystical insight. In the seventh house, for example, Neptune would indicate a blind spot about relationships or that the child approaches relationships with a mystical bent.

In the chart in figure 43-1, Neptune is in Capricorn in the tenth house of profession and careers. It suggests a career in the arts—film, theater, photography or a related venue. There may be a spiritual flavor to her work.

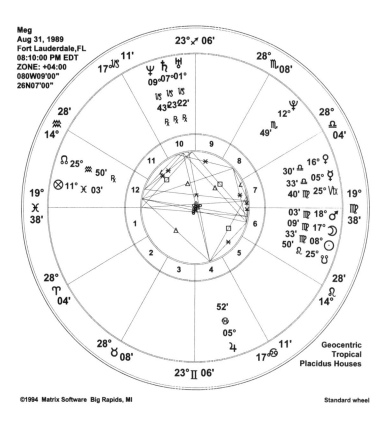

Figure 43-1

Neptune is conjunct Saturn in the tenth and Saturn is at a wide conjunction with Uranus, which is the highest planet in her chart. This combination suggests that she will bring originality and genius to whatever she does. She will have to work hard to achieve her potential and things will improve greatly after the age of forty. She'll always chafe at restrictions that are placed on her. But if she works within established parameters and brings her considerable intuition to bear against whatever she does, she will achieve her vast potential.

Notice that her Sun and Moon share a wide conjunction in Virgo in the sixth house of health and work. Since they're in the same sign, her emotions are never in conflict with her conscious mind. She's able to act with purposefulness.

Whenever the Sun and Moon fall in the same sign, the child was born under a new Moon. It means she's terrific at initiating things, but unless her interest is sustained, she moves on to something else.

The child's Moon and Mars are conjunct to within one degree in the sixth house and both are in opposition to the ascendant by one and two degrees. The conjunction indicates that she has a temper and it erupts swiftly, sometimes without apparent reason to others. As long as she's allowed to express the anger, she gets over it quickly. If she holds it in, it may result in health problems.

She's a fighter and doesn't give up easily when she really wants something. She fights in a Virgo way, through her intellect, her attention to details, and her communication skills.

The second aspect, the opposition, means that she may be combative with others. She also looks to other people for emotional support—her friends and family when she's young, partners and significant others when she's older. She isn't satisfied with casual friendships. She needs to know people on a deeper level—what makes them tick, what they feel and why.

44

Shapes & Stuff

Jones's Patterns

In *The Rainman,* the autistic character played by Dustin Hoffman knows in a glance how many toothpicks spill to the floor when a container is knocked over. He reads a *pattern* that yields very specific information.

In *Anatomy of the Spirit* and *Awakening Intuition*, medical intuitives Carolyn Myss and Mona Lisa Schultz describe numerous instances in which they read or tune into the energy *patterns* in their clients' lives that have led or may lead to illness. When you get a reading from a psychic, he or she reads the *predominant patterns* in your life at the moment of the reading and tells you how these patterns are likely to be manifested in the future. When you toss coins in accordance with the *I Ching* or pull tarot cards or lay down runes, they depict patterns. All divination systems, including astrology, are based on *patterns*.

Some astrologers shudder when astrology and divination are mentioned in the same breath; *divination* isn't as respectable as *science*. But astrology isn't like geology or medicine and never will be. Its closest scientific kin is probably quantum physics. Astrology, like every other divination system, is synchronistic. In the introduction to the

Chinese oracle, the *I Ching*, Carl Jung wrote, "Sychronicity takes the coincidence of events in space and time as meaning something more than mere chance, namely, a peculiar interdependence of objective events among themselves as well as with the subjective (psychic) states of the observer or observers." This means that, at the moment of your birth, a certain pattern of possibilities prevailed.

Some of the possibilities in that pattern are stronger than others, but the manifestation of any of them depend on your free will. One of the first obvious patterns in a chart is the shape formed by the way the planets fall. These are called Jones's Patterns, after the astrologer Marc Edmond Jones, who identified seven types of broad patterns in charts.

The Splash

In this type of pattern, the planets fall more or less evenly around the horoscope. I think of these kids as the

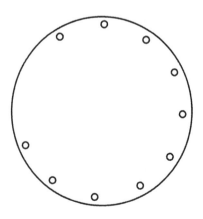

The Splash

type who enjoy a variety of experiences. Their interests are many, with their energy scattered among them all. They should be encouraged to concentrate on one particular interest or talent so their focus becomes more concentrated.

The Bowl

In this shape, the planets fall in half of the horoscope, with the other six houses empty. These kids are self-contained. Their lives are focused on the affairs of the occupied houses. The empty part of the chart symbolizes the challenges they face in their lives. The planet that leads away from the empty part of the chart (counterclockwise) symbolizes how the challenge is best met.

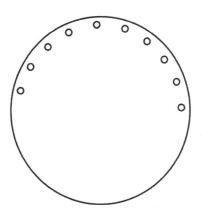

The Bowl

If Jupiter were leading, for instance, then the challenge can be met through higher education and the higher mind, expansion, and all of the things that Jupiter represents.

The Bucket

This pattern is one of the easiest to recognize. Eight or nine planets are concentrated in half of the horoscope, with one or two planets in the other half that form the "handle" of the bucket. If there's just one planet in the handle, it's called a singleton.

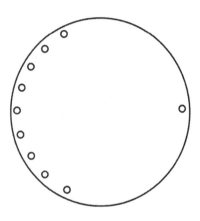

The Bucket

These kids live their lives primarily in the occupied part of the horoscope. But the handle is how that action is expressed. If Venus is the singleton planet, for instance, then the focus of the child's life is on relationships, romance, love, according to the house placement.

The Bundle

The shape is also easy to identify. All ten planets are bunched into one third of the chart, usually three to consecutive houses. Chase's chart in figure 31-4 is the bundle shape, with all the planets found in the third, fourth, fifth, and sixth houses.

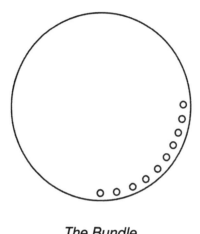

The Bundle

This child has a highly concentrated approach to life, with all of his concerns and activities occurring in the occupied houses. The concentration of energy is somewhat narrow but is very focused and powerful.

The Locomotive

In this shape, the ten planets fall within two trines (nine houses or 240 degrees), with one third of the chart empty. These kids are regular dynamos of energy, self-motivated and oriented toward achievement. The planet leading clockwise describes what motivates them. The house this planet occupies indicates where the child puts most of his energy.

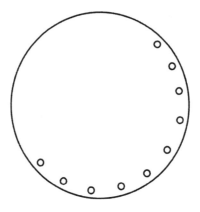

The Locomotive

The See-Saw

This shape looks exactly like it sounds; a cluster of planets on one side of the chart is balanced by a cluster of plan-

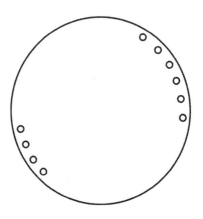

The See-Saw

ets directly opposite. The numbers of planets don't have to be equal. These kids share traits with Libras in that they look for balance. They can see both sides of an issue and instinctively weigh the pros and cons.

The Splay

This shape isn't easy to identify at a glance because it resembles the splash. It's distinguished by the irregular placement of planets around the horoscope. Kate Duffy's chart in figure 36-2 is an example of a splay pattern.

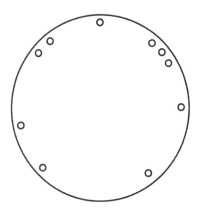

The Splay

These kids are Uranian in nature, individualistic, intense, and often eccentric. They live by their own code and set of rules.

45

Comparison Charts

Families & Friends

When charts are compared, the various patterns can be exceptionally revealing. Quite often, it explains why a child doesn't get along with a parent or sibling or why a child is especially close to one parent and not to the other. It may explain why your child is closer to a friend than he or she is to a sibling.

By comparing two or more charts, the dynamics of a relationship become apparent. A child with a fixed rising in Taurus, for example, may have outward conflicts with a parent whose rising is in cardinal Capricorn. But if they both have Moons in Virgo, then they click on an emotional level.

In the following chart comparisons, the mother's chart lies within the inner circle and the child's, in the outer. This shows how the child impacts on the mother's life.

One of the first things I look for in any comparison is the Vertex—Vtx. This is an imaginary angle of the horoscope that was popularized by astrologer Charles Jayne. It involves encounters or situations that are karmic or destined. I don't mean to imply any kind of predestination; this appointment was agreed to at a soul level by the individuals involved.

"Relationships that have strong Vertex ties have the strongest effects on the lives of the people involved," writes astrologer Robert Hand. "They . . . have a quality of portentousness."

The house placement for the Vertex in an individual horoscope indicates the area of life that will be most significant for the individual. It also describes how the energy should be expressed to further the person's growth. Aspects to the Vertex, particularly conjunctions and oppositions, and the planet that rules the Vertex, describe the kind of energy that influences the person's overall life path.

In the comparison charts in figure 45-1, the mother's Vertex lies in the eleventh house at 09℗18'. Her daughter's Sun sign (℗08°⊙) conjuncts the Vertex at slightly more than one degree. Her birth was certainly the mother's appointment with destiny. The ruler of Virgo, Mercury, is also the ruler of the mother's Sun sign of Gemini (⊙16♊12') in the eighth house. Mercury rules all kinds of communication; the mother is a writer, so this would fit.

The child's rising sign is Pisces at 19 degrees; the mother's is in Scorpio at 50 minutes. The water elements of the two signs mix well, giving them a natural affinity when it comes to the mystical and the strange. The mutable nature of Pisces, however, balks at some of Scorpio's fixed opinions on things, so they may find conflict there.

Their Sun signs are compatible; Gemini and Virgo are both mutable signs ruled by Mercury. This gives mother and daughter a natural affinity when it comes to books, learning, anything dealing with the intellect and communication. The daughter's rising sign also falls in the mother's fifth house of creativity, indicating that her mystical edge is a source of creative ideas for the mother.

The mother's Moon lies at the tail end of Capricorn; the daughter's Moon is in Virgo. Both are earth signs, yet their emotional makeup differs because Capricorn is a

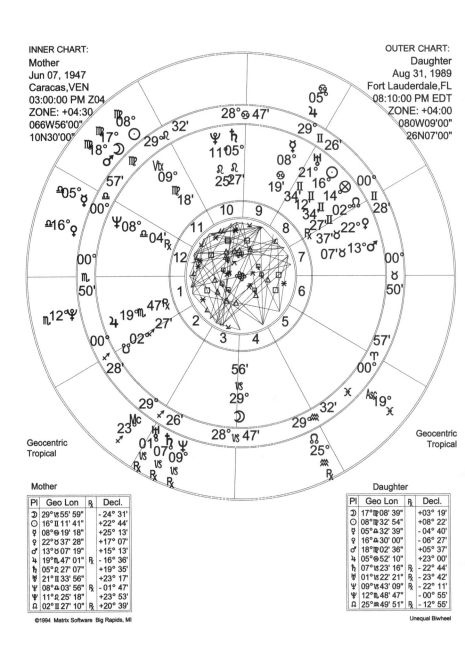

Mother

Pl	Geo Lon	R	Decl.
☽	29°♑55' 59"		- 24° 31'
☉	16°♊11' 41"		+22° 44'
☿	08°♉19' 18"		+25° 13'
♀	22°♉37' 28"		+17° 07'
♂	13°♉07' 19"		+15° 13'
♃	19°♏47' 01"	R	- 16° 36'
♄	05°♌27' 07"		+19° 35'
♅	21°♊33' 56"		+23° 17'
♆	08°♌03' 56"	R	- 01° 47'
♇	11°♌25' 18"		+23° 53'
☊	02°♊27' 10"	R	+20° 39'

Daughter

Pl	Geo Lon	R	Decl.
☽	17°♍08' 39"		+03° 19'
☉	08°♍32' 54"		+08° 22'
☿	05°♎32' 39"		- 04° 40'
♀	16°♑30' 00"		- 06° 27'
♂	18°♍02' 36"		+05° 37'
♃	05°♋52' 10"		+23° 00'
♄	07°♑23' 16"	R	- 22° 44'
♅	01°♑22' 21"	R	- 23° 42'
♆	09°♑43' 09"	R	- 22° 11'
♇	12°♏48' 47"		- 00° 55'
☊	25°♒49' 51"	R	- 12° 55'

Figure 45-1

cardinal sign and Virgo is mutable. At times, the mother's emotions may fixate on a singular direction or goal, while the daughter's emotions are changing by the moment. This can certainly be a source of conflict.

The daughter's Moon in Virgo falls in the mother's eleventh house (friends, group associations, ambitions, and dreams). This suggests that the daughter instinctively understands her mother's ambitions and supports them, even though she may feel that her mother spends too much time working.

In the comparison chart in figure 45-2, where the daughter's chart is within the inner circle, the mother's Moon in Capricorn falls in the daughter's eleventh house. This indicates that the mother lends emotional support to her daughter's ambitions and in some way provides a structure for her to achieve her potential.

In figure 45-3, the comparison chart is between the girl and her father, with the daughter's chart in the inner circle. The father's Sun in Taurus (♉25☉) and his daughter's Sun in Virgo are compatible because both are earth signs. They seek practical solutions to their problems. But Taurus is fixed, which means he has a particular, set way of doing things, while his daughter tends to get where she's going by adapting to circumstances.

His rising is also in Taurus, which reinforces the characteristics of the sign. The earth element is compatible with his daughter's earth Sun and Moon and her water rising sign. But his daughter has no planets in Taurus. The interesting thing is that both share a Virgo Moon. This gives them an easy, natural affinity on the emotional and unconscious levels. His Moon falls into her sixth house of health and work, indicating that any disagreements she has with him may inadvertently affect her health.

In comparison charts, when another person's planets conjunct any of the four angles in your child's chart, it's

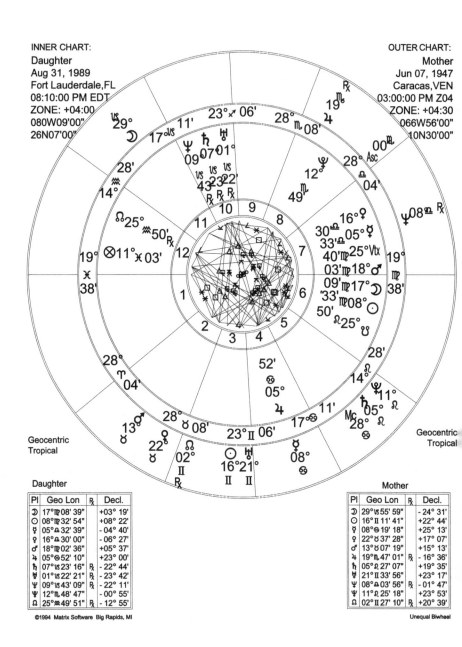

INNER CHART:
Daughter
Aug 31, 1989
Fort Lauderdale,FL
08:10:00 PM EDT
ZONE: +04:00
080W09'00"
26N07'00"

OUTER CHART:
Mother
Jun 07, 1947
Caracas,VEN
03:00:00 PM Z04
ZONE: +04:30
066W56'00"
10N30'00"

Geocentric
Tropical

Geocentric
Tropical

Daughter

Pl	Geo Lon	R	Decl.
☽	17°♍08' 39"		+03° 19'
☉	08°♍32' 54"		+08° 22'
☿	05°♎32' 39"		- 04° 40'
♀	16°♎30' 00"		- 06° 27'
♂	18°♍02' 36"		+05° 37'
♃	05°♋52' 10"		+23° 00'
♄	07°♑23' 16"	R	- 22° 44'
♅	01°♑22' 21"	R	- 23° 42'
♆	09°♑43' 09"	R	- 22° 11'
♇	12°♏48' 47"		- 00° 55'
☊	25°♒49' 51"	R	- 12° 55'

©1994 Matrix Software Big Rapids, MI

Mother

Pl	Geo Lon	R	Decl.
☽	29°♑55' 59"		- 24° 31'
☉	16°♊11' 41"		+22° 44'
☿	08°♋19' 18"		+25° 13'
♀	22°♉37' 28"		+17° 07'
♂	13°♉07' 19"		+15° 13'
♃	19°♏47' 01"	R	- 16° 36'
♄	05°♌27' 07"		+19° 35'
♅	21°♊33' 56"		+23° 17'
♆	08°♎03' 56"	R	- 01° 47'
♇	11°♌25' 18"		+23° 53'
☊	02°♊27' 10"	R	+20° 39'

Unequal Biwheel

Figure 45-2

308

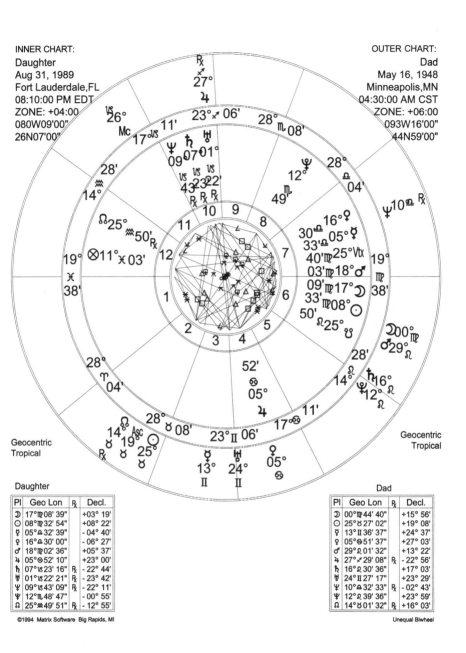

Figure 45-3

especially significant. In the father/daughter comparison, there are two such planets: Jupiter at the Midheaven (♃27♐R) and Uranus at the cusp of the fourth house (♅24♊).

Jupiter's position suggests that their relationship is expansive and fortunate for them both. The father will expand her career opportunities, perhaps through foreign travel and exposure to foreign cultures. Their relationship is about luck, synchronicities, and expansion.

Uranus's conjunction to the cusp is less than one degree. It indicates that the father brings an unusual and brilliant influence to the child's early life. He also brings sudden disruptions—an unexpected move, an innovative way of doing something. He may have an unusual occupation that involves computers or other high tech electronic wizardry.

Interestingly enough, his Midheaven in Capricorn (MC♑26), falls in his daughter's eleventh house, the same house where the mother's Moon also falls. This paints a rather fascinating picture concerning the daughter's aspirations. She not only has her mother's emotional support, but she also has her father's overall support in whatever she seeks to achieve.

Divorce and Death

There's no single aspect or planet placement that signifies divorce or the death of a parent. But the presence of Pluto or Uranus in the natal fourth house suggests upheaval early or late in life concerning one of the parents. It indicates numerous moves. If fiery Mars is tossed into the pot, it could mean the child experiences a disruption in a relationship with a parent through an accident or injury to the parent.

One woman whose chart I erected, a complete stranger whom I met over the Internet, had Mars, Uranus, and Pluto in Virgo, conjunct in the fourth house. To me, this meant a sudden and unexpected event that changed her relationship with one of her parents when she was quite young. I hesitated to say it was because of an accident or injury, but it turned out it was exactly that. Her father was killed in a car accident when she was three and a half.

A number of my daughter's friends come from divorced families. In some cases, the divorce doesn't seem to affect the child in an adverse way. When I do natal charts on such children, I sometimes find Jupiter or Venus on or near the cusp of the fourth house. This implies that the child's relationship with his or her parents remains largely unaffected by the divorce.

Identical Twins

When I was a child, I met a girl who was born on the same day and year and in the same place as I was. We were born about the same time, within two or three minutes of each other. In astrology, this is called "astral twins."

We didn't know each other very long or very well and lost touch when one of us moved. In all the years since, I have often wondered how her life differed from or ran parallel to my own. I imagine that the patterns in our natal charts attracted some experiences that are similar. But I also suspect our lives evolved very differently because we are different people. Our individual souls came in with different intentions. And, ultimately, the chart is only a blueprint; free will determines how the natal patterns manifest.

The same is true for identical twins. Research on twins has shown that even twins separated at birth and raised in different environments share similar experiences. One twin, for instance, might be married to a woman named Sharon, while the other twin has a daughter named Sharon. Both twins may love vanilla ice cream smothered in hot chocolate. But their lives are not the same because they are *two separate individuals.*

Skeptics, however, point at twins to disprove the validity of astrology. They reason that, if astrology works at all, then it must work for identical twins. The whole issue of identical twins becomes their litmus test for astrology. This bothered me until I realized that identical twins actually reinforce the concept of free will.

To use an analogy, think of a blueprint for a house. A developer builds a dozen houses from this blueprint. Even though the actual structures are identical, they may each be a different color. Or one house has a beautifully landscaped yard and the other has a yard straight out of a Stephen King novel. Or one house has a metal garage door and another has wood. Or one has a ladder to the attic and another doesn't. The differences among the houses result from the tastes and style of the people who inhabit them. Their free will.

The same is true for twins.

With the charts of identical twins born within minutes of each other, there usually isn't any deviation between the signs or houses in which the planets fall, unless a planet is in a late degree. The slower moving planets lie in the same degree and minute and so do the ascendants, unless they are in late degrees. The signs on the house cusps and the aspects are usually the same as well.

Astrologers have individual and often complex methods of interpreting the charts of twins. Most of these methods are beyond the scope of *Cosmic Kids*. I try to look for the simplest methods first, particularly with twins born only a minute or two apart. Since the degrees or the minutes of the ascendants and house cusps may vary, I look there first, beginning with the Sabian symbols.

Sabian Symbols

The genesis of the Sabian symbols goes back more than sixty years, to astrologer Marc Edmond Jones. He was intrigued by the work of John Thomas, a Welsh seer who had worked out symbolic interpretations of the zodiac degrees. Jones felt they were evocative but too moralistic and intended to request permission to reinterpret them.

At the time, he had an astrology student, Elsie Wheeler, who was a professional medium. He asked her if she would help him obtain 360 new interpretations for the zodiac degrees. They accomplished this in several hours, with Jones showing her a sign and degree and Wheeler giving him a corresponding psychic image. Jones subsequently sent astrologer Dane Rudhyar the interpretations.

Rudhyar considers the symbols to be archetypal in nature, representative of particular cycles in life. In his book, *An Astrological Mandala,* he explains how the Sabian symbols can be used not only to deepen the meaning of a horoscope, but as an oracle similar to the *I Ching*.

With this in mind, refer to the charts in figures 45-4 and 45-5. These twins were born two minutes apart. The only differences in their charts is in degrees. They are both Libras, with Moons in Sagittarius and risings in Cancer. Melissa, the oldest, has an ascendant of 10♋43 and a seventh house cusp in Capricorn in the same degree; Mandy's rising is 11♋09, with a seventh house cusp in Capricorn at the same degree. Melissa's Midheaven is in Pisces and her fourth house cusps is in Virgo, at 24 degrees and 27 minutes; in Mandy's chart, the signs are the same, but at 23 degrees

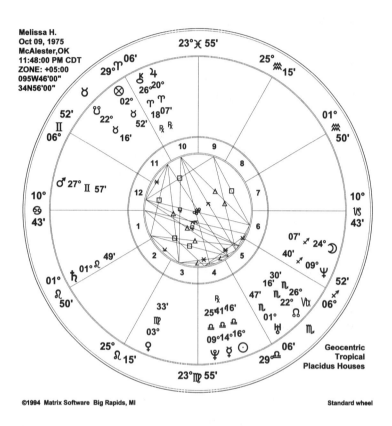

Figure 45-4

and 55 minutes. In other words, the four angles of their charts and all the house cusps differ by only minutes.

In terms of the planets, the only difference is a one-minute deviation in their Moons, not enough to make a difference. Melissa's Vertex is at 26♏30; Mandy's Vertex lies at 26♏50, a variation of twenty minutes. Their Parts of Fortune (⊗) in the eleventh houses vary by less than a minute; again, this isn't enough to make a significant difference.

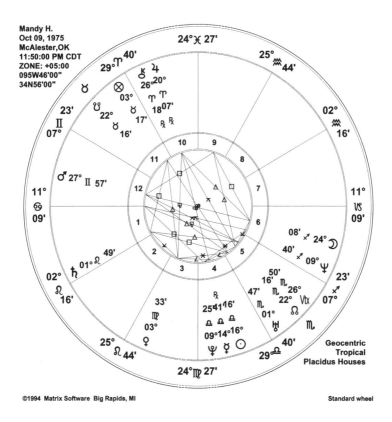

Figure 45-5

In interpreting these symbols for the angles in a chart, Rudhyar advises that the symbols should be interpreted in light of what the angles mean. He defines the ascendant as "what"; the fourth cusp, or IC, as "how"; the descendant, or cusp of the seventh house, as "where to"; and the Midheaven, or tenth house cusp, as "why."

So with the rising, the Sabian symbol addresses the types of experiences through which an individual can fulfill his unique potential. The Sabian symbol for the degree of Melissa's rising reads: "A clown caricaturing well-known personalities." This indicates that, through humor, she's able to develop the objectivity she needs to fulfill her potential. By laughing at herself and her own mistakes and weaknesses, she cultivates a deeper and more objective understanding of her own strengths.

For Mandy's degree of rising, the symbol reads: "A Chinese woman nursing a baby whose aura reveals him to be the reincarnation of a great teacher." This suggests that she must look past appearances to the hidden truths in life to fulfill her potential. This may be done through developing her intuition.

The fourth house cusp, the *how*, depicts our roots, our personal foundations. In the mimeographed version of the Sabian symbols that Jones gave to his astrology students, the symbol for this degree reads: "A large book for children is open at a colored page; Mary, with her yellow curls, feeds an immaculate white lamb." Rudhyar's version of this degree differs slightly: "Mary and her little lamb."

In either instance, the keyword is *picture*. It suggests that Melissa holds fond, innocent memories of her childhood and family. She should seek to cultivate this innocent simplicity within her own family when she marries and has children.

For Mandy, Jones's original symbol is: "A large, glorious public building is seen set in a spacious park; before it a flag moves with the breeze at half-mast." Rudhyar's interpretation varies somewhat: "A flag at half-mast in front of a public building." In both instances, the key is *respect*. Mandy has enormous respect for the traditions in which she was raised and will bring this same respect to her own family. It indicates that, at some point in her life, she will be recognized publicly for something she has accomplished.

The seventh-house cusp rules partnerships. As kids, these partnerships mean friends and peers; as adults, they are business and romantic partnerships. For Melissa, the Sabian symbol reads: "A large group of pheasants on a private estate." The key is luxury. This suggests that Melissa seeks a partner who reflects her desire for comfort and artistic fulfillment.

The image for Mandy's seventh house cusp is somewhat different. In the Jones version, it reads: "A student of nature is lecturing and conjures up dancing pictures of distant wonders before each listener." This indicates an intellectual curiosity about the fundamental mysteries in nature and the universe. Mandy seeks a partner who reflects her explorations.

The Midheaven refers to a person's achievements in the outer world, to their public life. The *why* of the Midheaven is the *big why* of life: "Why am I here? What role am I supposed to play in the larger scheme of things?" For Melissa, the image for the degree of her Midheaven is: "On a small island surrounded by the vast expanse of the sea, people are seen living in close interaction." The key word is centralize. This suggests that Melissa's career or profession may allow her to uncover her limitations so that she can focus her energies on her strengths to achieve what she wants. Her early childhood (IC) gives her a solid foundation from which to do this.

The image for Mandy's Midheaven, according to Jones's original information, differs considerably. "Ecclesiastical reform of drastic nature is in progress and a purged and purified priestcraft opens a new ministry." Reformation is the key word. This indicates that her profession or career may act as a catharsis to bring out the deeper creative urges in her personality.

When I told the twins' mother about these interpretations, she said the interpretations for the risings and the fourth house cusps were essentially correct and so was the "luxury" part of the interpretation for Melissa's seventh house cusp. She didn't think the tenth house cusp interpretations applied yet, but felt they might be more apt as the twins got older.

This kind of interpretation often allows an entrance point into twins' charts, then your intuition kicks in and delves even deeper.

For anyone interested in Sabian symbols, I highly recommend Rudhyar's *An Astrological Mandala: The Cycle of Transformations and Its 360 Symbolic Phases.* The book is particularly valuable in its depiction of Sabian symbols as an oracular device. There are also a number of sites on the Web where the symbols are discussed and where, if you're so inclined, you can choose your symbol for a particular day, project, or relationship.

To find related Web sites, you can conduct a broad search with "astrology" or a more specific search with "Sabian symbols."

46

Kids of the Millennium

What Kind of Kid?

When I was doing research for this book, several parents seemed baffled by the term "cosmic kids." Did I mean flaky kids? Eccentric kids? Little geniuses? Miniature Gandhis? Just what *is* a cosmic kid?

The title actually evolved from a conversation my daughter and I had one evening about dreams, which led to a discussion about telepathy and other psychic phenomena. I realized that, when I was her age, I experienced these things but didn't know what they were. Her generation, however, seems to have been born much more aware and, when they are exposed to these concepts at a young age, the awareness flourishes.

One of our favorite activities on rainy Saturdays is to get a group of Megan's friends together to do telepathy experiments. Each child chooses a crayon that none of the others see, then colors a sheet of paper, which is sealed in an envelope. On a corner of the envelope, the child jots his or her initials. The envelopes are shuffled, put into a pile, and each child chooses one. When a child selects your envelope, you try to "send" him or her your color. The number of hits, particularly in the beginning, before the game becomes repetitive, is astonishing.

Sometimes, we use animals instead of colors. Or shapes. It doesn't seem to matter what is used, as long as the "sender" sends vivid mental images of whatever is in her envelope.

Another game we play is seeing auras. Or we go to old places, like the fort described earlier in the book, and try to "read" the walls with our hands. Sometimes, we just sit around the kitchen table and talk about our dreams, sharing them in an attempt to understand what they mean.

Cosmic kids are open to this kind of thought, particularly when it's approached in a spirit of fun and adventure. Through these types of activities, they learn to trust their intuition, which is then permitted to grow.

Some cosmic kids bring in memories of their past lives. Chase Bowman is a prime example. Others have unusual musical or artistic talents, are gifted intellectually, or are flat out psychic. Every generation, of course, has its prodigies and fine minds. But never before has information been so accessible or has there been such an awakening to the call of the spirit. The children born since 1980 are a breed apart.

According to one survey, a mini baby boom occurred in the late eighties and early nineties, when some four million children were born. These are the cosmic kids, who have to be more aware than their parents were if they are to correct the results of our errors. They are the inheritors of the intuitive knowledge that today's pioneers are bringing to the rest of us. Visionaries like Robert Monroe, Jane Roberts, Carlos Castaneda, Ian Stevenson, and John Bell broke ground in the mid to late sixties and were, for years, considered heretics or weirdos. Then their ideas began to catch on and a momentum built.

Shirley MacLaine, with the publication of *Out on a Limb,* popularized New Age ideas to the point where publishers realized that New Age books were salable. Since then, the New Age genre has evolved into a spiritual genre that embraces evocative ideas from every field. I no longer have to go to a New Age bookstore to find what I like to read; my local chain bookstore carries the titles.

As a result, my daughter's search won't be as difficult as mine.

In 2020, my daughter will be thirty. I can't venture a guess at what her world will be like. I certainly can't guess whether my husband or I will be alive. But thanks to computers and astrology programs, I know the broad patterns that will be evident in her chart for that year. I know that, if my husband and I have succeeded at instilling in her a sense of her own uniqueness, that if her soul has begun to find the path to its greatest fulfillment, then she will have the intuitive knowledge and the left-brain tools to fulfill her potential.

In the end, we're all cosmic kids. We're here because we chose to be here. We're born into circumstances that we choose, to parents we select, with a soul blueprint that we have created. We're here to manifest the patterns inherent in that blueprint and how we do it is entirely up to us.

Cosmic kids recognize their divine spark and become conscious creators of their own destinies.

Index

About the Author

Born and raised in Caracas, Venezuela, Trish MacGregor became interested in astrology at the age of seventeen, after her family left Venezuela. MacGregor has been a professional writer for fifteen years and has authored nineteen novels and five works of non-fiction. Before becoming an author, she held various jobs, including prison librarian, social worker, Spanish teacher at the seventh grade and college levels, and English teacher for Cuban refugees. With her husband, Rob, she also led travel writing trips to the Peruvian Amazon.

The MacGregors have one daughter, Megan, who inspired *Your Cosmic Kids*. They reside in Florida.

The author can be reached at:

trmacgregor@worldnet.att.net

or

TJMacGregor@booktalk.com

Hampton Roads Publishing Company

. . . for the evolving human spirit

Hampton Roads Publishing Company
publishes books on a variety of subjects including
metaphysics, health, complementary medicine,
visionary fiction, and other related topics.

For a copy of our latest catalog,
call toll-free, 800-766-8009,
or send your name and address to:

Hampton Roads Publishing Company, Inc.
134 Burgess Lane
Charlottesville, VA 22902

e-mail: hrpc@hrpub.com
www.hrpub.com